Globalization and its Disconter

Globalization and its Discontents

The Rise of Postmodern Socialisms

*Roger Burbach, Orlando Núñez
and Boris Kagarlitsky*

Pluto Press

LONDON · CHICAGO, ILLINOIS

First published 1997 by Pluto Press
345 Archway Road, London N6 5AA
and 1436 West Randolph, Chicago, Illinois 60607, USA

Copyright © Roger Burbach, Orlando Núñez
and Boris Kagarlitsky 1997

The right of Roger Burbach, Orlando Núñez and Boris Kagarlitsky to
be identified as the authors of this work has been asserted by them in
accordance with the Copyright, Designs and Patents Act 1988.

British Library Cataloguing in Publication Data
A catalogue record for this book is available from the British Library

Library of Congress Cataloging in Publication Data
Burbach, Roger.
    Globalization and its discontents : the rise of postmodern
socialisms / Roger Burbach, Orlando Núñez, and Boris Kagerlitsky.
        p.   cm.
    Includes bibliographical references and index.
    ISBN 0–7453–1171–7 (hbk.)
    1. Economic history—1990– 2. Capitalism. 3. Post-communism.
4. Socialism. 5. International economic relations. I. Núñez Soto,
Orlando. II. Kagarlitsky, Boris, 1958–   . III. Title.
HC59.16.B87   1996
337—dc20   96–28837
                                                                CIP

ISBN 0 7453 1171 7 hbk

Designed and produced for Pluto Press by
Chase Production Services, Chipping Norton, OX7 5QR
Typeset from disk by Stanford DTP Services, Milton Keynes
Printed in the EC by J.W. Arrowsmith, Bristol

Contents

Contents

Preface

This book is a collaborative effort by authors from the First, former Second and Third Worlds. Roger Burbach is the principal writer and worked closely with Orlando Núñez to develop the main ideas of the book. Boris Kagarlitsky made comments on the manuscript and is the sole author of the chapter on the post-communist world. The views presented here have been profoundly shaped by the political upheaval and turmoil of the past decade and a half. Orlando Núñez, who participated in the Nicaraguan resistance to the Somoza regime, served as a leading strategist of the Sandinista government in the 1980s. With the defeat of the Sandinistas in 1990 he began searching for new approaches to democratic change at the grassroots, particularly among the peasants and agricultural workers. A member of the Sandinista Assembly, he now heads CIPRES, a center promoting agricultural sustainability and worker-run enterprises in the countryside. Boris Kagarlitsky, who was imprisoned under Leonid Brezhnev in the early 1980s, is deeply involved in constructing a new socialist project in the midst of a society that has suffered immensely with the collapse of communism. He participated in the resistance to the attempted coup against Gorbachev in 1991, and then was briefly imprisoned during Yeltsin's coup against the Russian parliament in 1993. He is also a founder of the Russian Party of Labor and served as an elected deputy of the Moscow City Soviet until Yeltsin abolished it.

For Roger Burbach, the third author charged with writing this Preface, the book is the product of a three-fold odyssey. The very fact that I enticed two others to participate in this project – Boris in Moscow and Orlando in Managua – gives some idea of the geographic odyssey. In addition to prolonged stays in the erstwhile Soviet Union and Nicaragua, my visits to China, El Salvador, Cuba, southern Mexico and half a dozen countries in Eastern Europe were critical in shaping this book – as was a summer spent in Amsterdam where the Transnational Institute allowed me to use their facilities.

Just as important has been the political odyssey that lies behind this project. I began to conceive of this book in 1989, the year that marked the collapse of "actually existing socialism." It is perhaps not too fanciful to think that the length of time and the numerous difficulties involved in producing this book are due in large part to the turmoil in ideology and beliefs that has taken place during this period. A more personal odyssey revolves around the spinal cord injury I suffered in Nicaragua in early 1989 that has left me partially paralyzed. Certainly this injury and my subsequent rehabilitation took their toll and attenuated the book's completion. However, my conviction that this book needed to be written helped motivate me to keep going and see beyond the pain and physical limitations I was experiencing.

Given these geographic, political and personal odysseys, I am indebted to an incredibly large number of people. I wish to thank all the people in Berlin, Prague, Budapest, Belgrade, Sofia, Moscow, Mexico, Nicaragua, Amsterdam, El Salvador and China who helped me with my wheelchair through train stations and on buses, assisted me in finding accessible hotels, or even let me share their homes. They made my life endurable and gave me new faith in the basic disposition of people to help their fellow humans who experience difficulties in their lives and travels.

Thanks to the following for discussing the books ideas, making comments on the manuscript, or providing research assistance: Marty Bennett, Raymond Barglow, Marie Nadeau, Carmen Diana Deere, Cecile Earle, Ed Colaianni, David Parkhurst, Dolores Plumb, Lea Guido, Trevor Evans, Marilyn McMahon, Peter Marchetti, Philippe Bourgois, Alejandro Bendaña, Marc Herold, Kevin Danaher, Judy Brister, Karen Judd, Robert Armstrong, Russell and Silvia Bartley, Jim and Judy Tarbell, Fred Goff, Noam Chomsky, Leo Panitch, Renfrey Clarke, Walden Bello, Steve Painter, Tracey Sorenson, Hank Frundt, Eric Holt-Giminez, Dick Walker, Kena Urrestarazu, David Hathaway, Marcos Arruda, Adriana Perez, Beca Lafore and Roger van Zwanenberg, our publisher at Pluto Press. We are also indebted to Robert Webb and Aleks Sierz of Pluto Press for their diligent work in guiding the manuscript through its final stages of publication.

Special thanks to Joel Rocamora, Andre Gundar Frank, Daniel Singer and Kees Beekart for their discussions with me in Amsterdam and Paris during the early stages of this book. Thanks also to Eric Leenson, Elizabeth Farnsworth, Susan Browne, Norton Tooby, Ethel Sajines, Melinda Delashmutt Altschul, and Carol Bernstein Ferry and her late husband, W.H. "Ping" Ferry, for support while working on this book.

I am especially indebted to my lifelong friends, Glenn and Marilyn Borchardt who assisted me during the worst days after my accident and who discussed many of the ideas in this book. Sharing life with my two children, Matthew and Alexandra, also provided me with inspiration and hope for the future.

This is the first is a series of books that will be published on the theme of globalization. Our belief is that globalization as most broadly defined – the breakdown of national boundaries in economic and political life – is at the center of much that shakes the world today. We are not opposed to globalization per se, in fact we would consider ourselves globalists in the sense that now more than ever a global perspective is necessary for humanity to grapple with many of the major problems it faces. But the economic forces that currently determine the direction of globalization adversely affect most of humanity and severely limit our ability to create a better world.

There is perhaps one longing that unites the discontents of the globe, those who are the principal antagonists of globalization. It is not a belief in socialism or even in democracy, but a desire for liberation. The international women's movement, the movements for racial and ethnic equality around the globe, the environmental movements in different regions – along with the ongoing struggles of the poor and impoverished everywhere – all these and others express a search for liberation from the conditions of oppression and exploitation that they see or experience. The authors of this book agree with the basic tenet of Marxism which asserts that the most pervasive form of exploitation and suffering in the world today derives from the economic system of capitalism. As long as greed, profit maximization and the accumulation of capital in the hands of a few are the predominant economic drives determining the direction of the globe, equality and real freedom cannot be realized. We are on the brink of a new stage in civilization. Globalization has been positive in the sense that it broke down provincialism and antiquated ways of thinking, but now that the human species has a common, dare we say global, awareness, we as a species are in a position to end many forms of exploitation.

We realize that many of the ideas presented here will be provocative and controversial. The particular analysis and use of postmodernism has been criticized as being anti-historical and anti-Marxist. We believe these assertions to be unfounded, but acknowledge that many of the concepts and ideas put forth here need to be critiqued and developed much more fully. We are witnessing a new stage in the world's development, and this requires that we be bold and experimental in our thinking. If nothing else, we hope that this book will provoke discussion that can further more advanced awareness and analysis about where the world is headed, and particularly about the role of the left and progressives in this turbulent epoch in humanity's history.

Roger Burbach,
June, 1996

Introduction: Back to the Future

It was the best of times, it was the worst of times.
Charles Dickens, *A Tale of Two Cities*

I may have thought that the road to a world of free and happy human beings shorter than it is proving to be but I was not wrong in thinking that such a world is possible, and that it is worth while to live with a view to bringing it nearer.
Bertrand Russell, *The Autobiography of Bertrand Russell*[1]

Humanity is at a tumultuous stage in its development. There are enormous possibilities for increasing the general well-being, and yet the globe is mired in an unprecedented era of misery, alienation and turbulence. The pages of this book have the difficult task of examining the root causes of this state of the world while probing for new actors and social forces that could enable humanity to break out of this impasse.

The principal problem for progressives around the globe is that they find themselves in this period with no worldview or political philosophy capable of galvanizing a mass movement. There is an ideological void. The decisive historic event of the late twentieth century is the collapse of communism and the triumph of Western capitalism. With this global realignment, revolutionary and progressive movements have entered a period of decline. The political playing field is now controlled by those espousing neo-liberalism and globalization, the secular creeds of the dominant classes.

Even liberal and social democratic forces, which for much of the post-World War II period offered a reformist approach to capitalism, are on the defensive and incapable of implementing policies that deal with the growing polarization of developed and underdeveloped societies. All the social and economic surveys of the past decade and a half reveal that we are entering a period in which capital is so powerful that its beneficiaries enjoy a "grand banquet" while ever-increasing numbers of the world's population are forced into poverty and misery. In this brave new world plagues and pestilences multiply while research and technology are harnessed by the rich and powerful in their own interests.

Globalization, a process spearheaded by the multinational financial and industrial conglomerates, is central to understanding

1

why the world is mired in this trough. As globalization advances it foments a diverse array of groups who are either marginalized or resisting the onslaught of modernization and globalization. Often reactive, and frequently inarticulate as oppositional movements, these are the discontents of the world, those who more often than not are lashing out or rebelling without a clear-cut cause.

Three paradoxes are critical to understanding globalization and the burgeoning army of discontents. Firstly, and most importantly, the destabilizing impact of late capitalism at the very time that capitalism has conquered the world. Secondly, the ideological impasse of liberal democracy at the moment when it has become ascendant. And finally the failure of socialism as a universal platform of struggle precisely when desperation and upheaval are as widespread and globalized as ever. These paradoxes compel us to look beyond what the modern world – or modernity – has bequeathed us, to search for new alternatives that are postmodern in the broadest sense of the word.

Freud, Marx and postmodernism

This book's title is an adaptation of Sigmund Freud's treatise, *Civilization and Its Discontents*. Freud believed that many are hostile to civilization because it "is largely responsible for our misery."[2] So it is today with globalization. At the turn of the millennium, the elites and rulers of the planet have made globalization virtually synonymous with civilization. In the name of progress and globalization, they plunder the world's resources, amassing greater and greater fortunes while propagating a global army of discontents comprised of the immiserated, the exploited and the dispossessed.

Neither these discontents, nor the other species who suffer from the rape of the planet's environment, can put up for long with this variant of civilization. The overarching conflict taking place in the world today is between the class interests that impose globalization and the discontented masses. By internationalizing economies, cultures and capital as never before, the dominant classes have inadvertently generated a growing popular awareness that leaps across national frontiers as people become increasingly conscious of their common rights, needs and interests.

Even though capitalism is hegemonic in this new epoch, the political and social foundations of the post-communist neo-liberal world are gravely flawed. The onrush of technology and capitalism makes it impossible to find stability. There is no "New World Order," as George Bush declared at the inception of the Gulf War, only growing instability and uncertainty. There is, however, an attempt to impose order from above through the use of economic and military violence, which is what Bush's New World Order was all about.[3] The rhetoric changed somewhat with Bill Clinton but the content of the world system did not. The United States and the other dominant imperial powers continue to rely on coercion and economic power to keep the other countries of the world under their control and influence. This domination from above is increasingly unstable and makes many parts of the world inherently volatile and potentially explosive.

This era of capitalism could drive humanity to the edge of a new barbarism, one in which the physical environment is destroyed, violence becomes endemic to virtually all societies, and the world's masses are impoverished while the elites set up privileged enclaves and guarded mansions to maintain their opulent lifestyles. We do not believe, however, that humanity is necessarily locked into this historic trajectory. There is another road that could be taken, a road that goes beyond the Marxist and communist experiences of the past century and a half and builds a world based on cooperation, participation and a real liberation of the human spirit.

We shall explore the new values and politics that are emerging as an alternative to modern barbarism. For want of a better term, we call the perspective we use in this endeavor "postmodern Marxism." It reaches beyond traditional left analysis to discuss the new forms of fragmentation, alienation and destruction begotten by modernism and global capitalism. We shall both negate and draw on Marxism. We reject the historic communist tradition that led to authoritarianism and an economic system not all that different from capitalism, with its destruction of the environment and the creation of new, alienated working classes. But our approach is Marxist in that we, unlike the relativist schools of postmodernism, remain dialectical materialists, believing a new worldview can be constructed to replace the ideology of capitalism and its system of exploitation.[4]

The particular variant of Marxism that became ascendant in the communist countries, Marxism-Leninism, erred fundamentally in asserting that a new order could be ushered in by taking control of the state, thus transforming the economy and society from above. This approach led to benevolent authoritarian governments at best, and harsh, violent dictatorships at worst. A new order cannot appear unless beliefs and values are changed in civil society – at the grassroots level – so that the state becomes a responsive apparatus rather than the principal agent of transformation.

Change at the base has been taking place since the watershed years of the 1960s, when social, cultural and political rebellion shook much of the developed and underdeveloped worlds. Contrary to Francis Fukuyama's widely discussed thesis that liberal capitalism represents the end of history, we believe that upheaval from below, with all its twists and unforeseen turns, is an ever more fundamental motor challenging liberal capitalism's control as we move into the twenty-first century. It is conceivable that over the long term, capital through its internationalization may be effectively digging its own grave, although in a way substantially different from that envisioned by Marx and Lenin. This time grassroots democratic and popular social movements, rather than vanguard political formations or state-oriented communist parties, may be setting the stage for an entirely new world.

Today's global crisis is similar to the age of the French revolution in that all the old ideologies are crumbling while new ones are struggling to emerge. The period from 1789 to 1815 too was tremendously chaotic and conflictual. No single ideological perspective predominated or proved capable of interpreting the multitude of events and developments. It was a period in which the modern ideologies were incipiently being formed – liberalism, conservatism and then socialism. But this was not at all clear in the midst of the French revolutionary process when Jacobinism, Bonapartism and restorationism competed to impose their respective political and world views.

At the end of the twentieth century new values are haltingly emerging as the old world order breaks down. However, there is no assurance that new progressive values will prevail. Capitalism, under the banner of neo-liberalism, may survive and even thrive as a system of and for the few while it forces most of the world's population to live in poverty, alienation and virtual barbarism. As Walden Bello notes in *Dark Victory*:

> Barbarism stares us in the face in many guises – in clean-shaven technowarriors who manage, from Washington, the death of hundreds of thousands in Middle Eastern battlefields that they experience as sanitized digital images in electronic monitors; in Christian Serbs who rape Muslim women en masse and depopulate Muslim villages in the name of "ethnic cleansing"; in neo-Nazi German Youth who burn down the homes of Turkish guest laborers; in French rightists who advocate mass deportation of undocumented Third World workers to preserve the "purity" of French culture; in American fundamentalists who have declared moral and cultural war on blacks, Third World immigrants, the women's movement.[5]

A major reason for the rise of these insidious forces is that the organized left is mired in a serious, worldwide crisis, and is largely incapable of providing leadership or alternatives to the diverse, ongoing popular upheaval. A major theme running throughout this book is a discussion of how the left can begin to construct new movements and visions that enable us to halt the slide into barbarism. Like Ronald Aronson in *After Marxism*, we believe that "We are on our own," that the specific Marxist historic project that evolved in the nineteenth and twentieth centuries is at an end.[6]

While Aronson rejects Marxism and approaches the crisis of the left and global disarray from a perspective somewhat different from ours, we find it an important sign of renewal that such works are now appearing. Another, edited volume, *Marxism Beyond Marxism*, contains an insightful article by Fredric Jameson in which he declares that "a postmodern capitalism necessarily calls a postmodern Marxism into existence over and against itself." Irwin Silber, a US activist in Marxist-Leninist organizations and parties for decades, has written another book of interest, *Socialism: What Went Wrong?*, that discusses the inadequacies of Marxist theory and practice from Marx and Engels to Stalin and Gorbachev.[7]

The postmodern economies

Our belief is that the left can develop alternatives to globalization and barbarism based on the emergence of new postmodern economic realities. The globalization process of transnational capital is both centripetal and centrifugal. It concentrates and integrates capital, commerce and trade in and between the metropoles, while at the same time casting off industries, peoples and even countries that it has no use for.

In the parts of the world that capitalism discards, a new mode of production is taking hold, which comprises what we will call postmodern economies. These economies do not and cannot compete head to head with transnational capitalism in the globalization process. Rather they lurk on the sidelines, seizing those activities that the transnational world decides to dispose of. This historic process resembles the transition from feudalism to capitalism. Then capitalism also first took hold in the nooks and crannies, slowly gathering momentum until it replaced feudalism as the dominant form of production.

The new postmodern economies are still incipient in much of the world, comprised of highly differentiated activities and economic islands that rise phoenix-like out of what capitalism discards. The most extensive of the postmodern economies consists of the informal sector – the ever more numerous street venders, the flea markets, petty family businesses, and even garbage scavengers who recycle aluminum cans, cardboard and bottles while consuming what they can of the refuse. On a larger scale, another economic sector is comprised of weak enterprises, like steel and airline companies, that big capital sells off to the workers because these businesses no longer reap high profits. Another postmodern economy in the developed world is comprised of the technical and skilled people who are spun off by corporate downsizing, forced to set up their own small cottage enterprises to subcontract at a lower income level with the big companies they once worked for. Although still very much a part of the global economy, these people are increasingly alienated and actual or potential antagonists of transnational capital.

The postmodern economies in Eastern Europe and Russia include the many enterprises where the workers have gained a significant stake in, or outright ownership of, industries and businesses sold off by their governments to appease the West's demands for "economic restructuring" and "privatization." Many of these industries will never compete in the global economy, but are defended and maintained by their workers, for whom they are the only source of livelihood available. In the many republics of the former Soviet Union another postmodern economy is located in the countryside, where a new peasantry consists of members of the old Soviet collectives, housewives who have lost their professional jobs and even university professors who have no work. These people now have no other option but to move onto the land to grow the food they need for survival.

The largest postmodern economy in the world is comprised of the little heralded township enterprises of China that are owned by the local communities and turn out one third of the country's manufactured goods and much of China's agricultural production. The Chinese government has unleashed the local forces of production in the countryside, and the rural township enterprises, many of which have roots in the era of Mao Tse-tung, have an economic dynamism as powerful as that of the large private companies or joint ventures that are favored by the Chinese government in the special enterprise zones.

In the Third World, postmodern economies are found in the mushrooming informal sector of the cities, in the numerous markets and micro-entrepreneurial activities in the barrios and favelas. A postmodern economy also exists in the countryside where peasants work barren lands. It is also emerging as plantations are taken over or sold off cheaply to peasants, agricultural cooperatives or small-scale producers because of the depressed international prices of sugar, cotton and bananas that have made these lands marginally useful for the oligarchs and latifundistas.

All these areas of postmodern economic activity grow in importance, not because they can compete in any significant way with transnational capital, but because they are the only option available to ever-increasing numbers of people. A subcontractor for a large corporation, a refuse scavenger, a micro-entrepreneur in the informal economy, a street vender or a peasant – none of them abandon their activities because there is little else they can do to survive.

The postmodern economies and their participants will ultimately become ascendant because global capitalism excludes more and more people, and also because of inherent crises and contradictions within the system itself. The very growth that capitalism needs to prosper is an increasing barrier to its survival. As Serge Latouche, a French critic of modern development points out, a 3.5 per cent annual growth rate for the next hundred years – the rate that economists generally argue is necessary to maintain stability in capitalist societies – would represent a thirty-one fold increase in global production.[8] By the end of the next century we would have something like thirty times more factories than we now have, thirty times as many cars and transportation vehicles, thirty times as many agricultural commodities produced and processed, and, even more importantly, the need for thirty times as much water and the spewing out of thirty times as much waste and garbage. Some may argue that there will be environmental technologies that will reduce the inherently pollutive nature of capitalism. But even if one were to halve the increment in waste and output to a factor of fifteen, the world would still be unliveable with this pace of growth and destruction.

Delineating past and future realities

To set the framework for understanding the postmodern economies and the values that are being forged in this period of upheaval, we will in the first two chapters look at the new world disorder and the discontented who are the main social actors at the bottom. Then Chapter 3 examines the current ideological disintegration, looking first at the limits of liberal democracy and then at how the authoritarian and top-down approaches of both the old communist world and the capitalist societies feed into the disarticulation of existing ideologies.

Chapter 4 probes the economic forces behind the global disorder. Capitalism has entered a new and more dangerous stage in which finance capital is ascendant. Often referred to as "casino capitalism," we contend that this volatile stage of capitalism will lead during the next twenty-five years to an economic catastrophe more severe than that of the Great Depression.

Then in Chapters 5, 6 and 7 we will focus on political and social realities in specific parts of the world. The view presented here is that while societies and economies are more globally linked than ever, there are also major regional differences and processes of social disintegration that need to be understood and incorporated into a new postmodern global perspective.

The Third World is of particular importance in our regional analysis, given the decline of the national liberation movements at a time when social upheaval and conflict are intensifying. The collapse of the Mexican economy in 1994–5 demonstrates that even the countries most favored by foreign capital are not about to escape from their subservient position in the global economy. Only a small number of people in these Third World countries, who dominate their political systems and are owners of the largest enterprises, are able to benefit from globalization.

In Chapter 6 we devote attention to discussing the social and political changes occurring in the United States. Just beneath the facade of a harmonious Western democracy exists one of the most conflictive societies in the world. The United States is an ever more violent country with a growing marginalized population. Its political system fails to address major strains and destabilizing tensions – in fact it accentuates them. The Los Angeles insurrection demonstrated that the underclass – which the US moneyed classes have written off completely – is capable of momentarily taking control of the streets and disrupting everyday life in one of the largest cities in the world.

The upheaval in the former Soviet Union and the limits of the aborted revolutions in Eastern Europe are the topic of Chapter 7. It is here that neo-liberalism has caused an unmitigated economic catastrophe by imposing its philosophy on the peoples of the region. This catastrophe is at the root of the political crises that are affecting most of the new regimes of the old communist world. At the end of this chapter, Boris Kagarlitsky discusses the future of Russian socialism, a future in which he sees the state playing a central role by "renationalizing" many of the enterprises that private speculators have taken over.

In Chapter 8 we discuss old and new visions in this age of dismay and disorder. New political and social conceptions are emerging that break with the pursuit and consolidation of political power as conceived of by Machiavelli and Western rulers since the advent of Western expansionism. Here we also look at today's ethnic and national movements, discussing their origins and what they may contribute to the construction of a better world.

In the final chapter, Roger Burbach and Orlando Núñez, unlike Boris Kagarlitsky, argue that grassroots economic endeavors and enterprises, what we call the postmodern economies, will gradually coalesce to form a new mode of production that will replace capitalism. Boris Kagarlitsky maintains that most of this economic activity is "a non-capitalist sector which is not opposing the development of the capitalist economy but is accompanying it."

However, we think that in many countries it is a necessary, transitory stage that will lead to a system of freely organized "associate producers" in opposition to the transnational corporations and their control of the global economy.

Roger Burbach and Orlando Núñez also emphasize a scenario that relies less on the state and focuses more on the social movements and the development of worker-run enterprises. Boris Kagarlitsky places little hope in the social movements and "is totally skeptical about worker-run enterprises. They can exist but this is no solution. They will be either a periphery of the capitalist production or a periphery of a socialist productive organization."

We agree that there will be a need for coordination and planning at a global level as well as a substantial role for state ownership and influence in the strategic sectors of the economy. But this planning, coordination and ownership will have to respond to democratic initiatives from below. It will be based on cooperatives, worker-run enterprises, forms of private and family enterprise that apply creative economic and financial skills for the greater good of society, and on the ever-expanding informal sector, which includes millions of petty-merchants and micro-enterprises. To rely principally on state control and ownership will lead us straight back to authoritarian socialism.

Roger Burbach and Orlando Núñez also believe that the new social movements – many of which have been around for a quarter century or more – are still potent political forces, and have been revitalized in the early 1990s due to intensifying social and economic contradictions. However we also recognize that a key issue is how these movements can link up more closely with the impoverished and marginalized underclasses.

The differing emphasis of the authors, as well as the tremendous political, cultural and economic diversity of the societies on this planet, accounts for why we employ the term "postmodern socialisms." A great deal of flexibility and experimentation will be needed as we search for new options in the wake of the collapse of communism. A major lesson of the Marxist-Leninist experience is that no singular model of socialism can be applicable to all societies.

It is necessary to begin articulating these new approaches so that progressive individuals and movements can once again feel empowered politically and ideologically with the demise of communism and the national liberation movements. As noted above, we should not forget that capitalism emerged over a period of centuries out of the old feudal system. History, of course, moves much more rapidly today. New postmodern social forces are slowly but surely building from within, tearing away at the established values and opening spaces and opportunities for the creation of a new, authentically democratic world. Whether or not they succeed in consolidating new postmodern socialisms will determine if we live in a state of virtual barbarism in the next millennium, or if we are finally able to break free and build a more egalitarian and humane world.

CHAPTER 1

The New World Disorder

The new world order is an old world lie.
> John Trudell,
> *AKA Graffiti Man* album

Capitalism has never been more prone to uncontrolled crises and disasters. It is an explosive mix which is everywhere polarizing societies on an unprecedented scale.
> Paul Sweezy and Harry Magdoff[1]

On the eve of the third millennium, civilization finds itself precariously straddling two very different worlds, one utopian and full of promise, the other dystopian and rife with peril.
> Jeremy Rifkin, *The End of Work*[2]

Capitalism has conquered the globe, the culmination of the process of expansion that began half a millennium ago. However, the very drive for a capitalist world order has begotten its opposite – global disorder. The Third World is fraught with turmoil, including famine and ethnic wars in Africa, the spread of AIDS and cholera in impoverished countries, and the failure of formal democracies to address popular needs and aspirations in Latin America, Asia and Africa.

Simultaneously, the collapse of the communist regimes has ushered in an array of new "free market" states that are proving incapable of consolidating stable economic and political systems. "Frontier capitalism" has taken hold in these countries as mafias and corrupt politicians build their fortunes at the expense of hundreds of millions of people who are worse off than they were under communism. The astounding drop in male life expectancy in Russia – from 65 years in 1991 to 57 in 1994 – bears testimony to the collapse of Russian health and living standards.

As impoverishment and strife accelerate in the Second and Third Worlds, the victorious powers, particularly the United States, find themselves unable to achieve internal stability. Governance in the societies of the developed world is increasingly pernicious and undemocratic. The neo-liberals cut taxes, gut the welfare state, and drive down wages by moving plants and businesses abroad, claiming that all this is necessary so that "the market place can operate more efficiently."

To distract their constituents from what is really happening, politicians whip up anti-foreign and anti-immigrant hysteria among the middle and working classes and sectors of the alienated youth. The crime, violence and poverty that are increasingly rampant in the major cities are blamed on the "lack of family values," or on inherent laziness and lack of initiative. Those who do not conform to the accepted mold of behavior are "disciplined" – thrown onto the streets or into the jails.

And while trying to keep their own populace in check through these means and others, the imperial nation states are often at each other's economic throats, attempting to gain advantage. GATT and international trade agreements may embody the new rules of the global economic game, but this does not stop each of the major capitalist nations from trying to manipulate or evade existent trade rules. They establish regional trade blocs, arrange barter agreements and engage in trade wars.

This current historical moment invites comparisons with the period leading up to World War I and the Bolshevik Revolution. Then also the world was unstable and conflictive, torn by major national rivalries and by economic booms and busts. With the decline of Great Britain – like the United States today – no single hegemonic power could simply impose its economic and political will on the other major nations of the world.[3]

The parallel with this earlier period breaks down, however, when one realizes that this time the conflict is global, not centered on the nation states of Europe and the Western world. Discontent and desperation are manifest in the massive migrations across national frontiers: from the south to the north as people seek to escape their dire poverty in the Third World, from the east to the west as Eastern Europeans flee from their imploding economies, and from one bordering country to another as ethnic conflicts erupt in places like Rwanda and the Sudan.

Even successful wars waged by the capitalist powers are not containable, producing shock waves that reverberate around the globe. The major conflagration of the post-communist era, the Gulf War, had repercussions far beyond the Middle East, forcing tens of thousands of oil workers to return to countries as distant as India and the Philippines. It also set in motion major internal political debates in countries as disparate as Japan and Algeria. And for George Bush the Gulf War turned out to be a largely pyrrhic victory as it did little to enhance his administration and did not usher in his much ballyhooed New World Order. Saddam Hussein remained in power, a corrupt monarchy was restored in Kuwait, and renegade countries, like Iran, refused to fall into line, even though they were antagonists of Hussein.

Technology and disorder

One can only comprehend the growing upheaval in the world by relating it to the profound technological transformations occurring under the aegis of capitalism. With the rise of capitalism in Western Europe, technological change has tended to accelerate, not at an arithmetic pace, but geometrically. This rate of change is reaching awesome proportions at the end of the twentieth century.

In communications, the transformation is perhaps the most astounding, altering the way capitalism operates on a daily basis. During the last two decades, money markets, stock exchanges and national banking systems have become intermeshed on a global scale. Twenty-four hours a day, 365 days a year, trillions of dollars in capital are transferred by electronic processes from one point of the globe to another.[4] In effect capitalism and technology are collapsing time and space.

This accelerating technological change, and its capitalist infrastructure, stand at the center of what shakes the world today. One pronounced effect, accounting for much of global instability, is the growing concentration of wealth and the spread of poverty. The decade of the 1980s was the most dismal in recent history in terms of the worldwide growth of an opulent and wealthy upper class alongside an ever more impoverished underclass. Since the advent of capitalism in Western Europe and the colonization of Latin America, Africa and Asia, fundamental inequalities have existed in the world system between and within the peripheral and core countries. But the accelerated integration of the planet in recent years has widened the gap between the rich and the poor.

For the affluent the 1980s was a splendid decade. The telecommunications revolution, the accelerated integration of the world's financial system, and the ability rapidly to move commodities and products around the globe enabled the corporate communities and the upper classes to expand their fortunes and their pleasures. In 1960, the richest 20 per cent of the globe's population had 30 times as much income as the poorest 20 per cent: by 1989 the rich had almost doubled that ratio, to 59 times as much.[5] In that same year, the planet hosted 157 billionaires and about 2 million millionaires.[6] These are the people who sup at the "grand banquet" served up by modernization and globalization.

But it is an entirely different story for much of the world's populace denied access to the grand banquet, the "castaways" of globalization.[7] In Africa and Latin America, in large parts of Asia and even in the core capitalist countries, the poor have suffered major reverses in their standard of living. Technological change driven by capitalism has produced growing unemployment, overproduction and the marginalization of increasing numbers of people.

By the beginning of this decade, the world had 100 million homeless, 400 million people so undernourished their bodies and minds were deteriorating, and over 2 billion people with inadequate or contaminated water supplies. In 1994, over one billion people lived on less than one dollar a day.[8] As the Worldwatch Institute declared in a *State of the World* report, "Following a business-as-usual course into the future could doom half of humanity to absolute poverty by sometime between 2050 and 2075."[9]

The growth in the disparity between the rich and the poor has also taken hold in some of the advanced industrialized nations, most notably the United States. As Robert Reich, the Secretary of Labor under President Clinton, has noted, "All Americans used to be in roughly the same economic boat ... We are now in different boats, one sinking rapidly."[10]

There is no longer one pattern of investment and exploitation for the Third World and another for the United States. International boundaries have been breached by the spread of technology and the quest for markets and cheap labor resources. Capital flight now ravages the United States as industries move southward, social services are gutted, and society stratifies into two tiers, one rich and opulent, the other increasingly marginalized and poor. In the last 15 years, the income of the top 5 per cent of the US population has increased by over 50 per cent when adjusted for inflation, while that of the lower 60 per cent of the population has declined.[11] While Clinton has addressed some of these problems rhetorically, his program offers little for the impoverished in the United States, other than "workfare" meaning subsistence jobs for a few while many others see their already impoverished lives worsened as the "safety net" continues to unravel. With the takeover of the US Congress in 1995 by the right wing of the Republican Party, all pretense of trying to rectify economic inequalities has been abandoned as the federal government turns the limited social programs for the poor over to the states.

The next sections of this chapter sketch the broad outlines of the unstable and conflictive world created by the rampant spread of technology and capitalism. We will explore the deterioration in civil society, the destruction of the environment, and finally the weakening hold of the capitalist state itself due to the onslaught of technology and globalization.

Fragmentation and civil society

Ours is a world more united than ever before, but also more fractionalized than ever. Capitalism has incorporated more and more people into its net through the veritable explosion of world trade and production, while at the same time it expels others, generating new divisiveness and fragmentation. Atomization on a planetary scale is pitting urban metropoles against the countryside while it divides cities internally into distinct self-interest groups.

People around the world react to the incursion of capitalism in different ways. With the collapse of communism as an alternative, there are no longer overarching ideologies or Cold War rivalries capable of mobilizing populations. In its place we are seeing diverse forms of rebellion and reaction. This growing lack of faith in state institutions accompanies the waning influence of ethical systems that previously governed people's daily lives.

In this process, traditional civil society is being shattered. The bonds of community and family used to be strong, the center of one's life. Now all this has changed. Alan Wolfe argues that the onslaught of the marketplace has undermined or destroyed many of the institutions of civil society in the developed world.[12] The family itself has increasingly become an extension of the market, rather than a social enclave set apart from it. Now more than ever, both adults in the traditional nuclear family sell their labor power outside the home, while child care, instead of being performed by a parent or grandparent, is often contracted out, usually to day care centers.

Even the institution of marriage is viewed as an economic relationship rather than as a personal or social bond. When marriages break up, the primary concern is often not for the emotional well-being of any children that may be involved, but over how the economic assets are to be divided up or over how much alimony or child support is to be paid. Many couples about to be married now recognize the centrality of economic issues by agreeing to "no fault" marriages, or by signing agreements that exclude certain assets from being considered in a divorce settlement.

While the monetarization of the marriage relationship and the family tends to be most characteristic of the middle and upper classes, the lower classes have also been hard hit by the penetration of the capitalist economy into family life. The extended family, which used to help a couple or a family member when they fell upon hard times, hardly exists today. Single-parent households, usually headed by women, have risen precipitously. This has led to the "feminization of poverty" in the United States and other countries, as the women and children have no means of support or a steady income.

In Third World countries, the spread of capitalism and capitalist relations has also taken a heavy toll on traditional civil society. As Oscar Lewis demonstrated three decades ago in his studies of poverty in Latin America, families that leave their villages to find work in the cities find themselves uprooted from their old community bonds. In the city the family may survive, albeit with less mutual help and support due to a scarcity of resources and jobs.

In many Third World cities, one of the appalling signs of the breakdown of the family and civil society is the thousands of urchins who live in the streets with no parents or adults to care for them. Orphanages, which the state or private charities used to fund, are few and far between. In cities like Tijuana, Mexico, Bombay, India, and Cairo, Egypt, children roam through the cities, scouring the garbage for food or engaging in petty thievery to survive. In La Paz, Bolivia and other cities children sniff glue, the cheapest drug available, to escape from their harsh daily realities.[13] And in some cities, like Rio de Janeiro, the authorities instead of building centers to help children, organize death squads to kill off the younger kids in the streets so that tourists or the upper classes will not have to deal with young beggars and petty thievery.

Ravaging the environment

The ravaging of the environment by modern industry and technology has dire consequences for all social sectors, rich and poor, urban and rural. This environmental disruption has generated the most cross-class, cross-cultural and transnational movement in the history of humanity. In the short span of just two and a half decades, environmental movements have been springing up and taking root around the world, in India, Brazil, South Korea and Chile, as well as in the advanced capitalist countries like Germany and the United States.

Yet in spite of these movements, the destruction of the environment has only quickened as capitalism spreads around the globe. During the years since the first Earth Day in 1970, the world has lost 200 million hectares of tree cover, an area roughly the size of the United States east of the Mississippi River. Deserts have expanded by 120 million hectares, and thousands of plant and animal species no longer exist.[14] Since 1970 the greenhouse effect has accelerated and huge holes have opened up in the ozone layer, causing a skin-cancer epidemic.

Many apologists for capitalism and even some environmentalists point to the environmental atrocities in Eastern Europe and the former Soviet Union to argue that it is human nature, or deeply ingrained patterns of human behavior, that lead to the destruction of the environment. The nuclear disaster at Chernobyl, the blackened mining towns of Romania, the polluted air of Sofia, Bulgaria, and the ravaged lands and rivers of Siberia are all examples of how communism has devastated large swathes of the earth.

But this argument ignores several fundamental realities. Firstly, the overwhelming bulk of the world's pollution and destruction is carried out by the dominant capitalist nations; secondly, the communist countries, in their drive to industrialize and survive, utilized techniques and practices developed in the capitalist world; and thirdly, communism and capitalism are *both* intertwined with modernism, the belief that nature exits to use and abuse at will. As such it is not human nature, but the logic driving these two systems that makes them unsustainable and globally destructive.[15]

Gorbachev, during his ascendancy as leader of the communist world, came to recognize that both systems were decimating the environment. In 1988 he declared that the world is not secure

> when currents of poison flow along river channels, when poisonous rains pour down from the sky, when an atmosphere polluted with industrial and transport waste chokes cities and whole regions, when the development of atomic engineering is accompanied by unacceptable risks.

To combat the ecological disasters that capitalism and communism had inflicted on the planet, he called for the United Nations to mount "a global strategy for environmental protection and the rational use of resources."[16] But it was too late for Gorbachev to act on these initiatives. The capitalist world refused to listen and the communist regimes he was the nominal leader of were by and large too encrusted and stagnant to deal with any "new thinking," particularly regarding the environment.

Some Third World revolutionary governments, like those of Nicaragua and Cuba, have acted in extraordinary circumstances to change abusive environmental practices that have been exported to Third World countries. The Sandinistas, for example, while under attack by US covert and counterinsurgency forces, began to eliminate the use of some of the agricultural pesticides that harmed the workers' health and contaminated the country's lands and rivers. And in Cuba the end of the flow of agrichemical and petroleum imports from the former communist countries combined with the US blockade has led to "the largest conversion from conventional agriculture to organic or semi-organic farming that the world has ever known," according to Peter Rosset of the Institute for Food and Development Policy.[17]

Today, it is the advanced capitalist economies that consume the bulk of the world's resources and drive the environmental devastation of the Third World. The industrialized countries use about two-thirds or more of the world's steel, aluminum, copper, lead, nickel, tin and zinc. They generate most of the world's hazardous chemical wastes, and almost 90 per cent of the chlorofluorocarbons that destroy the ozone layer. And, over the past century, their economies have pumped out over two-thirds of the greenhouse gases that threaten the world's climate. Today, the United States alone emits more carbon dioxide than Asia, Africa and Latin America put together.[18]

One interpretation of the degradation of the world's environment holds that it is due to overpopulation and the attendant pressures on available resources, particularly in the Third World. Certainly, some of the environmental destruction in the Third World is carried out by peasants and small farmers who are working new lands, often in rainforest areas. But they are given no alternative. Those who settle or work in these areas are most often impoverished people trying to eke out a living and maybe, if they are lucky, improve the lot of their children. Often they are only temporary squatters, opening up lands for large cattle-raising interests that ship much of their meat abroad.

The cause of rapid population growth in the Third World is attributable in large part to the specific form of economic exploitation carried out by the First World. As Barry Commoner points out, the Western European countries all underwent population explosions in the early stages of their industrial revolutions.[19] However, once the standard of living improved, the birth rates dropped off. The difference in the Third World is that due to the continued draining off of financial and economic resources to the First World, the Third World countries remain stuck in the early stages of industrialization. They are not able to give their populations the economic security and the standard of living that would enable them to cut back on their family size and their birth rates.

Moreover, a basic problem that many Third World countries encounter as they try to develop their economies is that the technologies and industries they get come from the core capitalist countries. The so-called "green revolution" for example, which was supposed to increase food production and alleviate hunger in the Third World, actually accelerated the introduction of environmentally harmful herbicides and pesticides and increased the use of chemical fertilizers, which damaged the rivers, lakes and water supplies.

Make no mistake about it. The capitalist world system and its attendant technological thrust are at the heart of the environmental crisis. As long as transnational corporations can move subsidiaries and products to any part of the globe in quest of maximum profits, they will continue to sack and plunder the world's resources. As Barry Commoner states:

> Substantial environmental improvement can occur only when the choice of production technology is open to social intervention

... Left to their own short-term profit-maximizing devices, future capitalists will make new environmental mistakes.[20]

In the long term, capitalism is destroying not only the environment, but also itself as it eats up its resource base and creates living conditions that are not even acceptable for the families of the ruling classes.

The decomposition of the old state system

Many orthodox economists and political scientists now recognize that the rise of the multinationals combined with the growing integration of the global economy has undermined the capacity of states to control their own societies. Even the central banks of the most powerful nations are held hostage to capital flows, volatile exchange rates and the determination of capital to move wherever it can find the most profitable investments.

Running parallel to the decreasing ability of the national states to control their national economies is the more general crisis of the international state system. Due to the spread of technology and the diffusion of economic power among the core states, the United States can no longer act as the hegemonic power, imposing its fiat and organization on the other major capitalist powers. Now without a hegemon, economic and financial markets are more volatile, and there is a growing and deepening economic rivalry among nation states that leads to calls for protectionism and the creation of regional common markets among the big powers. These economic and political tensions in the international arena will only grow in the coming years.

A provocative thesis put forth by the *Socialist Register* in its 1994 volume is that the decline of the state vis-a-vis the multinational corporation and international capital is highly exaggerated. As Leo Panitch argues in his article on 'Globalisation and the State,' "There is a tendency to ignore the extent to which today's globalisation both is authored by states and is primarily about reorganising, rather than bypassing, states."[21]

It is true that the core states are intricately involved as key agents in the process of globalization. However, in the regions where the bulk of the world's population lives – the periphery – governments find themselves increasingly weakened as international capital imposes its prerogatives on them. Moreover simply because the core states help foment the process of globalization does not mean that their economic powers go unchecked. Multinational capital is able to influence, and even dictate at times, the parameters within which the core states operate. The frequent failures of the most powerful central banks to halt the falls or rises of national currencies in Tokyo, Bonn and Washington are ample evidence of the limits of the financial authority of the leading nation states.

In effect, the modern state is becoming more and more of an administrative complex intent on performing the critical task of demobilizing the popular forces: sometimes through propaganda and ideological manipulation, at other times through direct repression. And while neutralizing the population, national governments sign new trade agreements and try to hold up the marketplace as the new utopia. This is the way they can best serve the increasingly powerful economic interests that dominate the world.

But by becoming an administrative and law enforcement complex for the neo-liberal marketplace, the modern state becomes increasingly devoid of any meaningful ideology. The state becomes brittle. It finds it more and more difficult to hold the loyalty of the masses, and it is susceptible to explosions or upheavals when difficulties arise, particularly in the urban centers.

In the past the ruling sectors have often turned to nationalism and chauvinism to hold their populations in check in times of crisis. But the end of the Cold War and the fall of communism as an enemy makes it more difficult than ever for the big Western powers to find the ideological glue to maintain the loyalties of their peoples. National chauvinist movements, which in the past were used by the capitalist classes to advance or consolidate their interests in times of crisis, have become contradictory and volatile forces from the perspective of big capital. As in Western and Eastern Europe, these extreme nationalist movements often oppose the free flow of capital and labor. They call for protectionist and anti-foreign legislation that restricts the globalization of the marketplace.

The resurgence of the nationalist movements also reveals just how limited the legitimacy of the modern state can be, especially if it tries to incorporate several different ethnic or national groups under its jurisdiction. Multinational states find it more difficult to survive today precisely because once external threats have subsided or the authoritarian structures break down, they are unable to hold their diverse nationalities together. This is what accounts not only for the break-up of the post-communist multinational states, but also for the rise of ethnic-political movements in the Third World, such as the Indian-based movements in Guatemala and Peru. Certainly the leading capitalist states are not about to collapse, but the surge in ethnic and nationalist movements does constitute a challenge to the existence of many Third World and new post-communist governments.

CHAPTER 2

The Discontents

Society waits unformed and is for a while between things ended and things begun.

Walt Whitman

The "new barbarians" will shake the very foundations of the empire with a creativity which is the evidence of a new society in the making. They are the new historical subjects, now emerging side by side with those who, in the bowels of the existing society, mobilise and struggle for a different social order.

Leonardo Boff,
Brazilian sociologist[1]

To live outside the law one must be honest.

Bob Dylan,
Bootleg Album

The discontented of today's world confront authority and the dominant ruling strata in many diffuse and disparate ways, breaking sharply with the organized revolutionary movements that have prevailed for much of this century. Among the new antagonists are radical environmental groups, militant feminists, indigenous societies and human rights organizations. The defiant also include fundamentalist religious movements – especially militant Islam – as well as the urban underclasses who engage in periodic revolts and pillage the properties and possessions of the well-to-do. All these challenges to the system of domination are "anti-systemic" in the broadest sense of the word. They shake capitalism at its roots rather than engaging in a frontal assault as the Bolsheviks and the Third World liberation movements did.

Here we will look closely at four major anti-systemic challenges. They are:

1) the growth of an underclass linked to crime and violence;
2) the ethnic movements based on race and nationality;
3) the Islamic fundamentalist movements; and
4) the urban rebellions, which are often driven by a mixture of the underclasses, the exploited nationalities and even the fundamentalists.

21

It is our view that with the collapse of Marxism and the traditional proletariat as the motors of revolution, new social actors for basic change are emerging from the growing ranks of these discontents.

Global crime and the global market

Globalization is spawning its own barbarians who are destroying it from within. The growth of a lumpen criminal class on a global scale is unprecedented. As Eduardo Galeano notes, "a culture of violence" has taken hold in our cities.[2] It is comprised of the disgruntled, the poor, the misfits, petty drug dealers and the alienated in general. Urban centers as diverse as Berlin, Managua, Moscow, Los Angeles, Nairobi, New Delhi and Caracas harbor destitute and growing social elements that live off criminal or illegal activities.

Reflecting the concerns of established society, a United Nations University study on urban crime proclaimed in its opening sentences:

> Ordinary crime is a pressing threat to life, personal integrity and property in most cities of the world. Its typically high incidence in urban environments not only challenges the very foundations of the social order, but carries with it a heavy toll of human suffering, economic waste, the despair of concerned citizens and general deterioration in the quality of life.[3]

The breakdown of civil society and traditional bonds as development occurs explains in large part the rise of violence and crime around the world. The United Nations University study notes that it is not simply the initial stages of development that cause crime. Rather crime tends to increase as "modernization" and "industrialization" advance and deepen. Thus the study found that crime rates against property were four times as high in the developed countries as in the newly developing societies.[4]

Aside from revealing the delegitimization and breakdown of authority, the spread of crime is a reaction to the crass materialism and fetishism of commodities that is at the core of contemporary capitalism. It is a major virus inherent in capitalism as it spreads to every nook and cranny of the world. It eats away at the very fabric of society, making people more and more cynical as they see that the rich take what they want, and then taunt the rest of society through the media, the movies and advertising with the "good life" of consumerism.

The old "work hard/get ahead" values are collapsing, undermining the Weberian belief that the rise of capitalism, hard work and the puritan ethic are all interlinked. A survivalist logic leads people to take what they need or believe they are entitled to instead of working for it. From Milikin's junk bond scams to the surge in petty crime at the grassroots, few respect the law. Laws are viewed increasingly as obstacles to be overcome rather than as binding rules.

The mass media through its enshrinement of consumerism has now so permeated virtually all societies of the world – First, Second and Third – that rampant materialism is the dominant ethos. Be it the advanced and hedonistic consumerism of the First World, or the migration of people from the Second and Third Worlds to the metropolitan centers, the goal and objective is the same – to gain access to material luxuries and the good life. Except for a very few isolated pockets, there are no longer totally separate or independent cultures and societies. They have now all been penetrated by a specific form of secularism, the market economy which drives people to possess commodities.

Even more traditional analysts who support capitalism as a system recognize that the spread of consumerist values is an integral part of the rise of criminality and global disorder. In his work, *Out of Control: Global Turmoil on the Eve of the 21st Century*, Zbigniew Brzezinski, asserts that a "permissive cornucopia" has become the new utopia replacing old religious and ideological values in the world. The Western world through the media spreads materialism and consumerism as the paramount values. In 1965, there were only 180 million television sets in the world. Today there are well over a billion. With one television for every five people, almost everyone in the world has a visual conception (colored of course by the ideologies and biases of the media) of what other people in distant countries or continents are doing and how they are living. Provincial, isolated views of the world are eclipsed, making interests more global and at the same time more insatiable.[5]

Those in a position to participate in the permissive cornucopia sold by the media orientate their lives around the accumulation of material pleasures and goods to the detriment of more important values that deal with the quality of life. Simultaneously, much of the world's population, unable to obtain many of these goods, grows frustrated, resentful and rebellious.

The ethnic challenge

A very different type of challenge to the existent order stems from the diverse ethnic movements. In earlier centuries, Indians, Negroes, Latin and Anglo-Saxon ethnic groups were distinct cultures, often largely isolated from each other. But Western expansionism during the past 500 years, facilitated by repeated revolutions in transportation and communications, has ended this isolation.

Racial and cultural miscegenation has occurred within every group, and more importantly, virtually all these groups interact with and influence one another. As Immanuel Wallerstein notes, "The network of groups is intricately cross-hatched. Some Blacks, but not all Blacks, are women; some Moslems, but not all Moslems, are Black; some intellectuals are Moslems; and so on ad infinitum."[6]

How then, given this mix, does one explain the surge in the nationalist and ethnic movements in recent history? According to Ernest Gellner in *Nations and Nationalism*, there are 200 states and at least 800 movements of effective nationalism, plus 7000 potential nationalisms if ethnic identity is taken as the premise.[7] This is another of the contemporary contradictions: while the global system throws distinct ethnic groups and cultures together, many of them step up their fight for autonomy and identity in a seemingly hostile, or at best, indifferent world.

Ethnic and national struggles have different roots and dimensions. But a central factor is the electronic globalization of the media, which gives peoples the capacity to understand their ethnic or national particularities and identities.[8] It also enables them to understand the exploitation they may be subjected to, and to begin sharing experiences and organizing in order to challenge that exploitation.

The national liberation movements have for much of this century constituted the most powerful form of national struggle. They combines an ideology along with a capacity to mobilize around national identity issues to challenge neo-colonial or colonial systems of exploitation. Revolutions and struggles in Vietnam, Cuba, Mozambique, Angola, Nicaragua, South Africa and El Salvador are classic national liberation movements. But they appear to have peaked, unable to overcome barriers to economic development. They have also lost much of their capacity to democratically mobilize the masses. (See Chapter 5 for a more extensive discussion of the national liberation movements.)

Other forms of ethnic and national struggles are the indigenous movements and the intra-ethnic rivalries. The Indian rights movements of the Western hemisphere are notable in that they raise issues that go beyond demands for mere changes in the existent nation states. These indigenous movements want to make fundamental changes in modern society, changes that often merge with the demands of environmental movements. As Russel Means, a founder of the American Indian Movement, notes, "It is only a matter of time before what Westerns would call a 'major catastrophe of global proportions' takes place. It will be the job of the Amerindian peoples, of all the 'natural' populations to survive."[9]

Both the Indian and environmental movements have gathered force since the 1960s and 1970s, and both have a fundamental critique of how contemporary industrial society is destroying the planet. The Indian movement in particular has put forth pre-modern values that are critical in the forging of a new moral and ideological framework for rescuing the world from destruction. The respect for nature, the understanding of life and death as part of a cosmic process, and the need to treat with respect all the living forms around us are among the values that will help us get beyond the current global destructiveness of capitalism.

A strong current within the feminist movement also identifies with the ethnic movements and the need to preserve the environment against the destructiveness of capitalism and modernization. As Lourdes Arizpe notes in the Preface to *Feminist Perspectives on Sustainable Development*, "A feminist perspective that looks at women not as victims but as agents of change has strong commonalities with other movements seeking a more sustainable future for humanity."[10] Several articles within the book portray women in ethnic or indigenous movements as providing alternatives to the capitalist development of the Third World.[11]

Intra-ethnic conflicts

A major scourge of the world in the 1990s is the intra-ethnic clashes. By and large they are not movements against capitalism or against Western systems of exploitation. The civil war in Ethiopia, the conflicts in India and ethnic cleansing in the former Yugoslavia – these are all conflicts with roots that cannot be blamed simply on imperialism.

Samir Amin however argues that even these conflicts do have links to the capitalist world system in that imperialism has fostered weak, ineffectual and economically insolvent states.[12] It is these weakened states which are subjected to military coups and to the repression of human and democratic rights. Stagnant or declining internal economies, often the product of conditions in the world market, help foster these conflicts, particularly when two or more ethnic groups live under the same state structure. Economic inequalities feed ethnic distrust, setting off battles that undermine or even destroy the central state.

While some of these ethnic rivalries are exploited and manipulated by imperialism, many of them actually run counter to the interests and needs of global capital. The ethnic fissures that have opened up in the former Yugoslavia and throughout Eastern Europe are generating significant dangers and problems for the developed capitalist world, particularly for Western Europe and the United States. A broader war could erupt in this region that draws in Greece, Turkey and even Russia, thereby compelling a response by the Western powers. Already, the flow of war-battered migrants from these ethnic wars is destabilizing Western European societies, as demonstrated by the violence perpetrated against immigrants in Germany. For Kohl, Clinton and other Western leaders, these are destabilizing conflicts, adversely affecting the continued expansion of the capitalist world.

The fundamentalist rebellions

With the collapse of communism and the decline of the national liberation movements, the most coherent challenge to the Western world comes from Islamic fundamentalism. One-fifth of humanity is Muslim, and the fundamentalism sweeping this religion is a powerful force in today's world.

Islamic fundamentalism is a complex and contradictory movement with reactionary and progressive tendencies. In Arabic and Middle Eastern societies it has galvanized the masses as no other ideology or religion in recent history. It draws much of its strength from the fact that it is challenging both Zionist and Western values. Not only Western interventionism, but many Westernizing influences, such as consumerism, the destruction of civil society and even the spread of capitalism in the Arab world are opposed by fundamentalists.

Islamic fundamentalism is not simply a reactive movement. In a number of Middle Eastern societies it has revitalized civil society, spawning a whole new array of social groups and organizations. Medical clinics, day-care centers, mutual support societies and small-scale commercial associations are some of the institutions that have flourished along with a renewed vitality and emphasis on "family values" and community cooperation.

Based on a reading of the Koran that prohibits "chasing money with money," or the earning of interest, some Islamic groups have placed an emphasis on productive and small-scale "working" investments. Speculative or banking capital is despised as immoral and exploitative. Most fundamentalists view with disgust the Western financial investments and the opulence of the Sheiks and the rulers of countries like Saudi Arabia and Kuwait. Many fundamentalists believe in a much simpler and more egalitarian society, one free of the extremes of wealth and poverty, and one not all that different from what many environmentalists in the Western world would advocate. They are not anti-technological, but they do believe in adopting only those technological advances that are compatible with a more just Islamic society.[13]

The problem is that these popular and egalitarian values are interwoven with a strong authoritarian and hierarchical approach that is often intolerant of other societies and religions. Women in particular suffer from a subservient status in the patriarchal Islamic order. Even more insidiously, fundamentalist leaders launch "holy wars" not only against Western interventionist forces but also in opposition to moderate political leaders and peoples within their own societies. As is demonstrated in the Gaza Strip and the West Bank of Palestine, the fundamentalists are willing to actively oppose secular liberation movements like the PLO when they pursue political paths with which the fundamentalists disagree. And in countries like Egypt and Algeria the fundamentalist movements are carrying out holy wars directed not only against governments that are corrupt and undemocratic, but also against innocent foreigners and civilians who are not involved with the governments.[14]

In Iran, the one country where the fundamentalists hold state power, they have repressed the more democratic tendencies within Islam. The Iranian regime may have stood up to Western imperialism, but it has also slaughtered thousands of leftists, many of whom were also opponents of the Shah and Western intervention. The Iranian state officially denounces communism, as it does the West, but in its effort to impose its religious worldview it has adopted an authoritarian system not unlike that of the old communist states.

The fundamentalist movement is extremely diverse, covering an immense area running from Morocco and Algeria to Pakistan and the Philippines. In Bosnia-Herzegovina, the Islamic Muslim movement is involved in the defense of its peoples and their very existence against reactionary, genocidal forces. So it is difficult to make absolute generalizations, even about how women are treated under Islam.

While Islamic women are formally relegated to a subservient status in the family, fundamentalism has in fact enabled many women to break their traditional fetters and to become active participants in their societies. Islamic fundamentalist women, while adopting the traditional Muslim dress, are quite often far more liberated than their mothers and other Muslim women who do not embrace fundamentalism. They help organize community groups, have a broad social interest, and participate in the political life of their societies. The repression of women in the Arab world is generally more absolute in traditional societies like Kuwait, where women cannot vote and are forced to stay at home.

Islam is more like Protestantism than Catholicism in that there is no single head of the movement nor a fixed body of decrees and moral statements that are handed down from above. The Western reaction to Islam does not recognize this, often portraying fundamentalism – like communism in the post-World War II world – as a monolithic, expansive and totalitarian movement, inherently "evil" and threatening to the rest of the world. Western progressive movements should not fall into this trap. While condemning the authoritarian and repressive tendencies of Islam, there is a need to understand the more populist currents of fundamentalism that are striving to develop their own identity in a world battered by the onslaught of degrading Western materialist values.

In spite of the Islamic movement's contradictory characteristics, it is an important social and political upheaval that is yet another deep-seated, systematic challenge to Western capitalism and many of the degrading values it represents. As such Islamic fundamentalism is part of the new polycentric world of values and beliefs that is taking shape as the capitalist world becomes more tumultuous.

The urban upheavals

The atomization of societies, the growing polarization of wealth and poverty, the ethnic disputes and rivalries, and the rise of fundamentalism are all most potently manifested in the urban areas of the world. Although peasant movements are still important, they are in decline. It is the cities where discontent and upheaval are most pronounced.

To understand this phenomena, it is instructive to begin by looking at two vastly different cities that have experienced major upheavals or rebellions in recent years. Lima, Peru, with over 8 million people, is a Third World capital steeped in poverty and political violence. In the northern hemisphere, Los Angeles, with over 10 million people and an economy larger than that of many Third World countries, is one of the principal cities of the developed industrial world.

In spite of their tremendous differences, both Lima and Los Angeles display similar social and economic characteristics. Both are swelled with immigrants – internal or international – who come questing for opportunity and a better life. And both cities are fully integrated into the capitalist world. The corporate and business elites, and even sectors of the middle class, of these two cities are connected to the world through modern telecommunications, computers and air travel.

Both cities also have their alienated underclasses who have become disillusioned and cynical about the old values of succeeding through hard work and diligence. And both cities are unable to control their increasing violence and crime. As any visitor or tourist who goes to Lima can testify, theft and robbery are rampant. And Los Angeles is also a violent city with an average of 35 crimes officially reported every hour of the day, of which 10 are listed as violent crimes such as murder, rape or aggravated assault.[15]

The Los Angeles uprising in April 1992 starkly revealed that many core capitalist urban centers are acquiring social and political characteristics that make them increasingly similar to many Third World societies. It is not simply the racial mix involved in the Los Angeles upheaval – Mexicans, Central Americans and Koreans as well as African-Americans – that gave the Los Angeles disturbances a Third World content. What went almost unnoticed is that the Los Angeles rebellion was part of a hemispheric, and even global, process of urban upheaval that has been going on for over a decade.

In the Western hemisphere, cities as divergent as São Paulo, Mexico City, Santo Domingo, Caracas and Guatemala City have all experienced major urban rebellions and riots in recent years.[16] While each of these urban uprisings has specific characteristics and causes, common factors have fomented urban unrest in over a dozen major urban centers extending from Buenos Aires in the south to Los Angeles in the north.

The first notable factor in these urban uprisings is that they have been a reaction to neo-liberal economic policies. In the early 1980s the Reagan administration began imposing its neo-liberal policies internationally, particularly through the International Monetary Fund. Hardly a country in Latin America was untouched as the IMF and US government agencies insisted on the implementation of austerity programs that slashed social spending in critical areas such as education and health care. State spending on public transportation as well as basic food subsidies was also curtailed or ended. Moreover, the IMF often insisted that "inefficient industries" controlled by the state be shut down or privatized, thereby increasing unemployment, particularly in the urban areas.

The result was a series of urban rebellions throughout Latin America. One of the more dramatic upheavals occurred in Santo Domingo, the capital of the Dominican Republic. When the government in 1984 doubled the prices of all imported goods and raised the prices on domestic foodstuffs, people took to the streets, igniting a massive wave of protests. Gangs of youths set up barricades of burning tires and pelted police with stones. Stores were looted, and even though the military was sent in, the riots continued for almost a week. The upheaval left 60 dead, hundreds injured and thousands arrested.

Variants of this urban upheaval subsequently occurred throughout Latin America. In 1985 Guatemala City erupted due to an increase in bus fares and steep hikes in the price of bread and milk. Public, primary and secondary students joined with people from the poorer barrios to protest the austerity measures. In Buenos Aires demonstrators took to the streets on a number of occasions between 1983 and 1985, protesting a series of IMF-dictated austerity measures. In Buenos Aires, often called the Paris of South America because of its relative prosperity, the hard-hit trade unions and the lower classes shut down the city and on some occasions looted stores.

The Los Angeles rebellion in 1992 was also a direct result of neo-liberal economic policies which cut social services, raised unemployment and forced many to live on the streets. In the wake of the riots, the Bush administration at first cynically tried to cover up the harsh impact of spending cutbacks and urban austerity policies by claiming that the riots were the result of the Great Society and the liberal policies of the 1960s. Then the administration declared that what Los Angeles needed was "free enterprise business zones" to deal with unemployment. In fact US census statistics reveal that between 1980 and 1990 the plight of US cities worsened dramatically, while "free enterprise" was more rampant than ever in the major metropolitan centers of the United States. Reaganomics and supply-side economics simply increased the wealth of the upper classes living in the suburbs as the budgets of the cities were slashed and the standard of living of the people in the core cities dropped precipitously.

Aside from being a reaction to neo-liberal economic policies, another characteristic that the upheavals south of the US border have in common with the Los Angeles uprising is that they involve the lumpen, the working poor and the most marginalized sectors of society. In some of these uprisings, trade unions, leftist political parties and even churches have also been involved in launching the protests. But the demonstrations frequently escape from the control of these organizations and become urban riots in which people rampage through the streets, sacking and burning stores. To use a phrase in vogue after the Los Angeles riots, it is the "urban underclass" that has become the most explosive element in these upheavals as they vent their anger, their desperation and their hostility towards the dominant society.

This dynamic was apparent in a string of urban protests in Brazil in the 1980s. They often began with the support of trade unions and some political organizations. But in cities like São Paulo and Rio de Janeiro the protests grew violent as people from the favelas, or poorer areas of the cities, moved in to loot food stores and confront the police and military. Protests in the mid-1980s in Santiago, Chile, and Port au Prince, Haiti, were similar in that the populace from the most marginalized barrios provided the raw kindling for the urban riots. They shook the dictatorial governments of both countries to their foundations and led to the eventual downfall of Augusto Pinochet in Chile and "Baby Doc" Duvalier in Haiti.

Although one certainly cannot compare the political impact of the upheaval in Los Angeles to the changes in Chile and Haiti, it is nonetheless important to note that these urban upheavals are often direct responses to repressive authority. In Los Angeles, it is the urban police force, in others cases it is the military that come under attack for having beaten and abused the poorer sectors of the urban population. In the early stages of the uprisings, the police and military authorities were often momentarily stunned, paralyzed and forced to withdraw by the hatred, anger and fury of the demonstrators.

These urban rebellions also tend to display a growing popular disgruntlement and alienation from all established political authority, be it elected or militarily imposed. People around the hemisphere are simply fed up with politicians and politics as usual, especially the political corruption that has come to characterize many of the new neo-liberal "modernizing" governments. Here the case of the urban riots in Caracas, Venezuela, in February 1989 is particularly revealing. A month earlier, Carlos Andrés Perez, a Social Democrat, took office after campaigning against the incumbent Christian Democrats on a platform of opposition to IMF policies. Once in power, however, he imposed a series of cutbacks in state social spending and raised prices on basic foods. The result was five days of looting and clashes in Caracas as tens of thousands took to the streets and 247 people were killed.

This sense of betrayal by the established politicians explains why large sectors of the populace of Venezuela were generally supportive of the military coup attempt in early 1992 by a group of young officers. Although Venezuela has the longest uninterrupted democratic rule of any country in South America, the Venezuelan people have simply had enough of civilian politicians who make election promises and then proceed to abandon them while enriching themselves at the expense of the rest of the country. This popular discontent was the motor that ultimately forced Andrés Perez out of office in mid-1993.

The riots in Santiago del Estero, Argentina, in December 1993 were also a reflection of the urban backlash against corrupt politicians. Carlos Menem, like Andrés Perez, had come into office as a reformist, pro-labor president, but he promptly proceeded to implement neo-liberal economic policies that produced prosperity only for the well-to-do. The conditions of the poor and working classes of Argentina changed little, while the politicians, particularly governors in the provinces, enriched themselves. When public employees in Santiago del Estero with monthly salaries of $350 were not paid for three months (while the heads of the provincial government continued to receive up to $60,000 per month) the employees set off public riots, sending political and economic shock waves throughout Argentina.

This process of urban upheaval against corruption, repression and neo-liberal economic policies is by no means unique to the Americas. The major urban centers of Morocco, the Sudan, Liberia, Turkey and the Philippines have also experienced severe urban disturbances in recent years. In the cases of Algiers and Cairo, urban inequalities and excessive government corruption combined with Islamic fundamentalism have precipitated urban revolts. And the urban riots in recent years in Seoul, South Korea, and Bangkok, Thailand, are also part of the global reaction to political and military/police repression in which the marginal urban underclasses, often with middle-class allies, are pitted against the dominant political and business classes that are intent on "modernizing" their societies.

As we move into the twenty-first century, the urban centers of the world will continue to be hotbeds of discontent and political revolt. It is here that progressive organizers must sink deep roots if they are to project a new political and social agenda with mass support.

The threat to authority

These diverse and diffuse challenges occurring throughout the world are not about to overthrow capitalism. They are too disorganized and disunited, they have different ends and means of struggle, and above all they lack a coherent unifying ideology. In a certain sense many of these anti-systemic challenges can be likened to the manner in which disparate forces, including lawless barbarians, undermined the Roman Empire. The drug dealers and common criminals along with the most repressed and marginalized sectors of the globalization process gnaw away at capitalist society from the inside.

The nation states are also being challenged by these and other social forces from below. As Richard Falk notes in *Explorations at the Edge of Time*, there are several different types of "evasion" practised by people against the modern state. There are "evasions across" boundaries, such as the international peace movements; there are "evasions within" a given state, such as the civil disobedience and war resister movements in the United States; and there are "evasions beyond" the control of sovereign states, such as drug exports from one country to another, or greenhouse warming.[17]

While Falk's three categories are useful, the content of each needs to be substantially deepened to understand why the modern state is facing major problems. The "evasions across" national boundaries also include the migration of peoples across borders, from south to north, and now increasingly from east to west. Even the most powerful states find it difficult to control these migrations. Big capital does not respect national boundaries as it searches for the best way to get the cheapest raw materials and the cheapest labor, nor do migrant laborers proclaim their state loyalty as they pass from one country to another in quest of better jobs.

The "evasions within" include not only militant pacifist actions but also the urban upheavals against the state and its version of law and order. They are dramatic illustrations of how tenuous ideological and even repressive controls can be over the more exploited and deprived sectors of a society. And the "evasions beyond" the modern state's control include forces like Islamic fundamentalism and Third World nationalist movements as well as environmental movements.

It is certainly possible to argue that all these anti-systemic challenges could lead to a modern form of barbarism as societies and the major urban centers of the globe degenerate under the strains of internal violence and civil conflicts. However, another view is that the very diversity of all these movements is their strength, that in the long run a new postmodern society will emerge that includes all these disparate and different groups that are the castaways of the Great Banquet.[18]

These postmodern cultures and organizations are so imbued and deeply entrenched throughout the world that today's dominant ruling institutions will never be able to reclaim anything akin to the relatively stable world order that existed from the end of World War II until the 1960s. Global capitalism is ulcerating, bleeding from internal wounds. The diverse challenges to the system will only grow in importance in the coming years, assuming directions that cannot even be envisioned.

free market → growth in unemployment
→ cut back in welfare

→ looting rioting

CHAPTER 3

The Crisis of Western Ideology

Of one thing we can be certain. The ideologies of the twentieth century will disappear completely. This has been a lousy century. It has been filled with dogmas, dogmas that one after another have cost us time, suffering, and much injustice.

Gabriel García Márquez[1]

This then is our challenge, the creation of a new left ideology in a time of disintegration of the historical system within which we live.

Immanuel Wallerstein[2]

The capitalist democracies have vanquished their twentieth century antagonist, communism, and with this victory the liberal democratic ideal has become ascendant. As Francis Fukuyama argues in his controversial treatise, *The End of History and the Last Man*, the model of liberal democracy with free markets has emerged triumphant. It is a "worldwide liberal revolution," he declares, as authoritarian governments of the right and left have fallen. There may be reverses in this or that country, as well as "peaks and troughs" of democratic change, but there is "a Universal History of mankind in the direction of liberal democracy."[3] Almost inadvertently Fukuyama does admit that "what is emerging victorious ... is not so much liberal practice as the liberal idea."[4] Herein lies the fatal flaw in the triumph of liberal democracy – the growing breach between the practice and the ideal of democracy. At its very apogee liberal democracy, due to its marriage to international capital, is becoming a shell.

Capitalist democracy may be ascendant but its denizens are increasingly disillusioned and alienated by their political systems. With globalization, the diverse societies of the planet are exposed to the ideology of liberal democracy but big capital and the transnationals are undermining it by stratifying societies and demanding the subservience of politicians and political parties to their global economic interests.

Formal democratic regimes have emerged in countries as varied as the Philippines, Russia and Nicaragua. However, for most of their citizens, democracy has little relevance as they struggle to survive amid the harsh economic realities of the free market. And in many of the old Western democracies, especially the United States, political institutions are largely unresponsive and political cynicism is pervasive. Meanwhile, the rich and powerful, who generally give lip service to democracy, have come to embody democracy's antithesis. They live increasingly in the modern equivalent of the old royal palaces and fortresses replete with retainers, guards and security systems. They isolate their children and families from the spreading misery and desperation of the masses, setting up private schools and hospitals, their own social clubs and privatized transportation systems including limousines and private jets.

New + top class

The collapse of the "isms"

Today all the variants of Western political ideology that trace their origins to the French Revolution – conservatism, liberalism and socialism – have exhausted themselves. They are no longer political philosophies capable of inspiring or captivating the imaginations of their peoples. As Edward Hyams notes, "Capitalism turns men into economic cannibals: and having done so, mistakes economic cannibalism for human nature."[5] All too many people, rather than being participants in a democratic community, have become economic automatons or, even worse, driven to crime and violence in order to survive. In this era of globalization, the crisis of liberal democracy has become the crisis of Western civilization itself.

Jack of flags

Sectors of the dominant classes, particularly the neo-liberals in the United States do call for the restoration of traditional "Western values," like hard work, order and discipline. But this is an ideological veneer used mainly to assault the bulk of the globe's marginalized populace in an effort to keep them in line so the elites can enjoy their privileges and pleasures undisturbed. Neo-liberalism's fundamental program on a global level is only that of more authoritarianism, using brute force and repression when necessary to contain the masses or any dissident movement. It is the most visceral pseudo-democratic philosophy put forth by the Western world since the age of laissez-faire capitalism in the late nineteenth century. Western political ideology as a force capable of advancing the common interests of the body politic is increasingly moribund.

Fukuyama, with his enshrinement of liberal democracy, fails to realize that historically it is just when political systems become pervasive that they begin to erode internally and new political organisms emerge. In the mid-eighteenth century, the monarchy in Europe appeared to be "universal" and the only viable system of political rule. Many of the philosophers of that century did argue for greater liberties to one degree or another, but few questioned the right of monarchs to rule and to pass their crowns on from one generation to another. In the early nineteenth century, Hegel, who Fukuyama draws on for the philosophical concept of "universal history," posited that constitutional monarchy was the ultimate system of government.

The problems and crises that capitalist as well as communist governments have faced during the past quarter century are fundamentally different from the crises that they have confronted in the past. It is no accident that intellectuals and commentators of diverse perspectives today speak of "post" or "end" societies: postmodernism, post-industrialism, post-Marxism and poststructuralism. These terms and perspectives, sometimes contradictory to each other, are used in an effort to explain or understand the difficulties that one or another of the political and economic systems are confronting at this moment in world history.

Western Europe, the birthplace of the "isms" that have driven the twentieth-century world, encapsulates the contemporary ideological crisis. There, anti-communism as a mobilizing force was in descent well before the collapse of Eastern Europe and the Soviet Union. The anti-nuclear and environmental movements by the early 1980s had mobilized large sectors of the Western European population to move beyond the sterile anti-communism of their governments and the NATO alliance. Then when Mikhail Gorbachev began to end the Cold War and to call for the incorporation of the Soviet Union into the "Common House of Europe," his popularity soared throughout Western Europe. Polls showed that he enjoyed more support than any of the national leaders of Europe. History, of course, has recorded his political failure to revive communism, but what his popularity in Western Europe and elsewhere reflected was the longing of peoples for a new politics and ideology that would end international conflict and enable humanity to construct cooperative, participatory and authentically democratic societies.

The Socialist, or Social Democratic, parties of Western Europe, like their Democratic counterparts in the United States, offer little that fills the ideological void of the late twentieth century. François Mitterrand in France and Felipe Gonzalez in Spain made a mockery of European social democracy with their efforts to appease private capital by cutting back on social spending while undermining the trade union movement. The British Labour Party in recent years has expelled or marginalized some of its militant and dynamic members, who were searching for innovative, grassroots solutions to Great Britain's many problems. Recently the party has even turned against the trade unions, substantially reducing their role in the party decision-making. + then there was Tony

The French Revolution, which enabled the bourgeoisie to secure political power and to consolidate bourgeois democracy, took as its principal slogan the refrain of "liberté, égalité et fraternité." Today one would be hard put in France or any other capitalist democracy to find a majority of the population that believes their governments are advancing the causes of liberty, equality and human fellowship. People are increasingly disenchanted and disgruntled with their governments and view them as governments "of, by and for" the dominant elites.

What are the roots of these difficulties and crises that afflict the post-communist and Third World countries, as well as the world's leading capitalist powers? Is it simply a historic coincidence that the two great ideological antagonists of the twentieth century, capitalism and communism, have reached a dead end or impasse at the same historic moment? Or is it due to some underlying forces that are at work in this era of globalization, forces that are laying the bases for a new ideological and political framework?

Immanuel Wallerstein argues that the demise of social democracy as well as communism is only logical given the fact that they – like liberalism and conservatism – have their ideological fountainhead in the French Revolution, which has spent itself on the global level.[6] This perspective however begs the question of why they have failed.

Wallerstein does not recognize that a fundamental defect of all four political variants is not simply their ties to liberalism and the French Revolution but the disposition of all of them to become ensnared in the quest for state power and the use of the state to advance their interests and political philosophies. It is the culture of domination – particularly as it manifested itself through state power and imperialism – that is under siege, not simply liberalism. Liberals, social democrats and communists as well as conservatives, all started in one form or another by opposing the existing state, but once they held state power they wound up reinforcing it in order to discipline or control vast sectors of the population.

The climax of Western civilization

The world is entering a new stage of history, one we choose to call the climax of Western civilization. (We use the word "climax" quite intentionally because it means that Western civilization may be exhausting itself at the same time as it is in full bloom in terms of its expansiveness and creativity – the same was also true of Greek civilization from about 350 to 250 BC.) Simply put, most of the values of domination and exploitation that have been at the core of Western civilization and the rise of capitalism for the past half-millennium are now under siege. There is a growing rejection and insurgency against the historic forms of domination, control and hierarchy that exist in virtually all societies. The challenge to these central characteristics of Western civilization has recently been most visible in the communist world, but it permeates the capitalist world as well, affecting both developed and underdeveloped societies. There is a global questioning of the current political and social orders to a degree that has not been witnessed since Western civilization began its outward expansion.

This new epoch of ideological, social and political upheaval began in the 1960s, with the year 1968 marking a historic turning point. In that year the world was engulfed in a series of political and social revolts of which the most dramatic were the Paris uprising in May, the Prague spring of "socialism with a human face," the student uprising in Mexico, and the political turmoil in the United States, which reached its peak at the Democratic convention in Chicago.

None of these movements or uprisings were victorious. Indeed they each met with defeat in the same year: de Gaulle weathered the general strike and remained in power in France, Soviet tanks rolled into Czechoslovakia, students were slaughtered in Tlateloclo Square in Mexico, and Richard Nixon won the presidential election in the United States. And yet the events of 1968 changed the world. They were similar to the revolutions of 1848 in Western Europe in that although they failed, they marked the beginning of a entirely new political era.[7] The social movements and political forces that were unleashed in 1968 could never be contained or eliminated. They questioned not only the existing political systems, but also the social values and relations that exist between races, sexes, communities, nations and individuals. Today we are witnessing the deepening of the struggles that burst into the open in 1968 as the old ideologies flounder and many of the central characteristics of Western civilization – its expansionism, its system of domination and its ruthless exploitation of human and natural resources – are being challenged as never before.

Three factors or forces produced the ideological upheaval and the generation of the 1960s. One factor was economic, but not the usually adverse one in the sense of a recession or economic slump. To the contrary it was the tremendous post-war boom throughout the developed capitalist world that opened up space and produced a generation of optimists who believed the world truly could be transformed. It seems almost implausible now, but in the 1960s there was a generalized belief in the Western world that economic growth and expansion could go on forever, producing prosperity for everyone. The United States still possessed the bulk of the developed world's wealth, but the astonishingly rapid recovery from the war in Western Europe created an aura of prosperity and the belief that a bright future lay ahead.

Secondly, the arrogance and miscalculation of US imperialism was also a central factor in creating the upheaval of the 1960s. The war in Vietnam was surely the biggest blunder by any of the big powers in the twentieth century. John F. Kennedy's refrain of "We will bear any burden, pay any price" reflects the imperial arrogance at work. It is little different from Kipling's nineteenth-century assertion that the British had to bear the "white man's burden." This attitude led the United States to totally enmesh itself in Vietnam, thereby leading to social turmoil in the United States, and to the undermining of its ideological leadership of the Western world.

The final factor behind the 1960s upheaval was the resilience of the Third World liberation movements. The Cuban Revolution in 1959, followed by a historic upsurge in Third World armed struggles in south-east Asia, Latin America and Africa made the decade in many ways the decade of the Third World. This Third World struggle became globalized as sectors of society within the First World were inspired by the liberation struggles. Important groups in the United States and Western Europe recognized the basic justice of the Third World struggles and challenged the imperialist policies of their own governments.

The culture of power in capitalist and Marxist societies

Since the 1960s, the crisis of the dominant social order has only deepened. The essence of the contemporary crisis lies not simply in the developments of that decade but in the erosion of the entire system of rule and domination that prevails in much of the world. It is a crisis not only of the state but of the entire culture of domination that is at the core of Western civilization.

Both capitalist and communist governments are in a certain sense authoritarian regimes, regimes that once in power, rule from above with the constant objective of manipulating society and the social forces below so as to remain in power indefinitely. The actual heads of government may change, but the regimes themselves remain intact until there is a massive upheaval or explosion, such as that which occurred in Eastern Europe in 1989.

The twentieth-century states, be they neo-liberal, social democratic or communist, have remarkably similar dynamics. They are all driven by a basic division of labor, between the rulers and the governed, between the central committee and the proletariat, or between the state and civil society. This does not mean that the socialist vision has no role to play in the future evolution of civilization, as will be discussed in Chapter 9. But it does mean that "actually existing socialism" has failed.

The socialism that sprang to life in the early twentieth century was severely crippled from the beginning, firstly because it emerged in the more underdeveloped countries and, secondly, because it was encircled and had to continually fight for its existence against a much more powerful capitalist world. In their struggle for survival, the new socialist societies more often then not borrowed many of the strategies, structures and tactics of the capitalist world. This is most evident in the fact that in communist as well as capitalist societies a fundamental division has existed between the rulers and the ruled. First the capitalist, and then the communist states, were able to generate a culture of political power that penetrated down to the grassroots or popular level. Any group that wanted to make changes generally looked upward, to the rulers for the ratification of such changes. The structure of power was vertical.

In communist and capitalist states some structures came into existence for channeling discontent or input from below. These channels included periodic elections for representatives, the ability to pressure for legislation, or the right to join a vanguard or political party. But these channels have always been controlled and limited: society, or groups from below, are never allowed to make radical changes, to legally question or overturn the basic structure of power.

Another common dynamic in both capitalist and communist states is the drive to accumulate capital. The disparities in income may have been somewhat less in communist societies, but both economic systems have rested on a division of labor that enables a small elite (the bourgeoisie or the state managers) to run and dominate the economic systems while the rest of the society is relegated to subservient roles. Once again, just as in the political system, people may be allowed to move up the economic, managerial or bureaucratic ladders, but only with the acquiescence of those who dominate the economic system and its enterprises. In the economic system, even more than the political, there is no real space for any authentic form of democratic or popular participation. Those who enter the economy, as workers, bureaucrats, teachers, and so on, must fully accept the authority of those in charge. Anyone who refuses to accept the "rules of the game" is simply discharged. Those workers who become too unruly in their complaints are blacklisted (under capitalism) or given the most menial and alienating jobs (under communism).

The challenge to communism and capitalism in the late twentieth century goes beyond a mere questioning of these vertical political and economic systems – it is also a challenge to the very values that these societies are impregnated with. This is why one can refer to this systemic challenge as a crisis of the Western culture of power. This culture of power permeates virtually all institutions and values of contemporary civilization. It is present in the exploitation of woman by man, in the heterosexual worldview and the repression of homosexuality, in the division that exists between physical and intellectual labor, and in the ruthless exploitation of the environment by industry. All these forms of exploitation go far beyond what Marx and Engels described and denounced in nineteenth-century capitalist societies.

The rise of the culture of power

This culture of power is rooted in the fifteenth and sixteenth centuries when Western Europe began its expansion and the nation state was consolidated. Its birth in the political form came with the rise of the national monarchies. The example par excellence is that of Louis XIV of France, who extended his power throughout the country, controlling the nobility, the peasantry, and even the merchants and the incipient bourgeoisie.[8] While these monarchical regimes were by no means capitalistic states, they did provide the stability and the conditions for capitalism to take hold in many nooks and crannies. The monarchical regimes did heavily tax the merchants and entrepreneurs, but the monarchs also enabled them to begin accumulating capital in local markets and to help build the emergent global system of exploitation.

The original political theorist of the emergent culture of power was Machiavelli. Anything was permitted to consolidate the "power of the prince." No action was considered immoral by the prince if it were carried out in order to assert his rule and extend his domain and power. This marks the conception of the secular state, the state in which the ends, political and economic power, justify any means.

The Western culture of power became internationalized with the outward expansion of Europe and the growing strength of merchants and capitalist production. The native peoples of Africa, the Americas and most of Asia were all forced to submit to European rule and economic exploitation in one form or another. And with this rule came the implantation of European "civilization" and its values.[9] The forms of exploitation and power the Western conquerors used were varied, some old, some new. But they were given a particular twist and intensity by the rise of capitalism.

The development of modern slavery in particular reveals just how capitalism in its phase of primitive accumulation took ancient and feudal institutions and reshaped them to its own needs. One of the oldest types of exploitation, the master–slave relationship acquired a particular ferocity in the New World with the drive of the new merchant classes to extract agricultural surpluses from first the sugar plantations, and latter the cotton and coffee plantations. It is true that eventually the English and then the northern US manufacturing classes came to oppose slavery, but not until after their national and regional economies had benefited enormously from slavery and had turned racism into an integral part of Western society.

In the sixteenth and seventeenth centuries, other basic international relationships of power were forged that also shape the world today. The modern dichotomy between the metropolitan centers and the periphery first began to manifest itself in the division between the colonizers and the colonies. Later with the rise of independence movements, the peripheral relationship assumed the form of neo-colonialism as the imperial powers used their ascendancy in the global economy to continue to accumulate wealth at the expense of the ex-colonies.

One newly independent country, the United States, escaped from its earlier peripheral relationship because many who settled there came from England, the European country in which the culture of power in its economic form (the ability to extract economic surplus) was most highly developed, thanks to the early English capitalist revolution. The US settlers and pioneers used these economic "skills" to exploit the continent's rich resources and to conquer native peoples and other early settlers (Mexicans, French, and so on) that stood in the way.

It was, however, the bourgeoisie of Western Europe that first truly consolidated the culture of power, both internationally and within their own nation states. Beginning in the late eighteenth and nineteenth centuries, the bourgeoisie of Europe had acquired sufficient economic strength to question the right of monarchs to rule. Having fed the coffers of the monarchs since the Renaissance, the bourgeoisie (beginning with the French Revolution) moved to seize formal power, and began to raise the banners of republicanism and democracy in opposition to the monarchies.

As nineteenth- and twentieth-century European history amply demonstrates, the bourgeoisie did not always view "democratic" or even republican institutions as capable of serving their best interests. Sometimes old monarchs or new dictators had to be installed (for example, Louis Bonaparte in mid-nineteenth century France) in order to provide the order and stability that the bourgeoisie craved.[10] Democratic institutions were permitted only when the bourgeois culture of power had been securely implanted and impregnated in these societies. And as fascism and Nazism demonstrate, the bourgeoisie would support even the most horrendous forms of repression if their power over society was severely threatened.

Marxist ideology and the culture of power

Marxism broke with capitalism in its assertion that capital's most basic power relationship, the exploitation of the working class by the bourgeoisie, had to be ended. Marx and Engels, in the *Communist Manifesto*, called for the establishment of a society in which the associated producers, that is, the workers, would exercise power instead of the bourgeoisie, thereby ending the exploitative relations and establishing a socialist system.

From its inception, however, Marxism incorporated much of the Western culture of power in the name of transforming society and eliminating the bourgeoisie. Marx and Engels believed that capitalism could not be ended unless state power was first seized. Lenin and the Bolsheviks drew directly on this fundamental premise, and set up the "dictatorship of the proletariat" to carry out the transformation of the economy and society from the commanding heights of the state. In subsequent Marxist-Leninist revolutions, once power was seized, it became the task of the state to pursue centralized economic development, while the Communist Party, often through control of state institutions (such as the education and health ministries) undertook the cultural and ideological transformation of society.

In reality, Lenin and the communist state were merely updating Machiavelli, as Antonio Gramsci recognized in his writings on the "collective prince." According to Gramsci, the party did not necessarily have a single prince or leader who would rule, but it did have a central committee, supposedly run by "democratic centralism" that would guide the revolution and move society forward. However contrary to Gramsci's hopes, socialist revolutions throughout the twentieth century, even when they enjoyed authentic popular and democratic participation at the moment of the seizure of power, moved to implant their rule from above, thereby perpetuating a culture of power analogous to capitalist societies.

Aside from Gramsci, Marxist theorists like Rosa Luxemburg, argued for the democratization of the political and economic systems once state power was seized. Before her death in 1919, Luxemburg disagreed with Lenin on the issue of the structure of the socialist state that was emerging in the Soviet Union. To this day, many Marxist theoreticians and intellectuals, along with Marxist parties that have never held power, critique most existing or former socialist states, asserting that mass participation and democracy should be the basis of decisions in the workplace and in the political system.[11]

But these positions have remained largely abstract theoretical arguments mainly because of the very dynamic of the revolutionary processes. Historically, up to at least the 1960s, virtually all revolutions, be they socialist or bourgeois, were in reality minority revolutions. At the moment when power was seized, popular participation was largely limited to certain social and politicized sectors of society. In the first bourgeois revolution, that of France, the revolution was fomented in Paris by a popular rebellion, but

the peasantry, which made up the vast bulk of 1
population, had virtually no role. And as the revoluti
it became largely a struggle among minority social s
small emergent bourgeoisie eventually establishing i.. ..
over the direction of the state and the economy. In the case of the
American Revolution, US historians concede that only one-third
of the colonists ardently supported the revolution, another third
was largely neutral and one-third was pro-British or fled to the
Canadian territory.[12]

In the Bolshevik Revolution, it was the small working class
combined with the remnants of the Tsarist army and a limited strata
of the intelligentsia that carried out the revolution and set up the
soviets. Once state power was seized in Russia, the Communist
Party, in the name of the small proletariat, began to transform and
impose its rule on the rest of society. The majority of the population
certainly acquiesced during the early stages of the French, American
and Bolshevik revolutions, but they were not active participants.

Socialist revolutions have faced one other obstacle that drove them
in the direction of verticalism, of change and revolutionary control
from the top down. Virtually all socialist revolutions have occurred
in the more underdeveloped regions of the world, not in the
capitalist centers as Marx envisioned, and this made it imperative
for the new revolutions to push for rapid economic growth if they
wished to survive. Given the hostility and aggression of the capitalist
world towards virtually all socialist revolutions, the new governments
had to extract a surplus, mainly from the peasantry, in order to carry
out industrial development. This is what happened in the Soviet
Union under Stalin's rule when he eliminated the Kulak class and
imposed forced industrialization on the country.

This economic phase was not much different from that of
primitive accumulation that has occurred throughout the capitalist
world. While this does not excuse the barbaric acts that Stalin
committed against sectors of the peasantry and even within the party,
it is important to remember that Stalin's actions are no more
horrendous than the brutal repression and exploitation the early
bourgeoisie carried out, through slavery, the eradication of native
peoples and the ruthless advance of colonialism. And one should
not forget that today's leading bourgeois democracy, the United
States, built its capitalist economic machine in the nineteenth
century by marching westward, annihilating the American Indians
and carrying out a genocidal war that was at least as horrendous
and costly as Stalin's oppression in the Soviet Union.

The mediating institutions of power

The capitalist and socialist states over the years have created an
array of bureaucratic, political and social institutions designed to

perpetuate their power by maintaining control over civil society. The bourgeois democratic state in particular has gone through a process of structural evolution in its efforts to contain and control popular movements and dissent from below. The first republican or "democratic" societies were actually run by elites, comprised of male propertied owners and the nobility who were allotted positions in the early parliaments or congresses. As other groups pressured from below, (non-property owners, women and minorities) the established bourgeois governments were compelled to accede, although they insisted that the new participants abide by the rules and institutions of the established order. Regional governments, political parties, the media, professional organizations, lobbies, government bureaucracies and ministries – all these institutions and others were forged to contain and direct civil society as it developed.

The rise of the middle class has facilitated the development of these mediating institutions. Marx and Engels portrayed capitalist societies as comprised of an ever-expanding proletariat and a dominant bourgeoisie. In reality, the class structure of capitalism grew increasingly complex, with an array of classes and class fractions emerging. The "middle class," a social sector that to this day confounds Marxists and leads to innumerable theoretical debates, has in fact become the predominant social group in the developed capitalist countries. Workers engaged in manufacturing, which the early Marxists envisioned as the principal political force for overthrowing the bourgeoisie, are now only a fraction of the entire work force, often constituting no more than 20 per cent of the gainfully employed in any given country.

While the new mediating organizations and institutions clearly did allow for greater participation and expression, they also served to divide, fractionalize and isolate different class sectors from one another. Plant workers, teachers, newspaper reporters and airport controllers can all technically be defined as "workers" since they are on the payrolls of giant corporations or state institutions. But in reality the latter three groups tend to view themselves as part of the middle class, and each of these groups pursues its interests through different and often competing mediating institutions. This institutional fractionalization of the middle and working classes makes it much easier for the state and the bourgeoisie to assert their authority whenever one or another social sector challenges the existent system by making economic or political demands upon it.

Today the structures of power and domination permeate all our educational, legal, economic and cultural institutions. In one form or another they hold back the full development of creativity by the individual and the group working together. Anyone who has worked in the educational or the corporate realm, for example, quickly comes to recognize that they are at the mercy of their superiors, who can dictate what they do, and how long they remain at their positions and jobs. There is no real democracy or group participation in decision-making in virtually all our key institutions.

However, it is these same mediating institutions that today are becoming increasingly important in the struggle against the state and the culture of power. Many environmentalists, for example, focus their strategies on penetrating, using and/or changing many of the key mediating institutions. They form lobbies and pressure groups, try to influence the media, pursue legislative changes at the local and national levels and even try to change the personnel in government agencies and bureaucracies. While these struggles do not alter the basic capitalist structure of society, they do raise consciousness and lead increasingly to the questioning of the very nature of contemporary society.

In addition to the environmental movement, the media provides another illustration of the reality that mediating institutions are not completely under the thumb of the dominant classes. Any study of corporate power reveals that all the major media institutions in a given country are controlled by big capital.[13] But the fact is that the ruling class has by no means been able to use the media to assert complete control over public consciousness. Polls reveal that large sectors of the public do not "trust" the media, just as they do not trust their political leaders any more. Individual rage against the media is often vented in letters to the editor which question many news stories and editorial opinions. And many of the people who work within the media themselves are cynical, and in some cases even directly challenge the control of the executives over what they say and write. The technological revolution in computers and mass communications has also enabled many small publishers, independent radio stations, alternative periodicals and newspapers to find special niches and political space where they can affect public consciousness.

The communist societies have collapsed before the capitalist countries in large part because of the failure of the intermediate institutions to control or channel public dissent. Most of these institutions in the communist world – the trade unions, schools, media, and so on – were under the direct control of the party or the state. In the capitalist countries control and influence over these institutions is much more decentralized, and thus they have a greater capacity to bend as dissent grows, thereby helping to coopt and contain any opposition movement. But in Eastern Europe, when the protest movement burst into the open, the mediating institutions with their "political line" had little or no capacity to halt or channel the popular rebellion.

Eastern Europe demonstrated that the more the political leaders try to manipulate the mediating institutions, the more acute is the public reaction. Here again, the media illustrates how tenuous the control of the state can be. The Eastern European communist parties held a virtual monopoly over the media. But this did not prevent the public from turning to other alternatives – international radio transmissions, underground articles and papers and word of mouth – to develop an independent consciousness and an understanding of what was going on in the world.

The postmodern quest

In 1982 Michael Ryan, in a book written to find common ground between Marxism and postmodernism, noted that "millions have been killed because they were Marxists; no one will be obliged to die because s/he is a deconstructionist."[14] A decade and a half later there are few who will die for Marxism. Postmodernism certainly has not replaced it as a banner for life and death struggles, but given postmodernism's impact on popular culture, it is conceivable that a larger number would rush to defend postmodernism than Marxism.

The crisis of Marxism and the rise of postmodernism compels us to look closely at the latter to draw out what may be useful to help revitalize the left. Postmodernity takes as its starting point "deconstructionalism," the effort to take apart the values of modernism and exploitation that are at the core of Western civilization. However, beyond this common endeavor there are many different tendencies in postmodernist thought. The most extreme argues for the rejection of everything that came from the Enlightenment and holds that thought cannot be organized or systematized in any useful way. For this school, everything is appearances, a collage of images, or the moment. There is no synthetic ideology or worldview that is relevant for all of humanity. Many postmodernists even assert that the very formulation of a universalist perspective leads automatically to repression of one group or another since there is no single philosophy that could possibly incorporate all the differences that characterize the disparate cultures, lifestyles and living conditions of humanity.

In some aspects, postmodernism draws on previous currents of thought that have reacted to rationalism and the idea of progress that flowed out of the Enlightenment. The first example of this is Romanticism. Later in the nineteenth century Friedrich Nietzsche also leveled a harsh attack on rationality and "modern man." Postmodernity in fact can be seen in some ways as a hybrid or variant of nihilism and modern existentialism. The point is that Western civilization in its moments of crisis has tended to throw up schools of thought which look to humanity's darker side and reject ideological constructs or the very idea of human betterment.

Much of postmodernist thought can be interpreted as yet another symptom of the bankruptcy of Western ideology. There is no overarching ideological unity for most postmodernists, which coincides with and reflects the ideological exhaustion of the existing order. All that the more extreme schools of postmodernism are doing is stating the obvious, that there is a crisis of Western thought, be it communism, liberalism or social democracy.

However, many postmodernists have put forth devastating critiques of Western domination and its culture of power while arguing for a new liberation of humanity. This is why we have chosen the concept of postmodernism as a building block for the construction of an alternative ideology. Postmodernity is strongly rooted in the call for an end to the genocidal destruction of "pre-modern" indigenous societies, in the demand for feminist liberation, and in the cry that militarism and the tyranny of the modern state must end. Moreover, we believe that the very term postmodernism should not be monopolized by those who are inclined to nihilism and a rejection of philosophic worldviews. Postmodernism can be a powerful concept to use against the existing order if one recognizes that capitalism is the essence of what constitutes modernity.

Two geographers, David Harvey and Edward Soja, published separate books in 1989 that have been particularly helpful in taking up postmodernity in a way that deconstructs modernity, capitalism and Western domination while searching for a new way of viewing the world.[15] Soja argues that four radical thinkers of the post-World War II era – Henri Lefebvre, Ernest Mandel, Michel Foucault and John Berger – were particularly important in breaking with the narrow historicism that had come to predominate much of Marxism as well as the established, highly compartmentalized, social sciences.[16] All four began to understand that the devastating impact of imperialism and capitalism could only be understood by placing them in spatial, geographic contexts. Harvey and Soja point to many ways in which Marxism narrowly aligned itself with modernism and a rigid concept of time, thereby making it difficult to provide a spatial, holistic view that could strike at the foundations of liberalism and provide a new integrative approach.

Richard Falk, in *Explorations at the Edge of Time*, also attempts to pull what is useful out of postmodernist thought by calling for a "postmodern globalism." He argues that a new "global civil society" is beginning to supersede the old traditional civil society of the Western world that has been destroyed by capitalist modernity. He points to "societal initiatives of transnational scope and dimension," such as "movements for democracy and human rights, for environmental protection and green politics, for feminist reinterpretation," as giving rise to a sense of shared human identity and the emergence of a global civil society.[17]

This view however may be "too rational, or too civilized." It attaches extraordinary importance to the social movements of Western Europe and the United States. While they are important, they are only one part of the global opposition to the Western capitalist world. And Falk does not take into account or deal with the barbarism that is being unleashed on the contemporary world. As Samir Amin points out in *Empire of Chaos*, this barbarism is not simply an innate characteristic of the dispossessed of the planet; rather it is rooted in the policies of the big powers and their associated economic and class interests. The destruction of the environment, the massive starvation of African populations, the growing disempowerment and impoverishment of the lower sectors of society, the increasing reliance on violence and force to control whole populations – these are some of the acts of barbarism perpetrated on humanity by Western capitalism and its culture of power. People are merely responding in kind when they besiege the citadels of Western power with ever-increasing violence and crime.

Amin, although not a postmodernist, puts forth a perspective that overlaps in many ways with postmodernism. He calls for a "polycentered world," one in which "Euro-centrism" will end and the peoples of the world will pursue their own ideas and development at the local and regional levels. As he declares:

> The only meaningful strategy for the progressive forces on a world scale – on whose basis the peoples of the West, East, and South could together draw new breath – must envision a polycentric world. The various components must be articulated in a flexible way, allowing for political, economic and cultural diversity. It must be acknowledged at the outset that the problems the people of the world must solve differ from one area to another.[18]

A polycentrism rooted in individual and group needs is the only approach that can challenge and replace the culture of domination that is at the core of Western expansionism.

The new individuality driving humanity

To understand the ideological upheaval in the contemporary world, it is necessary to go beyond even polycentrism. We need to incorporate the "new individuality" that is questioning the culture of domination and Western civilization itself. This new individuality is to be distinguished from the individualism that Western capitalism has nurtured over the centuries. Philosophically, it is juxtaposed to Adam Smith and his neo-liberal descendants who argue that whatever happens in the marketplace is good for the individual and good for the "wealth of the nation."

The new individuality, like the old individualism, is rooted in a personal quest. But the new individuality goes far beyond the economic sphere. It is the effort to define one's very being in relation to one's sexuality, to a particular social or ethnic group, or even in relation to other species and the environment. Indeed this new individuality is often at odds with the economic individualism of the marketplace, which tends to destroy individuality by turning us all into economic automatons as we purchase commodities or sell our labor.

This new quest for individuality runs right up against the efforts of the state and the existent powers to control one's life and identity, to limit the spheres in which one can express oneself. The women's movement is an example par excellence of how the new individuality is in direct conflict with the old values. At its roots, the women's movement is the assertion that each woman has the right to control her body and to fully develop her individual potential, be it in the personal, societal or economic spheres. The women's movement's first challenge is of course to the patriarchal system, because it asserts that women are subservient to men, that men have an inherent right of control over women's bodies and lives. Because patriarchal values are embedded in the social, cultural and economic systems around the world, it becomes essential for women to question and challenge the values and laws of the existent civilization itself.

What has not been generally recognized or discussed is that the social movements are rooted in this new individuality. Some scholars of the new social movements have asserted that the social movements are not "new" because most of them have precedents that go back centuries.[19] But we would argue that they are new in that they reflect a quest to satisfy individual needs and individual desires that is unprecedented in the history of civilization.

Because the old individualism was identified with capitalism and selfishness, progressives have ignored the powerful individual drive that is at the heart of the social movements. What are the gay and human rights movements, if not an attempt by each and every person to pursue his or her individual sexual identity? And what is the Indian rights movement, if not an attempt by individual Indians to reclaim their particular identity in relation to the ethnic group they are a part of? The environmental movement is also rooted in an individual, personal quest for a better life, a life free from visual, commercial and environmental pollution. And the environmental movement is also an attempt to define one's relationship and identity in relation to other species.

Individuality is also present in the movements that predominate in the Third World. Islamic fundamentalism, which is often portrayed as a new mass religious cult, actually draws upon the quest of individuals and peoples throughout the Muslim world to develop their own identities in reaction to values and political systems that have often been imposed on them in the recent past, especially from the West. Nationalist movements, in Eastern Europe and elsewhere, also draw on the quest of people for their own identity, that is for their own individuality and uniqueness in a world that is increasingly fragmented and chaotic.

The new individuality is also tied up with the quest for pleasure, another concept that many on the left have had difficulty dealing with. The gay rights movement is not simply an assertion of the right to one's own sexual preferences: it is also inherently a quest for what gives one the most sexual pleasure and satisfaction in life. The environmental movement is also ultimately a search for humanity to find harmony and pleasure with the natural environment, a pleasure that is much deeper and profound than that which comes with modernism's obsession with commodities at the expense of the environment.

The quest for pleasure in contemporary society of course goes far beyond the social movements, and in fact envelops many areas of life that the capitalist world manipulates or profits from. Pop music, mass sports, commercial movies, the use of drugs – these are all rooted in the quest for personal pleasure that modern technology makes available to humanity on a scale never envisioned before. Some purists put down many of these activities because they are part of a mass culture that is seemingly beneath them. But in most of these mass activities there is a certain quest for pleasure that is more advanced or sophisticated than comparable activities in the past. Take American football, for example, which to many modern cultural puritans is simply a brute sport in which men are knocked around. But there is far more to it than that. There is a precision to the varieties of play patterns that is not unlike a fast chess game, and there is a fascination for an adept quarterback who can avoid the rushing tacklers, and make sensational passes that fall into the hands of receivers who in turn are capable of running downfield and astutely sidestepping or dancing away from those who try to bring them down.

The growing fascination with the Olympics every four years is also a testament to how mass sports are becoming more sophisticated and even artistic in certain ways. And then there is the growing popular interest and participation in regular exercising, which is generally not based on the development of brute muscular force, but on aerobic principles and on making one's body more agile and flexible. These sports and activities are intensely exploited by commercialism, but this should not blind us to the fact that in most of them there is a basic human striving for beauty, for sound, healthy pleasures, and for the fullest development of the human body and mind.

CHAPTER 4

The Economic Shock of Globalization

The widely discussed "globalization" of economic life is largely a universalization of capitalism.

Arthur MacEwan[1]

You remember last year [1993] with all the flooding in the south and midwest [of the United States]? They discovered what a mistake it was to build all those levees so high, to dam up the river banks. Well the economy is just the same. The fed, and the banks, and the market have all built in a series of devices to prevent a crash in the system. And they've built them higher and higher, just like the levees. But one day they'll overflow, and when that happens, everything will be washed away, and we'll start building a sane society.

Carl Marzani,
The day before he died in 1994[2]

It is our contention that capitalism is in its final epoch, that it has already begun harboring in its bowels its antithesis – the postmodern societies and economies. A major reason why it is difficult for even critics of capitalism to see the impending demise of the system is because of its continued capacity to expand globally. Historically, economists and the public at large have identified economic crises with a depression, not with continued economic growth. But we believe that the very expansiveness of the system is creating ever-greater contradictions, contradictions that nurture the development of a new mode of production and will lead to major convulsions in the existent system within the next quarter century.

We do not have to look far even in our newspapers to detect deep-seated doubts and concerns about where globalization may be leading us. 'The New Strategy: Take Risks, Think Globally' – was the banner headline of a special business report by the *New York Times* in early 1994.[3] Implicit in the title is the belief that globalism is the cutting edge for any serious investor. This stance is absolutely correct. Capital, to survive and expand, now more than ever has to move globally. But to do so it must take more and more risks. *The New York Times* was upbeat about the US economy in its report, but the two other headlines on the same page summed up some of the immediate risks that capital faced: 'Wariness Grows

Amid a Dollar Cascade' and 'High Tech Surges, But Are Consumers Ready?'

Deeper into the survey on global business conditions, the *New York Times* reported many concerns about what could go wrong. One article wondered whether the approaching death of Deng Xiaoping would lead to the end of China's economic boom, thereby slowing down the development of the country's burgeoning demand for transnational capital. Other major worries included the fear that the free market business opportunities in Russia might come to an end with Boris Yeltsin's losses in the parliamentary elections, and questions about whether Western Europe and Japan would recover from their economic slump in 1994 or even in 1995. Latin America was labeled an area of opportunity and expansion, but it too had its risks as countries like Venezuela, Brazil, Mexico and Argentina confronted significant political and social problems that could easily spill over into the economic sphere.

Global disorder and instability are clearly major concerns of the business and governing classes. What none of the *New York Times* business articles pointed out was that capitalism has played the central role in the creation of this increasingly unstable and disorderly world. Three pivotal forces are fomenting its internal instability. Firstly, there is the very creation and integration of the global economy under capitalist hegemony. Secondly, there is the accelerated pace of technological change, and thirdly the increasing concentration of money and capital in the hands of the rich and powerful.

Neither the creation of a global economy nor the advance of technology are implicitly detrimental or destabilizing. However it is precisely the fact that these two forces are so tightly interrelated with the concentration of capital that promotes instability and disorder in the world today. The concentration of capital – meaning the ability of capitalists and capitalist enterprises to consolidate economic activities under their control and direction – has been going on for centuries, ever since the rise of commercial capital in Western Europe in the fifteenth and sixteenth centuries. But today, due to its ability to move in tandem with the advance of technology and the growth of the global market, the concentration of capital has reached awesome proportions.

It is this very concentration of wealth that is leading to misery and marginalization for ever-increasing numbers of the world's population. Today the ruling classes – particularly in the core capitalist countries – relentlessly accumulate riches on a global scale under the ideological banner of neo-liberalism, while the vast bulk of the world's population is experiencing growing poverty and deprivation. Even sectors of the First World's population are being forced downward into living conditions not all that different from those of the Third World.

This concentration is lead by finance capital and the big multinational enterprises that stand at the pinnacle of virtually all areas of economic activity, including banking, the mass media, transportation, manufacturing and electronics. The multinationals are the basic instruments used by capital to break down national economies and to build a global capitalist system. The very size of the multinationals, combined with their fierce drive for markets and new technology, unleashes intense competitive forces on a global scale that make for continual upheaval and instability. In the contemporary parlance of the capitalist world there are always new "winners and losers," meaning that companies, countries and social classes are continually being destabilized and torn apart by the global competitive forces at work.

This chapter will look at the fundamental tensions within the system, those that deepen the economic crisis and will lead sooner or later to an economic rupture. They are:

1) the growing unity and differentiation within the global economy;
2) the increasing rivalry among the dominant capitalist powers;
3) the shift of capital itself to a model of "flexible accumulation;"
4) trade wars;
5) the crisis of overproduction;
6) global unemployment; and
7) the rise of finance capitalism.

Unity and differentiation

The simultaneous development of unity and differentiation within the global economy makes it increasingly meaningless to use the terms First, Second and Third Worlds to describe the different economic regions of the globe. The Second World is gone, replaced by a wide variety of countries on varying paths of development. At the same time, the First and Third Worlds have become a pot-pourri of countries with an array of different economic groups and classes.

To understand this dynamic global economic system, it is still appropriate to use the core–periphery paradigm, although both the core and the periphery now have a somewhat different content than in the 1960s when these concepts were first developed. Then the boundaries between the core and the periphery were clear: the United States and Western Europe, followed by Japan, constituted the core of the capitalist world, while the overwhelming bulk of what was called the Third World – from Peru and Venezuela to Burma, India, Nigeria and Ethiopia – constituted the periphery. Some Third World countries, like Cuba and North Vietnam, escaped politically into the camp of the communist bloc, although, as history has demonstrated, they did not overcome the legacy of underdevelopment.

In the contemporary world, the old geographic boundaries between the core and the periphery have been breached. Due to the onslaught of technology and capital, the core now has islands of consolidated capitalist development in countries like South Korea, Taiwan, Mexico and Brazil. But simultaneously, the periphery has spread to the developed world as well. Cities like New York, Los Angeles, London and Paris now contain large areas where economic and social conditions are similar to those of many Third World countries, with people unemployed, hungry, illiterate, homeless and completely marginalized.

With the collapse of the communist societies, the same general dynamic is taking hold in the former Second World as pro-"free market" governments privatize their economies. From Moscow to Kiev and Budapest, the new bourgeoisie and its attendant economic and social strata is already emerging, demanding many of the privileges, powers and luxuries of their counterparts in the dominant capitalist countries. Simultaneously, large numbers of their populace are forced downward, compelled to live in conditions not all that different from the bulk of the populace in countries like Mexico or Algeria.

It is the very expansion and the universalization of the periphery in the First, Second and Third World that enables the postmodern economies to begin to take form. When the periphery was concentrated in the Third World, the underdeveloped economy was fairly simple. It was comprised of the impoverished peasantry, the large unemployed reserve army of labor in the major cities of the Third World, and the mining and plantation enclaves that were ruthlessly exploited by the early multinationals.[4]

Now, however, the universalized periphery, like the globalized transnational economy, has also become highly differentiated and complex. The informal sector of the postmodern economy includes an unimaginable number of micro-enterprises as well as the traditional poor who eke out a living on the streets. It also includes the growing number of worker-run enterprises – which are also highly diverse and differentiated among themselves, ranging from state industries now controlled by workers in the former Soviet Union, to steel companies in the United States that the workers have bought up at rock bottom prices, to former Sandinista state farms in Nicaragua that agricultural workers have forcibly "privatized" to grow staple foods and even some crops for exportation. It is the very diversity of economic activities in the universalized periphery that permits us to finally envision and articulate the rise of the postmodern economy.

Capitalist rivalry

Along with these transformations in the Second and Third Worlds, the capitalists classes are locked in an increasingly intense struggle among themselves. While the geo-political repercussions of the victory of the West in the Cold War are lauded by its political leaders and ideologues, few discuss the impact of the end of the conflict in the economic sphere. The post-World War II capitalist world was built around economic cooperation and a common enemy. The United States, Western Europe, and Japan to a somewhat lesser extent, were generally willing to come to an accord over their economic and commercial differences because of their underlying hostility to communism and the Soviet Union. The United States in particular allowed its old enemies, Germany and Japan, to rebuild as economic powers and even to capture US markets in the early post-war decades as long as they were strategic allies in the Cold War.

But, in the 1970s, just as the cycles of economic expansion and recession were becoming integrated on a global scale, competition and discord among the major capitalist powers began to grow in importance. Japan and the Western European countries, especially West Germany, were able to develop technologically, and to concentrate capital in their own multinationals, thereby enabling them to expand globally and cut into US markets. This led to the eruption of trade disputes which became increasingly pronounced in the 1980s.

A critical factor in the decline of US hegemony and the growing capitalist rivalry is the crisis of overproduction. This is another economic force unleashed by the spread of global markets, the advance of technology and the concentration of capital. Well before 1989 and the dismantling of the Berlin Wall and the Eastern European bloc, the markets of the capitalist world were increasingly saturated with a surplus of agricultural commodities, raw materials, and consumer and durable manufactured goods.

Between 1970 and 1990, global trade leaped in constant 1980 dollars from $3.3 billion to $3.5 trillion, more than a ten-fold increase.[5] What this increase in global trade reflects is a growing surplus of commodities as virtually every one, from the Third World agricultural commodity producers to the newly industrialized countries (NICs) and the core capitalist countries, stepped up their production and exports in the quest for markets and profits.[6]

Now, with the collapse of the Soviet Union, the tendency of the capitalist world to break up into competing trade and economic spheres in order to unload surplus commodities is a fact of international life. We are witnessing the full-blown emergence of a world in which the economic and commercial relations between the three major capitalist powers – Western Europe, the United States and Japan – are deteriorating as they increasingly view each other as antagonists rather than allies.

For the moment the central financial institutions created at the end of World War II, principally the IMF and the World Bank, are not vulnerable. But in spite of the conclusion of the new GATT agreement in late 1993, the "open markets" and reciprocal trade agreements of Bretton Woods that constituted the economic foundation of the post-war system are threatened by the emergence of distinct trade blocs and the efforts of the big powers to protect what they consider strategic areas of their economies.

Flexible accumulation

As David Harvey points out in *The Condition of Postmodernity*, modern capitalism in its expansionist drive has collapsed space and time.[7] The multinationals can tap productive centers around the world because of the revolutions that have occurred in transportation and communications. For a corporation like General Motors, the transportation costs have been so reduced and communications are now so rapid that it is no longer economically advantageous to have most of the components needed for a car produced in a limited geographic area. Harvey shows how this collapse of space and time has altered the very nature of capitalist accumulation. The age of the Fordist-like system of production, in which a corporation directly controlled the factors of production in its own plants and factories, has been replaced by "flexible accumulation." It is no longer necessary, or even financially desirable, for a corporation to run and own all the plants that provide the components needed for assembling a final product. Many corporations now engage in what is called "sourcing." They contract with producers around the globe for components, thereby maintaining maximum flexibility in their constant search for the cheapest possible commodity or source of production.

As Robert Reich declares in *The Work of Nations*, the multinationals' ability to establish a global web of flexible production means that the US-based multinational "is no longer even American. It is, increasingly, a facade, behind which teems an array of decentralized groups and subgroups continuously contracting with similarly diffuse working units all over the world."[8] The multinational constantly searches the globe for the cheapest producer of components and commodities. Reich gives the example of a Pontiac worth about $10,000 in the US market, of which about $3,000 goes to South Korea for routine labor and assembly operations, $1,750 to Japan for advanced components (engines, transaxles and electronics), $750 to West Germany for styling and design engineering, $400 to Taiwan, Singapore, and Japan for small components, $250 to Britain for advertising and marketing services, and about $50 to Ireland and Barbados for data processing. The rest, less than $4,000 goes to strategists in Detroit, lawyers and bankers in New York, lobbyists in Washington, insurance and health care workers all over the country, and General Motors shareholders – most of whom live in the United States, but an increasing number of whom are foreign nationals.[9]

Corporate "downsizing" is another manifestation of flexible accumulation. Major corporations spin off or subcontract for many of the goods and services that they once produced themselves, or else they lay off workers in the core countries and hire lower paid employees in the Third World. For example, ten years ago AT&T had only five dozen employees outside the United States; today it has 54,000 abroad, including 20,000 managers. Yet, it has gotten rid of more than 72,000 employees since 1984, mainly in the United States.[10] Between 1991 and early 1994, five major US-based corporations – IBM, GM, Sears Roebuck, GTE and AT&T – laid off a total of 324,650 employees.[11]

Agribusiness corporations were among the earlier multinationals to understand that it was not necessary to directly own the means of production in order to secure high profits. In the 1960s United Fruit (now United Brands) and Castle & Cooke realized that it was better to begin divesting themselves of their Third World banana plantations and turn them over to local producers. They would continue to buy and market the bananas, but by getting out of direct plantation production they would not be subjected to nationalist or trade union pressures. And if the costs of production from a given set of producers in a particular country rose significantly, the multinational could begin contracting with banana producers in other countries.[12]

The system of flexible accumulation also enables the multinationals to evade direct responsibility for many of the destructive consequences of their global expansion. By contracting out the production of commodities, from computer components to apparel products and bananas, the multinationals can claim that they are not responsible for the repression of trade union policies or the environmentally destructive practices of the local producer they are buying from.

Perhaps the best example of fin de siècle global capitalism is the high-tech sweatshop. Be it Mexico, Singapore or even Silicon Valley, computer firms set up plants that pay minimum wages to their workers (usually overwhelmingly women) to produce the most advanced microchips or to assemble the latest state-of-the-art computer. High-tech products can be produced virtually anywhere in the world. For a short time, IBM or Apple may be capable of extracting some high monopoly profits through direct production when they come out with a new commodity, but it is soon imitated or copied by producers in other parts of the world. Technology is quickly dispersed, often with the assistance of the technological innovators themselves who set up plants and production centers wherever the product can be turned out the most cheaply.

Here Tijuana and the Mexican border serve as an example of what is happening. Many of the *maquiladores* located there are not the direct subsidiaries of large multinationals. They are often small producers, in some cases even Mexican-owned, which manufacture products on contract with the multinationals. To keep their costs down, they repress union organizing and dump untreated plant wastes that contaminate the rivers and beaches all the way to San Diego. The multinational that buys the product disclaims any responsibility for these practices. And if questions are raised and pressures brought to bear on the multinational in its home country because of the supplier with which it is contracting, it can quickly shift its contract to another producer in another country.

One major effect of flexible accumulation is that it undercuts the power of trade unions. In today's world, the multinationals abandon plants in areas like Detroit or Los Angeles, where the workers are organized, and shift their operations to other parts of the world where there are no unions. Karl Marx asserted in *Das Kapital* that as the bourgeoisie expanded capitalist production, it would create its antithesis, organized workers in the factory who would eventually overthrow the system. Today flexible accumulation makes that scenario increasingly improbable. Although industry has spread around the globe creating an ever-larger proletariat, the workers are in many instances less organized and less able to resist wage and salary cutbacks than they were two decades ago. In the historic struggle between capital and labor, capital today definitely holds the upper hand.

And unlike the 1960s, when many Third World countries challenged the right of the multinationals to pillage their resources, there are today virtually no political or ideological challenges to their dominance. Few countries in the south or the east (the post-communist world) are questioning the multinationals' right to plunder the globe. Indeed the countries now compete intensely with each other to see who can be the most subservient and offer "advantageous" economic conditions to attract multinational investments.

Popular resistance and trade wars

But the multinational corporations through their expansion and the globalization of the world's economy have spawned a series of contradictions and problems. The global economy today, like the social and political spheres, has centrifugal and centripetal forces at work, factors that are pulling it together, and factors tearing it apart.

It is this ambience that explains the rise of the postmodern economies. Out of desperation, people are driven to find whatever economic activities they can when they are excluded from the formal or transnational economies. Simultaneously there are new postmodern actors in the social movements who fight against the excesses of globalized capitalism, including human rights and environmental activists as well as labor organizers.

Other contradictions arise because the multinationals are pitting countries and producers as well as workers against each other, thereby returning the world to the early twentieth century, when competition among the major capitalist nations was a decisive factor in global politics. The multinationals have created not only severe inequalities in the Third World, but also major dislocations within the dominant core countries that nurture the rise of protectionism and trade blocs.

The formation of cartels, the quest for colonial markets and recurring financial crises in the leading financial systems were all characteristics of the pre-World War I period. They have clear parallels in today's world, with the emergence of trade blocs, the levying of import sanctions, and the instability of the financial markets and national currencies. We have not reached the stage of conflict portrayed in Lenin's *On Imperialism*, where he described a capitalist world driven to war by its quest for markets. But the phrase coined in the early twentieth century, "Export or die," is now more apt than ever in describing the growing sense of desperation among the major capitalist powers as they compete for markets.

However, an important difference between today's economic world and that at the beginning of the century is that there is a tension in virtually every capitalist nation between the forces that favor the continued internationalization of the economy and those that are rooted more in the national markets. Computer firms, new biotech companies, and large multinational food processors tend to favor the continued opening of international markets, while agricultural producers, apparel manufacturers and steel producers are more generally in favor of protecting national markets.

But there are often few clear-cut lines dividing "national" and "international" capitalists in a given country. Some apparel manufacturers, particularly those which now have subsidiaries scattered abroad that export back to their home country, will often support the lowering of international tariff barriers rather than the protection of the home market. And the Big Three auto makers in the United States, which for decades have raced around the globe looking for cheap labor and resources, are an example par excellence of the conflicting tendencies at work often within the same industry or enterprise. Once leaders in lobbying for the development of a global economy, these firms in the 1980s began arguing for protectionism in selected areas. They have become desperate for market share and more than willing to encourage "Japan bashing" if it will help keep out Japanese cars and enable them to enjoy a protected market and higher prices within the United States.

Because of these conflicting tendencies the war for markets has few clear and consistent lines of battle. It is a slow, drawn-out war of maneuver with unexpected twists and turns. Developments in the European Economic Community (now European Union) illustrate this troubled and contradictory pattern of market consolidation and competition. The year 1992 was to be the "Year of Europe," as it dropped all internal tariff barriers, allowing for the free movement of most economic resources. But in fact 1992 turned out to be a year of disarray and disagreement within the EEC. First the rejection by Danish voters of the Maastricht treaty, which would have facilitated monetary union; then the depreciation of some of the weaker European currencies; and finally the clash among the major EEC powers over whether or not to yield to US demands to reduce agricultural subsidies – these were all serious areas of discord that revealed the limits as to how far and fast the EEC could move in becoming a single consolidated trade and financial bloc capable of displaying a united front against the United States and Japan.[13]

The disputes and disagreements at the top also enable popular forces to find space to undertake rearguard actions against the globalization process. The processes leading up to the final approval of the GATT (General Agreement on Tariffs and Trade) and the NAFTA (North American Free Trade Agreement) in late 1993 reveals the degree of popular distrust and disenchantment with the multinationals and the new international trade agreements. The open rebellion of French farmers in 1992 and 1993 almost led to the jettisoning of the entire GATT agreement. In the United States, trade unions and others in 1993 headed a national movement in opposition to the Congressional approval of the NAFTA treaty. Only an all-out campaign by a coalition of Clinton "New Democrats," big business and Republicans was able to secure the passage of the treaty.

While the contending powers try to extract the best terms possible during the negotiation of international trade agreements, they are also intent on creating new international trade and economic mechanisms that enabled them to evade popular pressures and democratic institutions.[14] The North American Free Trade Agreement is designed to make an end run around popular social and political forces bent on limiting the free reign of the multinationals. Once approved in the United States and Canada as well as Mexico, the NAFTA accord substantially reduced the power of legislatures to control their own economic development in response to national needs and interests. The belief was that even if a populist politician like Cuauhtemoc Cardenas won the presidency in Mexico, the country would be locked into adhering to the accords.

But this approach has not prevented popular pressures from building even after the accords are approved. In Canada, the Progressive Conservative government lost the elections in a landslide in 1993 in large part because of the adverse impact of the initial NAFTA accord within Canada. And in Mexico just as the NAFTA accord took effect there in early 1994, an Indian rebellion erupted in Chiapas that denounced NAFTA as "a death certificate for the Indian peoples of Mexico."

The crisis of overproduction

The deep-seated competition among and within trade blocs is linked to another central dynamic that is inherent in the capitalist system – the crisis of overproduction. The markets are increasingly saturated with goods and commodities, thereby driving down profits and intensifying competition among the capitalist powers. The problem is not a lack of potential consumers. As the global growth of malnutrition, poverty and hunger demonstrates, there is a tremendous need for increased production.

But the dominant capitalist classes have no interest in fulfilling these needs because there is no profit to be made by providing goods and commodities for the more marginalized sectors of the populace. As John Maynard Keynes pointed out during the Great Depression of the 1930s, there is a historic tendency for capitalism to face "realization crises," that is, the goods and commodities produced cannot be disposed of because capitalism so skews income in favor of those at the top of the economic ladder that there is no capacity for those at the bottom to earn the income necessary to purchase the essential goods and alleviate the problem of overproduction. According to David C. Korten in *When Corporations Rule the World*, "The world's 500 largest industrial corporations, which employ only

0.05 of 1 percent of the world's population, control 25 percent of the world's economic output."[15]

Related to the realization crisis is the growing importance of machinery, mechanization and automation in global production. A historic tendency of capitalism that Marx pointed to is the rise of "dead capital," that is, the increasing amount of capital that is tied up in machinery, equipment and infrastructure as capital grows and expands. With the enlargement of dead capital, fewer and fewer workers are needed to produce the same amount of goods. Of course new areas of production are increasingly being opened up, but today these areas also tend to be more and more capital intensive. Now there is a growing question as to whether the rise of dead capital, automation and new technologies are in fact generally increasing the ranks of the unemployed and the marginalized on a global scale.

Some new technologies do accentuate the overproduction crisis. In mid-1993, *Business Week*, in an issue called 'The Technology Payoff,' claimed that the information revolution was finally producing substantial increases in productivity in the corporate world. Companies were able to cut their labor costs with advanced computer and information systems, thereby increasing their productivity and profits. However, in an accompanying article titled 'Jobs, Jobs, Jobs – Eventually,' *Business Week* noted that in just the past year over half a million clerical and technical positions had disappeared in the United States. "It's no wonder that so many Americans are distressed: They see their paychecks lagging inflation, and they worry about joining their families and friends in the ranks of the employed."[16]

Business Week, however, refused to be deterred by this new development, the simultaneous growth of productivity and unemployment. It declared that "history offers striking evidence that technological revolutions eventually create many more jobs than they destroy." But, it went on to note, that "so far that isn't happening. Despite the recent gains in productivity, real wages and salaries have stagnated for the past four years, with high unemployment making it hard for workers to push for pay raises." What *Business Week* detected, but refused to explicitly acknowledge, is that the historic pattern may have been ruptured – new technologies are now leading to further concentration of wealth and income at the top while the wages of those at the bottom drop and the ranks of the unemployed and the impoverished grow.

The new army of unemployed

On a global scale, technology and the capitalist model of flexible accumulation are creating a huge army of unemployed. The

International Labor Organization, an affiliate agency of the United Nations, estimates that over 30 per cent of the world's labor force of 2.5 billion people are either unemployed or underemployed. Historically, this reserve army of labor is the product of capitalism's passage from an agricultural to an industrial economy, and then to our current information-based economy. From the nineteenth century until well into this century, industrial capitalism decimated agriculturally-based societies to get the manufacturing labor force it needed. Enormous cities and megacities arose, fed by waves of immigrants who left the rural areas.

Now with the rise of the computer/information age the need for mass labor has ended. In the era of automation, computers and simple robotic machines enable corporations and businesses to expel millions of laborers from the manufacturing, processing and services industries. Even government bureaucracies are downsized as data processing machines take over much of their work.

With the demise of the labor intensive industries and farmer/peasant agricultural systems, there are no employment opportunities available for the descendants of those who left the land for the cities. A vast, global pool of people now exists who are impoverished and marginalized. As Jeremy Rifkin declares in *The End of Work*, "Just outside the new high-tech global village lie a growing number of destitute and desperate human beings." It is this extensive community of outcasts from the global economy that has explosive potential and shapes many of the postmodern societies. As Rifkin goes on to note, a core part of this group already comprises a "new outlaw culture [that] is beginning to pose a very real and serious threat to the ability of central governments to maintain order and provide security."[17]

Earlier in this century, the solution that John Maynard Keynes and other economists hit upon to deal with the problems of unemployment and overproduction was deficit spending. By spending more than they take in, governments could pump money and jobs into the economy thereby enabling people to begin purchasing additional goods and commodities. As is commonly recognized, first World War II and then Cold War military spending continually "primed the pump" for the United States and most of the economies of the Western world.

The Reagan administration with its military build-up and deficit spending, managed to forestall the overproduction crisis for the US economy during much of the 1980s. And to a certain extent it also helped keep the global economy moving ahead. Increased deficit spending along with the growth of an enormous trade deficit allowed the US market to absorb more and more goods from abroad, particularly from the "Asian tigers," but also from Japan and Western Europe. The US economy in effect became a global economic locomotive, running on borrowed coal, that pulled the rest of the world forward.

But as is now patently clear the US economy can no longer continue on this track. The United States has become the world's leading debtor nation with a $5.7 trillion debt. The problem for capitalism is that the very measures which would begin to deal with the debt crisis, that is, the curtailment of deficit and government spending, will only make it more difficult for producers and factories in the United States and around the world to unload their wares and commodities. This is the central contradiction that the Clinton administration faces as it tries to curtail the deficit while resuscitating the US economy.

The realization crisis has also been accentuated because of neo-liberal economic policies during the 1980s that lead to a growing redistribution of income in favor of the rich within the United States and other developed countries. A similar phenomena took hold in much of the Third World, as IMF austerity programs were imposed that slashed social programs and the income of the poor and working classes.

Productive capital is caught in a vicious circle. It may have placed the working class on the defensive, but with the end of the Cold War and the collapse of military pump priming, the capitalist world and the multinational corporations in particular, are facing a realization crisis, one more severe than any they have faced since the Great Depression. They need to find new markets to dispose of the ever-expanding array of commodities produced around the globe. At the same time the big corporations in their drive to maintain profits and revenues are slashing real wages and pressuring governments to reduce their taxes and the amount of spending for the public sector.

This narrow, avaricious approach is contrary to what is actually needed – a dramatic redistribution of resources away from the very wealthy into the hands of the poor and the needy so that they can find meaningful and productive work enabling them to purchase the goods and commodities that they need to survive. But this approach is anathema to the capitalist classes, and as the Reagan–Thatcher years demonstrated, the drive of capital is in the opposite direction, one that the Clinton administration in spite of its limited populist rhetoric, is unable and unwilling to confront.

The rise of finance capitalism

Paul Sweezy in a *Monthly Review* article, 'The Triumph of Financial Capital,' argues that because of excessive production around the world, there is no profit to be made [by capital] from expanding the capacity to produce the goods that enter into mass consumption. To do so would be to invest in excess capacity, a patent capitalist irrationality. What then, are they to do with their profits? In retrospect the answer seems obvious: they should invest in financial, not real productive assets.[18]

This is precisely what capital has done from the 1970s onwards. Finance capital has ridden the wave of globalization and the new technological revolutions in computers and communications to become the most profitable, powerful and speculative actor within the capitalist world. Finance capital is commodifying money as never before, increasingly separating the capital and money markets from industry.[19] In other words, finance capital has forged its own instruments of expansion and a momentum of accumulation that are increasingly independent of what is happening in the sphere of production. Finance capital is begetting what is popularly called "casino capitalism," the rise of speculation and fast money-making on an unprecedented scale.

The very rise of finance capital is associated with the onset of slowed economic growth in the core countries and abrupt changes or shocks that hit the capitalist world in the 1970s. First in 1971, the United States renounced the convertibility of the dollar into gold because of the tremendous deficit it had been running in its balance of payments (due in large part to the funding of the Vietnam war and other Cold War expenditures). This ongoing outflow of dollars was in turn reinforced by the jump in oil prices in 1973 and the creation of a huge international pool of petrodollars.

During this period the large international banks used the excess dollars abroad to create an international capital market, first denominated "Eurodollars." In the 1970s the Eurodollar market lent heavily to countries and corporations in search of capital. A large portion of these petrodollars also began to flow through the new offshore banking centers set up to free the banks from the regulatory activities of their national governments. Many of the loans from this growing pool of international capital went to Third World projects and governments, particularly in Latin America.

When this uncontrolled lending resulted in the Third World debt crisis of the early 1980s, international capital turned its attention to reaping large profits by underwriting much of the merger and acquisition craze of the 1980s. Between 1985 and 1989, the asset value of world merger and acquisition deals rose from $300 billion to $1 trillion, providing ample opportunity for big banks, brokerage firms and junk bond dealers to move to center stage in the wheeling and dealing in the corporate world.[20]

Speculating in foreign exchange rates became another major area for finance capital when the United States went off gold-convertibility and allowed the dollar to float vis-a-vis other international currencies. By 1979 the turnover in the world's foreign exchange markets was around $25 trillion annually; a decade later it was over $100 trillion.[21] And by mid-1995, due in part to a boost in "computer driven trading" it was estimated that currency trading stood at $1 trillion per day.[22] As Gerd Sperder, a Paris-based currency specialist noted during the midst of the precipitous drop in the value of the dollar in early 1995, the floating exchange rate system "encourages enormous sums of speculative money to race around the world seeking hour-by-hour, even minute-by-minute profits. It's not so much a floating exchange rate system as a global floating crap game."[23]

Even when one sets aside these international exchange transactions, the advance of finance capital in the 1970s and 1980s is nothing short of astounding. The growth of international banking, the markets for international loans, the financing of merger and acquisition activity, and the markets for international securities all boomed: total external liabilities of international banks in these areas stood at $200 billion in the early 1970s, $1.3 trillion by 1980, and then reached $6 trillion in 1990.[24]

The biggest arena for finance capital in the 1990s is the global equities markets (the buying and selling of stocks), particularly in the Third World and the former communist bloc countries. Goaded by the IMF and neo-liberal policies, stock markets have been set up in virtually all the major country and regional markets of the world: thirty-five stock market exchanges now operate in developing countries alone.[25]

The purchasing of shares by foreign capital in national stock exchanges is labeled "direct foreign investment" in terms of international accounting. But this type of investment differs substantially from the direct foreign investments usually made by multinational corporations in factories and mines, that is, in areas of production. In contrast, direct investments in the stock market are volatile, do not necessarily go into productive activities and can be withdrawn from one day to the next.

In Latin America for example the alleged economic miracle of the 1990s (after the "lost decade" of the 1980s due to the debt crisis) is due mainly to the flow of capital into the burgeoning stock markets of Mexico and South America. In 1990 direct private investment throughout Latin America and the Caribbean stood at about $52 billion, in 1994 it reached $83 billion, a phenomenal increase of almost 60 per cent.[26] Meanwhile, the actual growth rates of these countries' economies have hardly been spectacular, running only at about an average of 3–4 per cent per annum.

So what's happening to all this foreign money, given that it has hardly touched off a revolution in manufacturing and commodity production? Simply put, it's used to speculate in the stock exchanges. International mutual funds, institutional investors and brokerage firms are all jumping into Third World equity markets, viewing them as the "hot buys" of the 1990s. In 1994, stock investors in Brazil saw their shares rise in value by an average 75 per cent while in Peru stocks increased by 56 per cent.[27] Clearly, the foreign investors are reaping hefty returns through the rise in stock prices, not through any significant increase in production. The volatility and ephemeral nature of these investments was amply demonstrated during the financial crisis in Mexico in December 1994, when many foreign investors pulled out of the stock market, thereby further accentuating Mexico's exchange crisis and the drop in the value of the peso. (In Mexico, offshore investors held half of that country's stock market shares prior to the financial crisis.)[28]

The growth in companies available for purchase in these stock markets has been spurred by the IMF policy of forcing many governments to privatize state enterprises at cheap prices in the name of "economic restructuring." From 1988 to 1992 the value of Third World privatizations in 25 countries totaled $61.6 billion.[29] These state divestitures have constituted some of the best buys for foreign capital intent on penetrating strategic, often monopolistic, sectors of national economies like telephone companies, banks, petroleum and mining enterprises.

The even darker side of finance capital is its setting of economic policies and financial priorities for the biggest nation states. Mitterrand's France in the early 1980s is a classic example of how finance capital decimated a social democratic government's policies. Elected in 1981, Mitterrand undertook a series of public expenditures designed to lower unemployment and revitalize many of France's lethargic industries, particularly those held by the state. Capital responded by driving down the value of the French franc and by raising the interest rates for government debt financing, thereby setting off a wave of capital flight and increased inflation. Caught in this pincer movement by capital, Mitterrand in 1983 abandoned the platform of social reforms that he had campaigned on – and for the next decade followed conservative economic recipes that were to the liking of international financiers.

In the 1990s finance capitalism appears intent on disciplining the few remaining avowed welfare states. In Canada, finance capital will only buy government bonds at the high interest rate of 9 per cent, in spite of the fact that inflation is less than 1 per cent. The reason for capital's penalization of Canada is due to the government's total debt being equal to its annual Gross Domestic Product (GDP) because of major social expenditures, including the financing of a national health care system. (Of course the financiers ignore the fact that the ratio of Canada's debt to GDP is about the same as that of the United States by the end of the Reagan–Bush years.)

In the case of Sweden, finance capital is also striking out at that country's welfare state, letting it be known that the Swedes can no longer expect financial "assistance" and capital flows unless the government begins to dismantle one of the most advanced and efficient social welfare systems in the world. As Walter Wriston, the former head of Citibank admitted, currency traders now "conduct a kind of global plebiscite on the monetary and fiscal policies of the governments issuing currency," exercising a control "far more draconian than any previous arrangement, such as the gold standard or the Bretton Woods system, since there is no way for any nation to opt out."[30] And in bland bureaucratic language, the *United Nations Perspective on the World Economy* stated: "Policy makers see themselves as operating in a relatively new environment in which maintaining the confidence of the financial markets takes high priority."[31]

The cracks in late capitalism

The rise of finance capital on a global scale has rendered capitalism more unstable in the past decade and a half than it has been since the early decades of this century. The Third World debt crisis of the early and mid-1980s marked the first major disturbance begotten by emergent finance capital. Then the stock market crash occurred in October 1987, in large part because capital from around the world had moved into the major stock markets – particularly the New York stock exchange – and overvalued many stocks. Major bank failures in the 1980s, like that of the BCCI, the collapse of the savings and loan industry in the United States, the boom and bust in financial rental markets, particularly in London and Tokyo, the financial meltdown in Mexico in 1994–5, and the fall of Barings Bank of London in 1995 are all linked to the mobility and ascendancy of finance capital.

Finance capital is driving late capitalism to the brink of a major economic disaster. Not since the late nineteenth century and the era of the robber barons has big capital been so unbridled, so able to indulge itself in financial greed and speculation. Then also Western capitalism experienced uncontrolled speculation in stocks, bonds and foreign currencies as well as precious metals. There were frequent booms and busts from 1870 onward, in the United States and Western Europe.

Interestingly, there was a period of consolidation around the turn of the century, when finance and industry established a working alliance that is aptly described by Rudolf Hilferding in his famous tome *Das Finanzkapital*.[32] At that time finance began to collaborate with industry in a process of consolidation, thereby benefiting capitalism as a whole as the big banks and the industrialists used their joint economic power to forge large corporations. Before this reorganization, many small companies had been competing with each other for the same markets, thereby leading to frequent business failures. With consolidation in steel, meat packing, chemical, food processing and other industries, the new corporations were able to open up national markets and to influence and control those markets.

The major difference between that era and today is that our finance capitalists are far bigger and more parasitical – they thrive on speculation and casino capitalism. They have little interest in organizing production. Except in the high tech and media areas of the economy, it simply takes too long to make a fortune by investing in an industry or a particular area of production. Some new fortunes are made by high-tech companies like Apple, Compaq, Intel and Microsoft. But just as many are being made by big currency speculators, merger and acquisition specialists, large stock brokerage firms and by "superinvestors." A leading example of the new superinvestor is George Soros, a post-war US immigrant from Hungary who has racked up a fortune by speculating in the stock and money markets. Since the collapse of the Soviet bloc, he has set up a foundation to spread the gospel of the free market in Eastern Europe.

Outright criminality has also taken hold in the highest spheres of finance capital, as is illustrated by the junk bond scams of Michael Milken and the insider trading of Ivan Boskey. These activities did not end with the downfall and imprisonment of these two financiers. In the United States in 1994 one-third of the 100 largest merger deals or tender offers were preceded by abnormal stock-price run-ups or increases in volume trading that could only be explained by access to inside information. During the fiscal year ending September 30, 1994, the US Securities and Exchange Commission filed a record number of 45 cases against insider traders, exceeding the previous high of 43 in 1989 when insider trading first captured public attention.[33]

Finance capital is largely beyond the control of the powerful central banks in Washington, Bonn and Tokyo, as their growing difficulty in affecting the foreign currency markets demonstrates. In mid-1994 and then again in early 1995 these central banks failed completely in their attempts to halt the fall of the dollar vis-a-vis the German mark and the Japanese yen. The amount of dollars the central banks sold, in the billions, was simply too small to make a dent in the multi-trillion dollar currency markets.

Moreover, the US Federal Reserve inadvertently precipitated an adverse reaction by international investors in the US bond market in 1994 by hiking interest rates at the same time as the dollar was falling in value. Raising interest rates, combined with the fact that many of the international bond buyers had bought their bonds with the now higher priced yen, led to a double squeeze on both sides of the Pacific. US bonds plummeted in value as international investors began a panic liquidation of their holdings.

The other financial jolt of 1994 that illustrates the volatility of finance capital occurred when Orange County, California, home to some of the richest suburbanites in the United States, filed for bankruptcy. The county's collapse came because it had put money into a little-known financial instrument called a derivative, which is one among many forms of speculation that has developed with the rise of finance capital. Today there are $20 trillion worth of swaps, options, caps, collars and other derivative products that circulate around the globe, beyond the control of most national regulators.[34] In the case of Orange County, the county's treasurer bet heavily on derivatives linked to low or falling interest rates. When the Federal Reserve raised interest rates throughout 1994, the county's portfolio collapsed. Of course the brokerage firm that had been advising Orange County, Merrill Lynch, made off handsomely, taking $80 million from the county in the two years before the debacle.[35]

The final crisis?

Given the series of jolts and scares that the capitalist world has experienced since the 1980s it is not unreasonable to predict that finance capital will provoke a major systemic crisis, one surpassing the Great Depression in its global impact. Too much capital is now tied to the financial sphere. It is on an uncontrollable roller-coaster ride that will end in disaster.

Is this crisis of capitalism the final one? Marxists, ever since Marx, have had the tendency to see the impending demise of capitalism as occurring just around the next historic corner. Lenin, for example, in *On Imperialism* totally misread what was happening in the capitalist world at the turn of the century. He asserted that the major corporations and trusts, by becoming monopolistic, were uninterested in and unwilling to expand production and advance technologically. For Lenin, imperialism, the final stage of capitalism, was characterized by "parasitism and decay" and would soon collapse. Lenin did not recognize that the large corporations of his time were in fact technologically and organizationally innovative, as demonstrated by changes in Ford and General Motors in the auto field, and by advances in chemical firms such as DuPont Siemans and Bayer. They were continuing to "revolutionize the means of production," bringing new vitality to the capitalist system as a whole.

But there is something that is very different about our period of late capitalism. Certainly, multinationals today are just as technologically dynamic, if not more so, than their early twentieth century predecessors. But, as we have argued, that very technology is now destabilizing. It leads to the constant increase in dead capital and the marginalization of more and more people who have no place in the capitalist system of production. Simultaneously, the rich and the powerful use their control of technology to concentrate even more wealth and property in their hands.

Even some enthusiasts of the new globalism are weary of what may be in store as finance capital takes over. *Business Week*, in a special report at the end of 1994 titled '21st Century Capitalism,' lauded the economy that has come about as a result of "borderless finance." This is the "fuel for growth" it proclaimed. However, on the downside, the report noted that "the markets will turn more cruelly efficient and risky than ever."[36] Finally *Business Week* declared: "It's clear that the sheer multiplicity of financial sources in an era of borderless capital will complicate crisis management," and that "the technology-driven 21st century money market will give birth to problems that are only beginning to become apparent."[37] Capitalism has simply become too unstable, too speculative, too greedy and too corrupt to avoid a major catastrophe before we get too far into the next century.

CHAPTER 5

The Trauma of the Third World

The Third World War has already started – it is a silent war, not for that reason any less sinister. This war is tearing down practically all the Third World. Instead of soldiers dying, there are children dying; instead of millions wounded, there are millions unemployed; instead of the destruction of bridges, there is a tearing down of factories, hospitals, schools, and entire economies.

Lula,
Brazilian labor leader

The Storm ... It will be born from the conflict of these two winds; its time has now come; the oven of history is now stirred. The wind from above now reigns, but the wind from below comes and the storm arrives ... and so it will be.

The Prophecy ... When the storm subsides, when the fire and rain leave the earth in peace once again, the world will no longer be the world but something better.

Subcomandante Marcos,
Lacondona Jungle, Mexico[1]

Although poverty and social decay now afflict the societies of the major capitalist nations, the regions of the world designated as the "South" or the "Third World" still possess distinctive characteristics that set them apart from the core capitalist societies. In a world dominated by the big powers, they suffer severe deprivation and exploitation. The economics of globalization have pushed them deeper into misery, violence, social decomposition, drug trafficking, ecological degradation and simmering or even explosive discontent. As Samir Amin notes, "The more the economic system globalizes, the more it generates frustrations in the peripheralized areas, thus constantly reanimating violent nationalistic responses."[2]

The end of the Cold War has not brought peace to these areas of the world, only more conflict as interventions by the Western powers assume new dimensions. It is no historical accident that since the fall of the Berlin Wall the big powers led by the United States have invaded four Third World countries: Panama, Iraq, Somalia and Haiti. Simultaneously, the United States as the globe's hegemonic military power has been particularly belligerent towards so-called rogue states, Iran, Libya, North Korea and Cuba, stepping up its economic aggression and raising the specter of new interventions.

On the surface, each of the four invasions was carried out for very different reasons: to remove a drug-dealing ruler in Panama, to roll back Iraq's takeover of the strategic oil emirate of Kuwait, to provide "humanitarian" assistance to the starving people of Somalia and to restore an elected leader in Haiti. Yet beyond these surface appearances, all four invasions had one single underlying explanation: they were undertaken because these Third World countries and their leaders ran foul of what the United States and its allies determined to be acceptable behavior in key or strategically located countries. These were by no means accidental or disinterested interventions. All occurred in countries where one Western power or another had been meddling for much of the twentieth century.

These invasions mark a continuation of the "rollback" offensive launched by the Reagan administration in the 1980s against Third World countries. As Susan George notes in the introduction to *Dark Victory*,

> Rollback meant an end to Third World pretensions. There was to be no more talk of a New International Economic Order, binding codes of conduct for foreign investors, mandatory transfers of technology or managed commodity prices. The South was to return to that quiescent state from which it should never have been allowed to emerge. The unruly would be disciplined and the rebellious cowed.[3]

Today many parts of the Third World are confronting severe crises of one form or another due in large part to the years of exploitation and subservience to big power interests. Africa faces famine and economic destitution; Latin America has just gone through a decade of negative growth rates and a surge in the ranks of the impoverished by about 40 per cent; the non-petroleum producing countries of the Middle East and Northern Africa are also afflicted with poverty, stagnant economies and rapidly growing populations; and many parts of Asia, from Afghanistan and India to Bangladesh, Vietnam and Indonesia, are home to some of the poorest people in the world.

Dashed hopes

When the United States and the Western powers are not threatening or cajoling Third World countries, their approach is that of disdainful neglect now that the Soviet Union is no longer an international competitor. Guy Arnold in a book aptly titled *The End of the Third World* points out that Third World countries are "largely expendable" and have "nowhere to go" as the North refuses to alleviate their debt burden, relies less and less on their resources as new products (like saccharin and sucrose) enter the market, and embarks on racist campaigns designed to control immigration from the South and/or justify Western policies of intervention or neglect. With the termination of the Cold War has come "the disappearance of any independent capacity to bargain on the part of the old Third World," and a "growth of neo-colonial controls exercised by the North."[4]

Many Western writers and ideologues of the 1990s, when they do turn to discussing conditions in the Third World, wring their hands in anguish and largely portray the poorest of the Third World countries as lost to the cause of modern civilization. Robert D. Kaplan in 'The Coming Anarchy,' an article in the *Atlantic Monthly* magazine, proclaims that "scarcity, crime, overpopulation, tribalism, and disease" in Africa and much of the Third World are "rapidly destroying the social fabric of our planet."[5] His argument is that many Third World societies are ungovernable and the West can do little to assist them. These countries are losers because they have forsaken civilized values. At one point Kaplan asserts that there are no "social anchors" in West Africa because religions are "undermined by animist beliefs not suitable to a moral society." These societies are supposedly doomed to a choice between "totalitarianism (as in Iraq), fascist-tending mini-states (as in Serb-held Bosnia) and road-warrior cultures (as in Somalia)."[6]

Any objective effort to understand what is really happening in the South must start out by realizing that the Third World is by no means a uniform entity. It contains a tremendous diversity of races, cultures and societies with widely disparate economies. It is for example impossible to compare the Philippines, a complex country of almost 70 million people, with the former English colony of Belize which has about 200,000 inhabitants. And India with its 890 million people and rich history and cultural diversity has little in common with Angola, the former colony of Portugal that has one of the lowest population densities in the world.[7] But for many of the approximately 4 billion people who live in over 110 Third World countries there is one deplorable reality – they live in poverty, face a dismal economic future, and are at the mercy of global economic forces that serve the interests of the dominant capitalist powers.

It is also important to recognize that the current despair and hopelessness expressed about the Third World did not characterize attitudes and positions in decades past. Once there was hope in the Third World, first in the 1940s and 1950s with the independence movements in Africa and Asia, and then in the 1960s and 1970s with the triumph of a number of national liberation movements. A sense of optimism prevailed as most of the Third World believed that it was seizing control of its destiny and that sustained economic development was within its grasp. This is the legacy of governments extending from Nkrumah of Ghana and Nasser of Egypt to the revolutions in Cuba, Vietnam and Nicaragua.

But virtually all the hopes of these movements have been dashed. What has happened? A nexus of factors and forces have come together to make the future of the Third World so bleak. First and foremost is the continued intervention of the dominant capitalist powers and their determination to perpetuate a global economic system based on inequality and exploitation. Secondly, related to this is the legacy of the Cold War which has had devastating consequences for the Third World as the two big power blocs, the East and the West, used much of the Third World as their proxy battlefields. Finally, the failure of the alternative model – that of the national liberation movements – to generate economic growth has thwarted the hopes of a large portion of the Third World that sought a non-capitalist path of development.

Malthus and technology

Any assessment of the South must acknowledge that there are of course internal dynamics at work throughout the Third World countries that feed the economic and political crises. Paul Kennedy in *Preparing for the Twenty-First Century* depicts a Third World on the brink of a neo-Malthusian disaster. The population explosion in the Third World is indeed daunting. By 2025, in about thirty years, the population of the Third World could almost double, producing widespread poverty, ecological disasters and social upheavals.[8] Kennedy is of course aware that in the past Malthusian and other pessimistic interpretations of the world were proven wrong by the development of new technologies and revolutions in agriculture and manufacturing. But Kennedy correctly points out that today there is a fundamental division in the world between the haves and have-nots that makes it extremely difficult to reproduce a similar type of transformation. The countries that are developed and have fairly stable populations monopolize most of the world's technological and capital resources, while those with exploding populations have neither capital nor technology.

In many cases, the development of new technologies may even worsen the plight of the Third World. As a World Bank report on biotechnology points out, small-scale impoverished farmers "are most likely to be adversely affected by the social and trade changes" that accompany modifications in agriculture through biotechnology.[9] Because the results of biotechnology will predominantly be employed in the core countries, it means the prices of primary agricultural commodities produced in the Third World will drop even more. At the same time the use of robots and automation in manufacturing enables some multinationals to turn out their products with very few workers, thereby permitting them to cease paying even the miserable wages they are accustomed to paying in the Third World.

The technological fix of recent decades pushed by the developed countries, the Green Revolution, did nothing to resolve the problems of Africa or any other regions of the Third World. Michael Lipton, in a study supported by the International Agricultural Research Centers, the very research institutes that backed the Green Revolution, concludes that the "greening has not been revolutionary."[10] Throughout the Third World, the seed varieties increased agricultural output, but they have not alleviated poverty or provided the people at the lower tiers of society with better diets. Meanwhile the heavy use of fertilizers and pesticides associated with these new seed varieties contributed to the accelerated degradation of the environment. Lipton does acknowledge that "poor people's purchasing-power did not increase to buy the extra food," but he refuses to admit that the very structure of capitalism with its highly skewed income levels is the root cause of the failure of the Green Revolution.[11]

While Kennedy and Lipton recognize that the control of technology and many global trends emanating from the core countries adversely affect the Third World, they, like many of today's developmental analysts, do not recognize that the big powers relentlessly pursue policies that reinforce the internal conditions of underdevelopment and keep most of the Third World impoverished. Kennedy for example discusses at length the developmental barriers posed by large illiterate populations and a vast untrained labor force as if these were autonomous conditions, unrelated to the history of colonialism most of these countries experienced. And when he bemoans the lack of an entrepreneurial spirit and the existence of cultures that do not encourage productive work beyond subsistence activities, he is ignoring the fact that the ruthless advance of global capitalism has destroyed the self-sufficiency of innumerable societies and cultures.[12]

Kennedy does critique conservative economic policies and their insistence that only the free market will change these conditions. But what Kennedy, most liberals and many so-called "development experts" do not acknowledge, especially now with the end of the Cold War, is that there are systemic forces at work that run much deeper than the mere issue of what particular type of capitalist model is being applied in the Third World.

The invasion of Somalia by the United States and the Western powers in December 1992, brought out this fundamental ideological unity between liberals, conservatives and even social democrats in their view of the Third World. They backed Bush's portrayal of the invasion as "humanitarian," as a Western effort to "save" the Somalians from themselves. Only occasionally would it be mentioned that most of the arms used by local Somalian leaders were provided by the United States when it swung its support to the dictator Mohammed Siad Barre to win him away from his former Soviet backers. In effect the First World invaded Somalia because of the conditions of war, poverty and underdevelopment that it had been instrumental in creating.

Even more significantly, much of sub-Saharan Africa, which is not involved in local wars, faces deteriorating economic conditions similar to those of Somalia. Throughout the 1980s, this region suffered a greater loss of export revenue than any other region of the Third World, not because of drought or internal conflicts, but simply because the prices for most of its commodities dropped on the world market.[13] Kennedy and others who buy into the existent global economic system argue that this is the cold-hearted reality of today's world, that there are "winners and losers" and that sub-Saharan Africa has simply had the bad luck to be among the losers in the late twentieth century. This disingenuous interpretation enables the developed world to wash its hands of responsibility for what is happening in sub-Saharan Africa.

The legacy of the Cold War

With the end of the Cold War, a common view put forth is that the Third World will fall even more into the pit of poverty and under-development. For about four decades, the argument goes, many Third World countries were able to play off the Soviet bloc against the Western world and gain enormous amounts of aid and development assistance.

While it is certainly true that the Western world is even more tight-fisted in its disbursement of economic aid in the Third World now that the Soviet Union is gone, the reality is that much of the Third World is on the brink of disaster precisely because of the legacy of the Cold War. All too many countries – in Africa, Asia and Latin America – became politico–military pawns in proxy wars carried on by two great superpowers who were too terrified to use their nuclear arsenals against each other. These wars exacted a heavy toll, sucking up enormous quantities of Third World resources, resources that could have been better used for internal development.

Entire regions, particularly in south-east Asia, were decimated. And many other countries from Ethiopia and Somalia in Africa to Guatemala and El Salvador in Latin America developed politico–military regimes in alliance with the big powers that sucked up resources and divided people in Third World countries into warring factions bent on destroying each other.

In the heat of these regional conflicts some Third World countries, like the Arab petroleum producers, spent billions of their wealth on buying advanced military systems from the Western world, particularly the United States. Another group of Third World countries, which weren't able to pay for military supplies, were given huge military "loans" and sometimes outright grants. Small countries like Nicaragua and Honduras, and larger ones like Egypt and Angola, developed obese military structures under Western and/or Eastern bloc auspices. While the military supplies were subsidized, the focus on militarism distorted the development of all these nations. The education of efficient public employees, skilled technical personnel, and qualified economic and business administrators often took second place to the budgets and demands of the local militaries. Simply put, the militarization of countries in the Third World sucked off a large portion of their internal resources and people's productive capacities.

One consequence of US intervention in the Third World was the destruction of the most democratic tendencies in the socialist movements. The Chilean Popular Unity government under Salvador Allende (1970–3) tried to pursue a democratic path to socialism, mobilizing the workers and appropriating the means of production while abiding by the Chilean constitution. But the right wing in Chile, allied with US imperialism in the persona of Henry Kissinger and Richard Nixon, refused to accept this democratic process. They sabotaged the economy, mounted paramilitary activities in the streets and ultimately staged a military coup that led to the slaughter of thousands. Allende could have prevented the downfall of the Popular Unity government only if he had been willing to forsake his democratic principles. He would have had to purge the military, suspend parliament and issue presidential decrees that violated the constitution. These steps and others would have been necessary to control and repress the opposition. But these measures would have also meant the abandonment of democracy, and a clear decision by Allende to opt for a more typical, neo-authoritarian form of socialism as in other Third World countries.

Crisis of the national liberation model

It is important not to lay the blame for the plight of the Third World solely on the doorstep of the capitalist system or the capitalist powers. What is clear from the perspective of the 1990s is that the communist model of development as well as capitalism have failed the Third World. The national liberation movements in power were generally effective at redistributing wealth and providing some minimal necessities for the population, like access to education and health care. But, with a few exceptions, they were unable to unleash the forces of production.

The national liberation movements in Africa, Latin America and Asia have suffered or are experiencing severe economic and political crises. The Cuban Revolution is in a serious crisis, the Mozambique and Angolan revolutions have suffered severe reversals, the revolutionary movements in Central America have been decimated and, in Asia, one can hardly argue that the Chinese communists, or even the Vietnamese, are advancing the banners of socialism and national liberation. The crises of these Third World countries and their movements cannot be simply attributed to the fall of the Soviet patron or to the drying up of Soviet assistance – it is due mainly to the tensions and shortcomings of the economic and political models these national liberation governments adopted and internalized.

The collapse of the communist parties and the crisis in the Third World movements have the same common roots – the lack of an authentic and deep-seated commitment to democracy, both within their political movements and their forms of economic organization. The fundamental premise of the national liberation movements, once in power, was that the way to change society and run the economy was from the top down, by using "the commanding heights" of the state.

The centralism practiced by traditional national liberation movements in both the party and the state overshadows any democratic tendencies. As Samir Amin notes in *Maldevelopment*, the "national popular revolutions," instead of pursuing "political democracy and a mixed economy" to deal with "the effects of polarization and peripheralization produced by the global expansion of actually existing capitalism," opted instead for "statism, thus reflecting the reconstitution of privileged class interests."[14]

Cuba's situation today illustrates the consequences of pursuing this path of development. One cannot deny that Cuba's statist economy did bring substantial economic growth to the island during the 1970s and 1980s. The country made progress in developing its industry, in producing a sophisticated medical sector linked to pharmaceutical export production, and in building up a tourist industry that became the major earner of foreign exchange after sugar cane. But when Soviet assistance collapsed, the external dependence of the economy and its statist-orientation had dramatic consequences. The Cuban Communist Party had grown accustomed to running the political system and the economy from the top down. The trade unions, the country's plants and industries, the women's association, the educational system were all controlled by the dictates of a highly centralized party apparatus that dominates the state and society. Many people at the base level did not believe they were participating in the building of socialism, nor did they feel that they were responsible for the government.

Thus when the economic problems hit due to the cut-off of Soviet assistance, the people naturally blamed the government for their plight. Their response is entirely different from that of the 1960s, when economic conditions were much worse in Cuba, but the Cuban people still had a sense that they were participating in the political and economic development of the country. Today they feel powerless to deal with the situation, and thus when conditions worsen instead of getting better, it is perceived to be the fault of Fidel Castro or the leadership around him. These leaders chose the path that placed the emphasis on a command economy and led Cuba to an historic dead end with the collapse of the Eastern European communist bloc.

The Central American case

The Central American experience in the 1980s demonstrates even more conclusively the shortcomings and exhaustion of the "actually existing" national liberation movements. In 1981, it appeared that revolutionary movements were ascendant in the region. The Sandinista movement had taken power in Nicaragua, the popular struggle was growing in intensity in El Salvador, the guerrillas in Guatemala were stronger than they had been in a decade and a half, and in Honduras guerrilla movements were making their first real impact on the national political scene.

Almost a decade and a half later, depending on which country one looks at, the national liberation movements are moribund, in a state of disarray, or in largely defensive positions. In Honduras the guerrillas have been wiped out, in Nicaragua, the Sandinista Front has been voted out of power and is divided, in Guatemala, the guerrillas have been reduced to rural-based groups with little impact on national politics, and in El Salvador, the FMLN, although it has survived a dozen years of civil war and made the transition to electoral politics, is also fractured and by no means on the brink of taking power.

None of these setbacks or defeats in Central America can be blamed simply on the curtailment of Soviet bloc assistance. In the case of Nicaragua, where the Sandinista Front was dependent on external assistance for its survival, the electoral debacle in February

1990 occurred when aid from the communist countries was flowing in at significant levels. In 1989 figures from the Organization for Economic Cooperation and Development (OECD) show that the economic aid received and committed from the Eastern bloc countries stood at all-time highs.[15]

The problems of the national liberation movements in Central America are rooted in the fact that they began to loose touch to one degree or another with the popular classes on behalf of which they were supposedly making the revolution. The vanguard organizations in all of these countries in effect became highly centralized politico–military organizations whose primary function was that of conducting armed struggle against US imperialism and its allies in Central America. By focusing on armed conflict and violence, they in effect became voluntaristic, that is, they came to believe their own rhetoric that the masses would be supportive of a long drawn-out struggle for "national liberation." But they were wrong. The bulk of the population – particularly in Guatemala, El Salvador and Nicaragua – grew tired of war and violence. They wanted peace and increasingly turned away from the national liberation movements as the 1980s wore on.

The same happened in large parts of Africa, particularly in Angola and Mozambique, where the internal civil wars resolved nothing. Mozambique today is the poorest country in the world, and in Angola, the per capita income stands at less than it did in 1976 when the country won independence from Portugal. In the case of Angola there is no doubt that the flight of the Portuguese colonists, combined with the intervention of the South African government and the United States exacted a horrific toll. But the Angolan governing national liberation movement, the MPLA, must bear major responsibility for the economic decline of the country. Until 1988, it tried to run the economy from the top down, "ordering" economic growth and government-run development projects that did not have the trained or skilled personnel to implement them. These policies led nowhere as the country lapsed into economic chaos with much of the populace surviving only by turning to subsistence agriculture or other rudimentary economic activities.[16]

Some may argue that this crisis of the national liberation movements is principally attributable to the intervention of imperialism. This is true in part, but one has to recognize that from its inception, the theory and practice of national liberation has been rooted in the very idea of a confrontation with imperialism. If anything, one could argue that big power intervention in Central America and Africa was quite limited, given the fact that neither US nor Western troops were ever deployed in direct combat against these revolutionary governments or guerrilla movements. The

United States did pump in economic and military assistance to sustain local reactionary elites but these social forces were supposedly part of the discredited old order that the national liberation movements had declared they could easily sweep away as "ancien regimes."

From Angola and Mozambique to Laos and Central America the national liberation movements became rigid and locked into old ideological formulas. Along with a commitment to armed struggle, they continued to view the worker–peasant alliance as central to the liberation struggle. That formula may have been effective in earlier decades but it no longer worked by the early 1980s. Society had become far more complex, even in the most undeveloped Third World societies. Professional associations, religions sects and groups, community organizations, women's movements, cultural and ethnic groups – these and many others were part of the development of civil society that has occurred in recent years.

Imperialism in the short term has managed to adjust to these new realities because it operates in a more decentralized manner, allowing a variety of groups and organizations to work under its banner without being formally tied to it. Fundamentalist missionaries, non-governmental organizations, private business associations, non-profit foundations and others have facilitated the development of pro-capitalist societies without being directly under the control of imperialist governments. The vanguard parties, on the other hand, with their politico–military orientation and their top-down structures were simply incapable of incorporating or responding to the new developments in civil society. They tried to adjust by setting up new fronts or popular organizations, but it proved impossible to use this approach when a bewildering array of new organizations and movements with highly diverse goals and interests were emerging at the grassroots level.

The neo-liberal disasters

Now with the end of the Cold War, the problem is that the old centrally planned economies are being driven to adopt an economic model of development that will prove just as disastrous. Instead of being allowed to decide what system or mix of systems is best suited for their needs, the international financial institutions are forcing the entire Third World to open up their weak economies to the global economic system dominated by the big powers.

The tragedy is that neo-liberal economics, as well as command communism, need to be thrown into the historical dustbin. A NACLA Report demonstrates that even the two major "success cases" of neo-liberal economics in Latin America, Costa Rica and Chile, have produced a concentration of wealth at the top of society while hunger and malnutrition have grown at the bottom. Costa Rica, which received major US subsidies in the mid and late 1980s to support non-traditional exports and a neo-liberal economic policy, has seen a jump in those living below the poverty line, from 18.6 per cent in 1987 to 24.4 per cent in 1991 alone.

And Chile, which has now practised one form or another of neo-liberal economics for over two decades, has also experienced a substantial increase in the ranks of the poor during these years. About 42 per cent of the country's populace now lives in poverty, a dramatically high proportion, given the fact that Chile once prided itself on having a fairly equitable distribution of income compared to other Latin American countries.[17]

Even *Business Week* has come to recognize that neo-liberalism has largely benefited a class of nouveaux riches and the multinationals. In an article on Mexico's economic boomlet before the crash in December 1994, *Business Week* noted that Mexico was largely dominated by "a continental network of Harvard, Chicago and Stanford grads [who] are back home atop businesses and government ministries spreading a new market mind-set ... These MBAs and PhDs are not afraid of bonding with the U.S." The article went on to note that there have been few improvements in the lot of the poor, with "the immense underclasses still untouched by the bonanza."[18]

Delinking

Almost simultaneously with the rise of neo-liberalism has come the economic reality that the Third World is delinking from the First World, not voluntarily as many socialists once hoped, but because the core capitalist countries have proportionally less use for the resources of the South. In recent decades the Third World has come to occupy a diminished role in the international economic system and has attracted a smaller proportion of total foreign capital. In 1967, 31 per cent of the total foreign investment was located in the Third World. By 1989, it had dropped to 19 per cent. For the United States, which has led much of the developed world in its Third World investments, just one quarter of its total foreign capital in 1990 was found in the underdeveloped countries.[19] In the 1990s, there has been a surge in foreign investments in Third World stock markets, but these are highly speculative and are not producing sustained economic growth.

Rosa Luxemburg in the early twentieth century argued that the imperialist nations needed the underdeveloped world in order to export their capital surpluses. If there were no Third World markets, then the high rates of profits would fall. Luxemburg's thesis is sustained by economic development during the immediate post-World War II decades, when the Third World did occupy a fairly important role for the United States and Western Europe, as they dumped surplus capital and commodities into Third World markets as never before. But in the last decade and a half the Third World has proven far less viable as an outlet for investments and commodities. New technologies in the core countries combined with declining rates of profit in the Third World have rendered it less lucrative for the multinationals and international capital. But this new trend does not necessarily refute the core of Luxemburg's thesis. Delinking the Third World actually does pose major problems for the dominant capitalist nations. On one level it can be argued that a large part of the realization crisis of the First World (discussed earlier) may be due in part to the decline of lucrative markets and investment outlets in the Third World.

There are other more specific reasons why the First World needs the Third World. Above all it is critical as a massive reserve army of labor. Every year the Third World sends more and more immigrants to work in the developed countries, either legally or illegally. This flow of immigrants does cause conflicts and social tensions in the First World, particularly as a result of the recent economic recessions in much of the capitalist world. But these immigrants continue to arrive because the core capitalist economies need them to help keep wages down, as immigrants take on a variety of low-end service jobs, working as gardeners, fast-food employees, mechanics, caterers and maids. They are also a critical labor source in the sweatshops of major cities like Los Angeles, New York and London.

The developed countries also use the Third World as a source of skilled labor. The United States is especially adept at this, having rewritten its immigration laws in recent years to favor the entrance of professionals ranging from doctors and nurses to scientists, professors and computer experts. Many of the most talented people in the Third World countries are drawn to these opportunities, hoping to encounter a more rewarding material life in the United States than in their own unstable and undeveloped countries.

The teeming millions that remain at home in their impoverished countries also serve as a reserve army of labor for the development of significant pockets of industrial and export production in the Third World. The *maquiladores* across the US border, the multinational food processing plants that develop and market Kellogg's cornflakes, Heinz ketchup or Pillsbury muffins, as well as Japanese and US auto manufacturers with subsidiaries scattered throughout the Third World – all these transnational enterprises and others benefit enormously by being able to pay wages that are only a small fraction of what they are in the core countries.

The Third World is also still important to the core countries as a major source of resources and primary materials. Western developmental economists correctly assert that many Third World countries are growing poorer because they produce agricultural products like coffee and sugar, or raw materials like tin, copper or iron ore that pay badly on the international market. But what is not pointed out is that many of these areas of production were initially encouraged through direct investments by multinationals and foreign investors. Now, as part of the process of flexible accumulation, multinationals have pulled out their investments in many of these areas of production. With a surplus of these commodities on the world market, multinationals can buy them up at cheap prices on the open market and lower their own costs of production with inexpensive inputs.

Many commodities from the Third World may no longer be "winners" in the international marketplace, but if they were to dry up, the Western countries would find themselves in difficult straits. The point is not that international capital could be expected to do anything different, but that it is benefiting from and needs the Third World countries to keep providing cheap raw materials and commodities, even as these countries fall deeper into poverty and bankruptcy by doing so.

The shift of big capital away from fixed production to flexible accumulation is also the key to understanding how international capital exploits the Third World today in less visible forms. The sale of large-scale production units with fixed capital (like banana plantations), the rise of *maquiladores* (sometimes under the control of local capital), the importing of non-traditional and traditional agricultural exports (often by subcontracting with local producers) are all illustrations of how the multinationals are using more flexible and less visible forms of accumulation to take advantage of the Third World's human and material resources. To obtain these resources and commodities, the spheres of commerce and finance are increasingly used by transnational capital. US statistics show that 40 per cent of its foreign investments in 1990 in the underdeveloped world were in banking, finance and insurance, while these types of US investment in the industrialized countries constituted only 25 per cent of the total.[20]

There are other, more negative, reasons why the big powers will not delink, or simply ignore the Third World. The flow of drugs and the rise of terrorist activities drive many core countries to constantly watch over and meddle in the activities of many underdeveloped countries. Also the outbreak and spread of deadly diseases, such as cholera and AIDS, have direct repercussions for the core countries. Precisely because the Third World languishes in poverty and miserable living conditions, it serves as an incubator and breeding ground for these and other diseases that can and do spread to the developed world.

The destruction of the globe's environment also compels the core countries to pay attention to what is happening in the Third World. The world's rainforests, most of which are located in the underdeveloped world, combined with the biodiversity of these areas makes it imperative for the First World to try to find ways to preserve these resources, even as they act as the primary motors of global environmental destruction with their capitalist driven, industrialized economies.

The limits of the NICs

The conventional wisdom is that the most advanced newly industrializing countries, or NICs, meaning South Korea, Taiwan, Hong Kong and Singapore, have opened up a new path for development in the Third World. These countries are the alleged success cases of Third World development, showing that there is hope for the Third World and that countries can lift themselves up from abject poverty to be a dynamic part of the global economy while moving down the road to developed status.

However, with less than 2 per cent of the world's population living in the NICs, serious questions are now being raised as to whether new global economic trends will enable other countries to follow the NIC model of export-led development. As Walden Bello and Stephanie Rosenfeld demonstrate in *Dragons in Distress*, the existent NICs may have even reached an economic dead end in their development strategies.[21]

The NIC model of development in Asia has a triangular base, involving Japan, the United States and the repressive conditions in the individual NIC countries themselves. Japan provided technology, capital goods and trading companies for these countries to launch their export-led growth, the United States provided the massive consumer markets, and the NICs themselves acted internally to hold down wages by repressing the working class and controlling social discontent. This was a system of "command capitalism."

Now there are problems with all three of these pillars of the NIC export model. US efforts to protect its own markets are not only directed against Japan but also at the four NICs, particularly South Korea and Taiwan. And neither Western Europe nor Japan are prepared to open up their markets to absorb anything like the proportion of goods that are going to the United States.[22]

In recent years the NICs have made concerted efforts to move into more high-tech, high-value-added production. One multinational executive, commenting on Taiwan's efforts to enter high-tech production, stated that its advantage "has shifted from cheap labor to cheap brains."[23] Neither the Japanese corporations, the traditional purveyors of technology to the Asian NICs, nor the multinational corporations in general, are willing to turn over the patents and technology free of charge. And with the approval of the newest GATT accords that enable the multinational corporations to wrest monopoly profits from their control of technology, it will be even more difficult or impossible for the NICs to simply take and use technology that they have been accustomed to getting in the past. Now the production of clone computers, for example, will be severely restricted, unless the NICs are willing to pay high fees to obtain the necessary licenses and patents.

The final, and perhaps most critical, base of the export tripod that is crumbling relates to the conditions within the NICs themselves. The regimes of South Korea, Taiwan and Singapore have all faced serious political and social disturbances in the last half decade. Worker and student strikes, peasant movements, grassroots environmentalists and reformist opposition parties have taken on in one way or another the tight-fisted repressive policies of their governments that secured cheap wages and subservient societies.

The peasants, particularly in South Korea and Taiwan, are agitating against their governments' policies. These peasant revolts are due in part to the fact that the United States in recent years has insisted that the governments drop their agricultural import restrictions. Now US agricultural commodities are flooding many of the local markets, driving many of the peasants into bankruptcy and insolvency.

Along with rapid economic growth in the NICs has come the rapid destruction of the environment. Taiwan in particular has become an environmental nightmare. Its rate of industrial density is 75 times that of the United States, with an average of 3 factories per square kilometer. The few existing environmental regulations have gone largely unenforced as unprocessed industrial waste is dumped into the nearest body of water. Twenty per cent of the farmland is polluted by industrial waste water and 30 per cent of the rice grown in Taiwan, which is its staple crop, is contaminated with heavy metals including mercury and arsenic. Cancer is Taiwan's leading cause of death, having doubled over the last 30 years. The island's water supply is also polluted by raw sewage, and Taiwan has the world's highest rate of hepatitis infection.[24]

What all this means concretely is that the glory days of the NICs are over. This model of development is being defrocked, mainly by the peoples within the NICs. And simultaneously multinational capital is searching elsewhere, for more easily exploitable resources and labor. The big corporations, with their capacity for "sourcing" and flexible accumulation, are beginning to look to other countries for cheap manufactured commodities. In south-east Asia, Thailand, with its cheap and abundant labor force, is the new "boom country" for foreign capital.

South Korea, Singapore and Taiwan will in all likelihood languish at about their present status in the world market. They will continue to serve as manufacturing feeder lines to one degree or another, but they will not join the ranks of the developed countries under the existent global economic system. None of them will become a Belgium, Switzerland or even a Luxembourg. Their populations will maintain barely adequate early industrial standards of living – not facing a Malthusian disaster, but also never commanding the living standards of their working-class counterparts in the Western world. Annual per capita income in Taiwan is about $10,000 while that of South Korea (by far the most populous country of the four NICs with about 45 million people) is $6,800, less than one third that of the United States.[25] Given the relatively high cost of living in these countries, this is hardly an income that enables one to live well.

Meanwhile their own economic groups and elites will continue to haggle with the dominant capitalists in the global economic system over how much of the wealth they can keep for themselves. They will live opulently and have a certain status in the global international order. But their countries will remain at best in the global economy in a secondary position. All this does not bode well for heavier populated Third World countries like Thailand, Egypt and Mexico, which are hoping to become the new NICS.

Of course this does not negate the fact that new economic groups in Asia, Latin America and even Africa have been able to incorporate themselves into the "webs" of international development. Virtually all the major Third World countries have nuclei that are part of the new international system of flexible accumulation: Colombia, Nigeria, Venezuela, Argentina, Thailand, and so on. However, as in the United States, it is only the upper tier of these societies that is able to incorporate itself in this international web. And of course this tier is much more limited in proportion and numbers in the Third World countries than in the core countries.

The Chinese models

In a world where many of the Third World countries are in the throes of economic disaster and much of the former Second World is on the brink of economic collapse, the substantial growth of the Chinese economy during the past decade and a half merits special scrutiny.[26] Has the country found a new path of development that can serve as a model for other countries? Or is the Chinese model wracked with contradictions – such as the dictatorial role of the Chinese Communist Party and the use of capitalist mechanisms and incentives – that reproduce the extremes of wealth and poverty that afflict other developing societies?

There is no doubt that much of Chinese development can be characterized as raw, primitive capitalist accumulation. In the new free enterprise zones and the urban centers of China, the power of the trade unions is diminished, the workforce suffers from increasingly exploitative conditions, and the growing extremes of wealth and poverty makes Beijing and other cities look increasingly like many Third World urban centers. Guangdong province for example, China's most rapidly growing urban and industrial center, has a burgeoning middle class, a new bourgeoisie and a sprawling urban populace, many of whom lead marginalized existences. As even a US consular report from China notes, the boom in Guangdong has meant "population congestion, criminal activity, prostitution, vagrancy, drug use and the rise of contagious diseases."

However, there is another face to Chinese development that has gone virtually unnoticed. Most discussions of China's double digit economic growth focus on the economic zones set up to encourage foreign investment, the use of capitalist market incentives, and the general pursuit of Western-style industrial growth. In reality China with its enormous population and tremendous economic diversity does not have one single model of development but "two, three, many models of development."

Alongside the urban economic boom and its attendant problems has come an economic miracle in the countryside. Since 1978, it is estimated that the real incomes of people in the Chinese countryside have quadrupled and the standard of living has risen dramatically. About 900 million people are classified as rural inhabitants in China, meaning that almost 17 per cent of the world's population has been affected by the Chinese rural economic miracle.

There are two major pillars of the rural economic miracle. Firstly there has been the opening up of the market, thereby stimulating the peasants to produce more. Secondly, since the beginning of the 1980s, rural township enterprises, which have received public financing, have boomed throughout the countryside with many of them involved in some form of manufacturing. China's rural development has now advanced to the point that a new rural development model can be articulated. Key to the Chinese model is the trinity of village–town–city. In the 1930s the famous Chinese sociologist Fei Xioatung argued that the towns should serve as the critical link in Chinese economic development. Based in part on 600 years of Chinese development, Mao Tse-tung after 1949 did look to the towns and villages as centers of development. But the heavy emphasis on state planning and collective agriculture limited the Chinese peasantry's ability to develop the countryside's full potential.

Since the start of the reform period in 1978, the towns, via the township industries, have become a central element in Chinese rural development. These township industries are generally owned by the communities. Although there are cases where groups of local investors have set up township enterprises and in some instances foreign investors are also involved in township industries as co-investors, the overwhelming emphasis is on local involvement and the development of the local economies.

It is estimated that one quarter of China's rural labor force is now employed in township industries. They provide about one third of Chinese manufactures, producing everything from bricks and processed foods to electrical and computer components. What is important about these township enterprises is that unlike every other development model, they are bringing industry to the countryside, thereby providing the world with an alternative to the sprawling, congested megacities where most of the globe's industry is presently concentrated.

In peasant agriculture itself, the Chinese have clearly moved away from collectivized agriculture. However, it is notable that the Chinese have steered clear of the IMF/World Bank neo-liberal economic approach that has devastated much of Third World peasant agriculture and even helped precipitate the collapse of the old Soviet system through its excessive emphasis on the marketplace. The Chinese alternative has combined market incentives with a strong governmental role that protects and encourages the development of small-scale peasant agriculture.

A related lesson of the Chinese experience is that the land has not been turned over to the peasantry. The peasants are free to work the land as they see fit, but by preventing land from being bought and sold, the Chinese have avoided the emergence of a real-estate market in which many speculate and grow rich off rents while producing little of real value. This approach to land is clearly at variance with the neo-liberal model, and merits careful study to understand how it could be applied in other parts of the world.

However in the last year or two, the traditional urban-based industrial model of development is coming into increasing conflict with the more grassroots model of the countryside. Although land is not bought and sold on the open market, the gargantuan land needs of urban industries and the sprawling cities has swallowed up more and more of the productive agricultural lands. In a country that has less than one acre of cultivable land per inhabitant this has already had an adverse impact on agricultural production. For the first time since the onset of the modernization program, China is being forced to import large amounts of grains, particularly from the Western countries.

What will happen in the huge nation of China in the future is virtually impossible to predict. But regardless of the fate of the rural areas and the township enterprises, their past and recent experience merits the close scrutiny of most Third World countries whose agricultural systems are in crisis or collapse due to globalization and the growing domination of much of the world's food markets by transnational agribusiness corporations. Chinese agricultural development in the past decade and a half reveals that viable peasant-based food systems can be created if the peasants receive fair prices for the commodities they market, have access to credits, and enjoy a certain degree of protection from foreign exports and dumping as they strive to augment their output and productivity.

Forms of political struggle

Immanuel Wallerstein sees three different forms of political struggle emerging in the Third World with the collapse of socialist and national liberation movements.[27] One he calls neo-Bismarkian, which is represented by Iraq and Saddam Hussein. These are strongly armed Third World regimes that try to use whatever power or leverage they have to assert themselves on the global scene vis-a-vis the big powers. The second trend is the rejection of the Enlightenment worldview, as exemplified by Ayatollah Khomeini and much of the Islamic fundamentalist movement. They repudiate the very basis of the rationalist enlightenment of the eighteenth century, which proclaimed Western individuality and its faith in the idea of secular progress. The final form of reaction is that of socio-political mobility, the migration of peoples from the South to the North. They can no longer tolerate the living conditions of their own countries, and because of their awareness of other opportunities, they opt to search for better opportunities through migration.

Wallerstein, in his attempt to categorize the types of Third World struggle, underestimates the raw, explosive power of rebellion that exists in much of the Third World while he overestimates the importance of the neo-Bismarkian struggle given the weakness of most Third World states vis-a-vis the dominant powers. The central importance of the urban explosions discussed in Chapter 2 are virtually ignored. Principally a reaction to neo-liberalism and IMF-imposed austerity programs, these urban insurrections, or riots, do frighten the dominant classes of the world and even wring concessions from them. It is true that these rebellions are generally leaderless and lack a clear ideological orientation, but they are fundamental forms of class struggle that will probably grow in importance in the coming years.

These types of rebellions are typical of transitional periods in history when there is no defined ideological leadership. The slave rebellions throughout the Americas in the eighteenth and nineteenth centuries are perhaps comparable. People rebel in desperation and anger, and they do threaten and destabilize the existent order. Above all they reveal that neither the imposition of the dominant ideology nor the use of force and repression is sufficient to contain or delude important sectors of the downtrodden masses. These are dangerous instabilities in the capitalist system that do indeed threaten to engulf and afflict the developed world.

Postmodern politics and the Zapatista rebellion

One should also not ignore the importance of new politically articulated forms of rebellion like the Zapatista movement in Chiapas, Mexico. Led by the Zapatista National Liberation Army (EZLN), the Indian uprising in Chiapas that burst upon the world scene in January 1994 can be characterized as a postmodern political movement. The rebellion is an attempt to move beyond the politics of modernity, be they of the Mexican government or of past national liberation movements. And even more fundamentally, it seeks to end the victimization of Indians by centuries of Western modernization. Particularly during the past quarter century with the onset of the oil boom in southern Mexico, Chiapas has experienced economic upheaval and new dislocation that has pushed the Indians and peasants of Chiapas to organize and rebel against the government.[28]

What distinguishes the Zapatista movement from previous national liberation movements is that it is not bent on taking power in Mexico City, nor is it calling for state socialism. Its objective is to spark a broad-based movement of civil society in Chiapas and the rest of Mexico that will transform the country from the bottom up. This is a rebellion against a government that has nominally proclaimed its commitment to revolutionary reforms and democracy while actually using repression and the free market to consolidate the position of a new ruling class. The Zapatista movement's familiarity with the limits of taking state power in the name of revolution explains why its platform and politics focus on civil society and the demand for authentic democracy.

This postmodernist perspective permeates even Indian villages in the rainforest that had no contact with the EZLN before the January 1 uprising. In March 1994, as part of an international delegation that went to Chiapas, I visited the Indian village of Cascada, near Palenque, the site of the magnificent old Mayan ruins. In a meeting with many of the community members, it was striking that the women's organization took the lead in discussing the community's needs and plans as well as the obstacles it faced. They wanted decent schools, medical services, assistance so they could attend nearby technical colleges, and the right to elect their own representatives at the municipal and state level. They also wanted lands from the nearby cattle estate to augment production on their own marginal ejido the government had granted them back in 1960. But as the ecological representative of the community pointed out, they were fully cognizant of the fact that these lands could only be farmed with appropriate technologies to avoid impoverishing the delicate soils of the region.

One should not fall into the trap of romanticizing the EZLN or the struggle of the indigenous peoples of Chiapas. But the community of Cascada, like hundreds and even thousands of other villages and towns in Chiapas, in the forefront of the global effort to search for alternative paths of development. The movement in Chiapas has already shaken Mexican society and pushed the country's political discourse to new levels. The movement's success or failure in resisting the onslaught of the global market, mobilizing civil society and stopping government repression and manipulation will be critical in determining the pace of authentic change in Mexico and serve as an example for other Third World societies.

CHAPTER 6

Decomposition in the United States

The American beacon helped to teach people everywhere to aspire to self-realization and to rebel against powerlessness. Now, it seems, the former students must re-educate Americans in the meaning of their own faith. Perhaps that is when the American moment will begin.

William Greider,
Who Will Tell the People[1]

Whoever our leaders might be as we approach the twenty-first century, their challenge will be to help Americans determine whether a genuine multiracial democracy can be created and sustained in an era of global economy and a moment of xenophobic frenzy ... Either we learn a new language of empathy and compassion, or the fire this time will consume us all.

Cornel West,
Race Matters[2]

There must be something rotten in the very core of a social system which increases its wealth without diminishing its misery, and increases in crimes even more rapidly than in numbers.

Karl Marx,
New York Daily News,
September 16, 1859

In 1992 the Mall of America opened on the outskirts of Minneapolis. The largest shopping and entertainment complex in the United States, it is five times as big as Red Square and 20 times larger than St Peter's Basilica. Anchored by three retail giants, Sears, Macy's and Bloomingdale's, the mall contains virtually every conceivable consumer product known to humanity. When one isn't busy shopping and buying, one can get a hamburger at McDonald's or Burger King, or take a ride on Paul Bunyan's Log Chute or the Pepsi Ripsaw. With 109 surveillance cameras to monitor the activities of its shoppers, the mall, according to one commentator, is "monolithic and imposing in the manner of a walled city," and has "the disturbing magnetism of a mirage."[3] This consumer extravaganza stands in sharp contrast to the urban deterioration in recent years of the Minneapolis–St Paul region, long known as one of the most progressive and trouble-free urban areas of the United

States. While the big banks and corporations were busy pumping $625 million dollars into building the mall, public investment and funding for the Twin Cities declined precipitously, particularly for social programs assisting the poor and most needy. During the decade of the 1980s, the poverty rate in Minneapolis rose by 37 per cent, while that of St Paul jumped by over 50 per cent.

Hardest hit were its four major minority groups: African-Americans, American Indians, Asians and Chicano-Latinos. In St Paul in 1990 all of these minorities had unemployment rates in double digits, with that of the Indians running at over 20 per cent. In Minneapolis, the employment conditions were slightly better for Asians and Blacks although they were worse for Indian and Chicano-Latino males. As a 1993 report by the Urban Coalition notes, "The Twin Cities metro region is increasingly divided into two separate and unequal worlds."[4]

In the Twin Cities as well as the United States at large, it is now widely recognized that the gulf between the rich and the poor widened significantly in the 1980s. Noted figures and publicists from the liberal economist John Kenneth Galbraith to the Republican political analyst Kevin Phillips have pointed to the growth of upper-class wealth and the decline in the income of the bottom 80 per cent of US society as one of the pivotal dynamics of the decade. Already in the mid-1980s, the United States had the highest disparity of income between rich and poor of any major industrial power. As Galbraith and Phillips both point out, by 1990 the salaries of the average corporate chief executive officer were more than 100 times that of the average worker, while a decade earlier there was only a differential of about 29 times.[5] A 1993 US census report showed that these disparities continue to worsen. From 1992 to 1993, median household income declined by about $300, when adjusted for inflation. From 1989 to 1993, the typical American household lost 7 per cent in real income. While average per capita income was up by 1.8 per cent, most of the benefits flowed to the wealthiest Americans. In 1993, the top fifth of American households earned 48.2 per cent of the nation's income, while the bottom fifth earned just 3.6 per cent. Over 15 per cent of the population lived below the poverty line and more than a million Americans fell into poverty in 1993 compared to the previous year. Felix G. Rohatyn, a senior partner in the investment firm of Lazard Freres, acknowledged that "what is occurring is a huge transfer of wealth from lower-skilled middle-class American workers to the owners of capital assets and to the new technological aristocracy."[6]

The consequences of these disparities are many fold. Compared to other economically developed countries, higher incidences of crime, violence, teen suicides and drug abuse pervades US society, especially among the poorest social sectors. The decline in the welfare of children in the United States is particularly appalling with more than twice as many US children living in poverty compared to Western European societies. The United Nations Children's Fund found that even some developing countries rated better than the United States in specific indices of child care. Mexico, for example, bests the United States in the area of vaccinations, while Turkey rated higher than the United States in children who completed the first four years of primary education.

Reflecting the poor quality of life and desperate conditions, the murder rate for children in the United States is 5 to 10 times higher than in the other developed countries. Even before the cutbacks in child and welfare assistance by the Republican Congress of 1995–6, the United Nations reported on the dismal plight of US children due to the failure of the US government to take action to assist the poor. Tax and transfer payments to poor families and their children in the United States in the early 1990s were less than half those of England, which had the next highest incidence of impoverished children among the developed nations.[7] Today almost one in four children live in poverty in the United States.[8]

What explains the increasing opulence of the American rich, while the most important asset of a nation, its children, are allowed to go hungry and live in miserable conditions? The common belief is that it was the permissiveness of the Reagan years towards the wealthy, specifically, the passage of regressive tax legislation, deregulation, and in general the laissez-faire atmosphere. Certainly, the Reagan era played a role in the decline of the welfare and living conditions of many Americans. But there were deeper, more profound forces at work that enabled the dominant classes to consolidate their hold, forces that predate the laissez-faire years of Republican rule.

The demise of trade unions

One central factor was the gutting of the US trade-union movement. It is easy for Americans today to forget that in the aftermath of World War II, the unions were a powerful economic force in US society. Their clout enabled US workers to bargain for a significant share of the expanding economic pie. When necessary they could bring big industry to its knees as they did in major strikes in the auto and steel industries, the railways and the coal mines. In the mid-1950s about 33 per cent of the workforce was unionized.[9] Even more important than the percentage, was the fact that union workers, by driving their wages upward, had a "pull" effect on the salaries of non-unionized workers and helped create a large middle-income tier in US society, comprised of many who were blue-collar workers.

It can even be argued that the trade unions, more than any other trade or class organization, strengthened and facilitated the consolidation of a "middle class" as the predominant socio-economic phenomenon of post-World war II America.

But today the unions are no longer a powerful force. The percentage of the unionized non-agricultural work force now hovers around 16 per cent, a dramatic plunge in a few decades. Even more importantly than their decline in numbers is the fact that the unions, even when they are predominant in particular industries, are strategically on the defensive, unable to strike and bargain successfully, forced to accept major cutbacks in salaries and benefits in industry after industry. Moreover, much of US society, even many workers, have turned against the unions, regrading them as ineffective and even corrupt organizations, capable only of garnishing a portion of their salaries for the union bureaucracies and incapable of helping workers advance their legitimate interests.

The reasons behind the decline of trade unionism in the United States are several. For one, as John Sweeney, the new reform-minded president of the AFL-CIO argues, the union leadership itself over the past three decades has become entrenched and unimaginative, practicing a form of "business unionism" that is often more concerned with satisfying its own bureaucratic interests and cutting deals with management than with ardently pushing workers' demands. But even more important than the lethargy of union leadership is the ability of capital in recent decades to concentrate its economic power, to internationalize its operations and to turn technology to its almost exclusive advantage. The concentration of capital in ever larger blocs in the United States has given big business greater power to maneuver and drive down workers' salaries. This concentration of capital should not be confused with centralization. In fact big corporations while becoming more and more concentrated have actually decentralized their operations in order to have more flexibility in dealing with trade unions.

Developments in the meat-packing industry are an example of this process. Earlier in the century the industry was highly centralized in big plants in Chicago and Kansas City. But today this is no longer the case as the meat packers have decentralized their operations throughout the Midwest and the United States, breaking many of the meat-packing unions that were once powerful advocates of their workers' interests. Simultaneously the meat-packing corporations have merged with other corporations or diversified, thereby making it easier for them to weather long strikes. In the late 1960s and early 1970s Swift and Armour, once the two giants of the meat-packing industry, were taken over by two conglomerates, Esmark and Greyhound respectively, which because of their diversified activities, had the power to hold out against workers' demands or strikes.[10]

Then in the 1980s the unions in the meat-packing sector were dealt a new series of blows by another round of buyouts, mergers and plant closures. Today two of the biggest meat packers are Cargill and Conagra, both vertically integrated agribusiness companies that are aggressively anti-union. These changes in the industry have made it virtually impossible for the workers to negotiate collectively at the national level or to carry out coordinated strikes. And when the workers do strike at individual plants they are often defeated, as occurred in the case of the strike by workers at the Hormel plant in Austin, Minnesota.

This concentration and decentralization of capital, which has happened in industry after industry, is often closely linked to the internationalization of industries. Even the beef-packing industry which deals with a perishable product that should have an inside track in serving the internal market, is affected by the move of multinationals abroad. McDonald's and Burger King contract abroad for huge quantities of frozen beef for their fast-food chains, thereby undercutting the US meat-packing workers.

Capital today is highly mobile, able to search for the lowest wages and the most favorable economic conditions around the world. In the United States in particular the once powerful unions in the auto and steel industries have been undermined by the movement of investments and subsidiaries abroad. In many US industries, it is now commonplace for the corporations to merely threaten to move abroad in order to dampen wage demands or forestall strikes.

The technological fix

Technology is also used by US capital to consolidate its economic power and to undermine the trade-union movement. The telecommunications and computer revolutions demonstrate in particular how corporate capital has used technology to its advantage. Lester Thurow, a well know mainstream economist, points out that the introduction of modern communications and the computer into the workplace in the 1980s was extensive but did not increase white-collar productivity in the United States. In fact white-collar productivity actually declined by 3 per cent between 1980 and 1990, while it rose by 28 per cent for US blue-collar workers.[11]

So why were managers, executives, professionals, financial managers, and so on, so successful in accumulating wealth in the 1980s when in fact their own strata, the white-collar worker, was stagnant in terms of productivity? The reason is simply that management and the entrepreneurs used their power and control over certain types of information and technology, not to increase their productivity, but to extract wealth from the other sectors of society.

In a book written before he became Secretary of Labor in the Clinton administration, Robert Reich goes deeper than Thurow in demonstrating how the top tier of US society consolidated its position through the use of technology. In *The Work of Nations*, he shows that the "symbolic analysts," the group of workers and executives who use the most advanced technology, are the ones who now dominate economic activity, not only in the United States but in the rest of the world as well. The symbolic analysts for Reich are investment bankers, lawyers, real estate developers, advertising executives, corporate head hunters, and consultants of all kinds as well as research scientists, software and biotechnology engineers.[12] They manipulate the flow of information and knowledge in the business world with technology, and they do it in a way that guarantees that they garner the highest incomes and salaries, often to the detriment of those who work under them or in other positions in society.

Reich defines two other tiers in the workforce – the productive workers, meaning mainly blue-collar workers, and the in-person service personnel, such as nurses and elementary school teachers. They have seen their incomes decline in relation to the symbolic analysts, primarily because they are not in a position to manipulate the telecommunications and computer revolutions to their advantage. Factory and blue-collar workers in particular have the added disadvantage that big business and the multinationals use technology to shrink the globe and access cheap labor power, pitting the different national workforces against each other to lower wages.[13]

The gutting of urban America

Along with the decline of the trade unions has come the decay of the inner cities and the growth of the "underclass." The breakdown of living conditions in the urban centers is particularly pronounced in the United States compared to Western Europe and Japan. The rhetoric of the Reagan and Bush administrations, and even that of Bill Clinton, would have us believe that this crisis is largely the fault of those who live in the inner cities, of those who are unemployed, engage in criminal activities, receive welfare payments and are uninterested in improving their lives. This is the logic behind the workfare program that Clinton proposed even before Newt Gingrich and the Republicans took control of Congress: those on welfare are to be given "opportunities" to educate and train themselves, and if they fail then the welfare payments are to be curtailed or cut off. Simultaneously the Clinton administration has dramatically expanded federal funding for local police forces in the cities so that those who "get out of line" can be repressed and thrown into jail.

But the reality is that many who live in the urban centers are despondent, feel helpless, or turn to illicit activities because their lives' experience has taught them that they cannot find regular jobs and make a decent living. In the poorer areas of cities like Los Angeles, Chicago, Miami or New York the sense of desperation is palpable. The violence, fear, crime, alcoholism and drug abuse that grips the underclasses of these cities is directly linked to this despondency and hopelessness.

The seminal work of William Julius Wilson, principally in the ghettos of Chicago, shows that the growth of the underclass is rooted in structural forces, most notably the disappearance of blue-collar jobs. In the greater metropolitan area of Chicago, for example, there were 616,000 jobs in the manufacturing industry in the mid-1950s, but almost three decades later the total had shrunk to 277,000, a decline of 63 per cent. Some of these factory jobs went to other cities where labor was unorganized and cheaper, others were lost to automation, and in other cases major corporations abandoned the city and the country entirely to employ workers in Third World countries.[14]

While the corporations were pulling out of the urban centers, the federal government was also intent on slashing its support for the cities. Even before the advent of Ronald Reagan, the politicians had begun to cut back on urban federal programs such as housing, job training and education. In 1977, 20 per cent of Philadelphia's and Baltimore's city budgets came from the federal government: by 1984 these figures had declined to 8 and 6 per cent respectively.[15] The Clinton administration, even before the Republicans took control of Congress in 1994, made no serious effort to reverse these figures. As a representative of the "New Democrats" who are bent on building a strong suburban base, Bill Clinton has dealt with the cities principally as major crime centers, funneling new appropriations into urban police forces, while providing little for programs that deal with poverty and unemployment, the real underlying causes of crime in the United States.

The commercialized American Dream

The African-American community has been hardest hit by the gutting of the inner cities, mainly because it is the largest single group to reside in most of the old urban centers. Cornel West, one of the most insightful commentators on American race issues, describes how the commercialization of America combined with the inability of most blacks to buy into the materialist dream has led to a pervasive nihilism throughout the African-American community. Familial and community bonds which once helped sustain African-Americans, even in the face of bitter racism and repression, have been decimated by the onslaught of commercial America.

The images that corporate America uses to sell its culture of consumption to the public are those of comfort, convenience, machismo, femininity, violence and sexual stimulation. As West notes, the primary motivation of the corporate world

> is to make profits, and their basic strategy is to convince the public to consume. These institutions have helped create a seductive way of life, a culture of consumption that capitalizes on every opportunity to make money. Market calculations and cost-benefit analyses hold sway in almost every sphere of US society.[16]

Corporate commercialism feeds on and develops some of the basest tendencies of human nature. It fetishizes love, foments rank consumerism, generates mediocrity, augments selfish tendencies and encourages aggressiveness. These values, while edging out non-market values that are more community and family oriented, play upon and accentuate the individualism that has permeated US society throughout much of its history. And for those groups at the lower income end of American society, like Afro-Americans, their inability to purchase many of the pleasures and goods hyped by rampant commercialism leads to deep-seated despair and nihilism. They feel that their situation is hopeless, that they are doomed to live on the margins, denied access forever to all that corporate America holds up as the "good life."

African-Americans are by no means the only group victimized by the onslaught of corporate America. On the east coast, particularly in New York, Puerto Rican immigrants numbering more than a million who have arrived during the past 30 years have the worst poverty and income statistics of any ethnic group in the United States except for American Indians. In New York, they have the highest welfare dependency and poverty rates, and the lowest labor force participation. Broken families, substance abuse and devastated health conditions are all rampant among Puerto Ricans.[17] The tragedy of the Puerto Rican immigrants is that their arrival in New York largely coincided with the restructuring of industry and business. From 1950 to 1989, manufacturing suffered a three-fold decrease in its share of New York jobs. The service sector grew, virtually doubling its proportion of the labor market, but these jobs have tended to pay less, are more insecure, and are often located in smaller businesses where the worker has little or no defense against racism or anti-immigrant abuses.

Given these poor employment prospects, it is small wonder that many young Puerto Rican males in New York have turned to drug dealing, particularly the sale of crack. It is one of the few ways Puerto Ricans can advance themselves and tap into the dream propagandized by commercial America. These Puerto Ricans are simply doing what immigrants to the United States have done historically – searching for the best way to get ahead and accumulate wealth. The big difference is that the economic opportunities are no longer found in agriculture or industry as they were for many earlier immigrants, but in the ghetto streets pursuing high-risk, high-return activities like drug dealing.[18]

The existence of up to 3 million homeless people in the United States is also a product of the structural changes in the US economy and the gutting of the cities. The major factor that distinguishes the homeless from others in the underclass is that they have been deprived of the so-called "safety net," be it public or familial. About three quarters of the homeless receive no regular welfare payments, have no housing subsidies of any sort, and are unable to get even occasional jobs.[19]

The plight of the homeless and the underclass in general makes their living conditions increasingly indistinguishable from those living in the Third World. In all the major cities of the United States one commonly sees people begging in the streets, scouring garbage for bits of food, and living in squalid sub-human conditions, making their lives similar to many in cities like New Delhi, São Paulo and San Salvador. The percentage of the destitute may still be larger in Third World cities, but as the corporate and financial elites of the United States internationalize their activities, the numbers and percentages of the dispossessed and downtrodden in American are increasing.

The rise of the right

Coinciding with the growth of poverty in the United States is the rise of the Republican Party under the dominance of its right wing. The takeover of the House of Representatives by Newt Gingrich and the Republicans in the 1994 elections revealed that the Reagan years were by no means an anomaly. The conservative right is now well into the second decade of its campaign to liquidate the liberal welfare state and the political coalition that emerged during the Great Depression and the presidency of Franklin Roosevelt. The demise of liberalism and consolidation of the right wing in US politics is directly linked to the decline of US industry and the trade unions. Big labor, with all its flaws and problems, was the cornerstone of the New Deal Coalition and welfare politics. It mobilized workers for elections, contributed mightily to the Democratic Party's coffers, and worked to cement the support of working-class ethnic groups.

Economic marginalization in the United States, rather than leading to an expansion of the welfare state as one might logically expect, has facilitated the rise of the conservative right. As Thomas Byrne Edsall notes in *The Rise and Fall of the New Deal Order:* "Under American democracy, those who are unemployed or marginally employed are weakest politically."[20] The poor and working poor are far more difficult to organize and are increasingly disenfranchised, often correctly perceiving that voting in a particular election will do nothing to change their lot. In the 1994 elections only one third of the US potential electorate voted, with the highest incidence of voter participation occurring in the upper income brackets, and then tapering off at the bottom. In effect the United States now has a "virtual democracy:" regular elections and all the formal institutions of democracy exist, but people at the base participate less and less in its mechanisms and institutions.[21]

A financial and lobbying infrastructure has also emerged in US politics that undermines political activity by the poor at the grassroots level. The rise of the Political Action Committees, or PACS, as the principal source of funding for political candidates has dramatically skewed the political structure. Most political candidates – Democrats as well as Republicans – often spend more time seeking out and speaking to fat cat financiers than they do campaigning among voters. Over a billion dollars was spent in the 1994 elections, of which $700 million went to TV ads.[22] An array of right-wing think tanks, like the Heritage Foundation and the Enterprise Institute, have also been set up with corporate support to put out right-wing position papers that influence policy and shape legislation. Within the Republican Party these financial outlays by big monied interests are complimented by the rise of a right-wing evangelical movement. This group of voters plays a role in the Republican Party similar to that which labor played in the Democratic Party. It provides a mass base, even among some lower income people, that makes it difficult to simply label the Republican Party as the party of the rich and well-to-do. Due in large part to this base, the Republican party apparatus is able to raise three-fourths of its money from a 900,000 person small donor base while the Democratic Party is still tied largely to big-money donors.[23]

The rise of the evangelical right is linked to economic insecurity and growing social instability. Outside of the south, religious fundamentalism is often found among many of the white ethnic groups that once supported the Democratic Party. Feeling squeezed by the collapsing American Dream as the middle class shrinks, many

Christian fundamentalists direct their anger at "moral decay," crime, minorities and the welfare system. The presidential bid of Patrick Buchanan revealed that right-wing sectors of the Republican Party are even willing to direct this anger at the multinational corporations that are "downsizing" and abandoning US workers. As *Business Week* editorialized during the early primaries,

> There's no question that a lot of people have serious economic problems, to which Pat Buchanan is giving voice … The voters attracted to Buchanan haven't had a real raise in 20 years, and even white-collar professionals are being downsized from their corporate perches.[24]

The so-called New Democrats, led by Bill Clinton and the Democratic Leadership Conference, have responded by staking out largely defensive political positions. There is no philosophy or ideology driving Clinton, unlike the right-wing Republicans and the evangelicals. The term "New Democrat" does not carry the same forceful resonance as the terms "New Right" or "conservative." The Clinton administration is often accused of devising major policies "on the fly," with no basic philosophy. It stands for little beyond the search for a centrist political strategy to hold onto political power, as Clinton's acceptance of a largely Republican "welfare reform" legislation in 1996 demonstrated. This is why Clinton is largely perceived as an opportunist.

At the same time, the Clinton Democrats espouse an economic strategy tied to globalization, moving in step with the multinational corporations. The party of Franklin Roosevelt may still not proclaim "What's good for business is good for America," but the new pro-business Democrats are light years away from the Democratic Party of the New Deal that tied its destiny to the urban masses and launched the welfare reform state. Gone is the integral alliance with labor and the trade unions as the Clinton administration enacts programs to curtail government spending, appeases big business and pushes international trade agreements like NAFTA and GATT that favor the multinationals to the detriment of US labor.

Clinton's much lauded tax increases on the rich in 1993 meant that the wealthiest lost a maximum of 4 per cent of their income to the federal government, that is if they did not augment their use of tax loop holes. The administration's only early program that appeared vaguely analogous to New Deal polices was the $30 billion fiscal stimulus program proposed during the administration's early months in office. However, this bill was dumped by Clinton when the Republicans dug in their heals with a Senate filibuster. There was no public campaign or effort to mobilize the public against the "gridlock" actions of Senate Republicans.

The Clinton administration, with its call for "reinventing government" is actually doing little more than applying the regressive labor policies of the corporate world to the federal government. Millions of workers are to be dropped from the payrolls, to be replaced by the latest labor-saving technology of the communications and computer revolutions. As in the private economy, the dynamic of government is to be that of labor displacement with no serious effort made to fund the plethora of jobs and programs that need extensive public assistance such as urban renewal, day care centers, libraries, community social services, and so on.

The Clinton administration's call for a communications superhighway with generous government subsidies will only help ensure the concentration of wealth and technology. Except for the corporate high-rise buildings, the superhighway makes it even easier to bypass the delapidated inner cities and to provide the suburbs with cheap high-tech services so that the typical suburbanite can have as little contact as possible with the inner city. Two Americas – one well-to-do and "plugged-in" technologically, the other poor, neglected and technically disenfranchised – will face each other across an increasing social and economic chasm.

Symbolic analyst or new robber baron?

Robert Reich as a member of the Clinton administration is pushing for policies that tend to favor the so-called symbolic analysts. In his book he portrayed them as the most innovative and creative sector of society; they have to be encouraged and stimulated because they are creating the new "global webs" that are producing the most "value added" in the world market. Reich does in one section of his book recognize that the symbolic analysts have separated themselves from the rest of society,[25] creating their own clubs, gilded ghettos and private schools. But this is not reconciled with his assertion that this group is now the key to the continued integration of the globe and the new high-tech world order. He refrains from discussing the fact that most of the symbolic analysts are intent on maintaining and expanding their privileges as a class at the expense of other social groups and classes.

The wealthiest strata in the United States is using its dominance of technology and capital to return the country to a stage akin to that of the robber baron era at the end of the nineteenth century. Much of the populace is being brutalized and cast aside as is demonstrated by the demise of the US farming class, the elimination of millions of jobs through deindustrialization, the abject impoverishment of the ghettos and the growth in the ranks of poor whites stripped of the dignity they once held as members of the middle or working classes.

This brutalizing phase of US capitalism has one salient characteristic that distinguishes it from the earlier era of the robber barons – it is rooted in the decline rather than the ascent of the US economic system. In the late nineteenth century, the new US bourgeoisie was building an industrial and economic machine that would soon surpass that of the European powers. The capital accumulated through ruthless exploitation of the US working class was by and large reinvested in steel mills, railroads, oil wells, factories and large grain exporting firms, all of which created jobs and stimulated the rapid expansion of the US working class.

In the late twentieth century, US workers once again feel the tightening exploitation of US capital, but this time the new surplus is as likely to go to support the opulent and ostentatious lifestyles of the rich as it is to be reinvested in productive enterprises in the United States. Supply-side economics, the pro-business policy of the Reagan years, did not stimulate investment – it merely enabled the rich to get richer. In the corporate world, merger mania, financial speculation and green mail became the buzzwords as young business executives became intent on making quick fortunes at the expense of the rest of society.

Reich, as Secretary of Labor, is arguing that the retraining of the US workforce is the key to dealing with its declining importance. A nation is only as competitive in the world market as its workforce is skilled, he argues. This is true only to a limited extent. The problem is that there are only a certain number of skilled positions, or "symbolic analysts" that are needed in the corporate world. More education often does not mean a better job. As one wag put it, Reich is living in "a field of dreams" if he thinks job retraining means jobs. Reich is also up against the real world of "downsizing" by the big corporations as they try to secure their profit margins by getting rid of blue-collar and middle-level management workers. Even computer and technologically skilled employees are laid off, often forced to become "independent contractors." In this position they compete with each other for contracts, usually earning incomes well below their former levels as corporate employees.

What this means is that the so-called "exceptionalism" of the United States is at an end. In the nineteenth and much of the twentieth centuries it was argued that America escaped from the class conflict of Europe because of its extensive natural resources and the upward mobility of the immigrants and the poor. This is no longer the case. In the United States the struggle is now overwhelmingly a class one, a struggle over wealth and power, with the poor being treated with ever-increasing cold-heartedness and cruelty. The classical Marxist critique that the rich take what they can from the working class and the poor is more valid than ever. Able to neutralize the trade unions and cut support payments for the poorest, the dominant classes are hoarding wealth and pushing policies that undermine authentic democracy. It is now widely recognized that wealth is used to buy political power in the United States. Multi-billionaire Ross Perot, who portrays himself as a political outsider, is an example par excellence of how those who have money and power are able to function in US politics, while those who do not are relegated to the sidelines.

This exploitative approach feeds the overproduction/underconsumption crisis that is gripping the capitalist world. The corporations have no problem in producing a plethora of goods and commodities. But the problem is increasingly one of finding markets. Keynes and the New Deal economists realized that the way out of the overproduction/underconsumption crisis of the 1930s was through increased government spending, particularly on programs that employed or assisted those with the lowest income. Ronald Reagan inverted this approach in the 1980s, when he increased the national debt three-fold, but insisted on cutting social spending while reducing taxes for the rich and pumping billions of new spending into military programs. This policy has been correctly dubbed "military Kenyesianism." The deficit spending did stimulate the economy, but it was primarily the rich who benefited rather than the workers and the most needy.

The international context of US decline

One of course cannot say that the United States stands alone in the deterioration of its social and political life. The Western European nations and Japan are also experiencing their own particular crises and problems. Japan in 1993 underwent a major political upheaval when the ruling liberal party lost power. Its high economic growth rates, based on burgeoning export markets that are now challenged by the other developed powers, have dropped precipitously since the heady days of the post-war years. And given the housing and environmental problems of Japan it is questionable if high Japanese incomes really translate into a good quality of life.[26]

The dynamics of late capitalism in Western Europe, just as in the United States, are also producing a growing economic stratification of society, although the divide is not yet quite as pronounced. Unemployment in Europe in recent years has reached unprecedented post-war levels, often hovering around 10 per cent. Even countries like the Netherlands and Sweden, which have advanced social policies, have begun cutting their state programs designed to assist the unemployed, the poor and the most disadvantaged in their societies. Daniel Singer, a leading commentator on Europe notes that Western Europe is now being visited by "the US nightmare. It's the US model with the huge and growing gap between the haves and the have nots, with its 'working poor,' with its absence of a national health service, and its terribly deficient welfare services now under constant attack."[27]

The growing insecurity of sectors of the working and middle classes in Europe has opened up a reactionary political space for the resurgence of neo-fascism and a new racism. Throughout Western Europe, racist campaigns are taking hold that exclude and expel racial minorities who have come from Turkey, the former Yugoslavia, Algeria, Morocco, India, Hong Kong, and so on. In Germany the anti-foreign sentiment has become extremely virulent as the riots in 1992 demonstrated. Many of the members of the ethnic or national groups under attack are actually nationalized or second-generation Europeans. Simultaneously in France and Italy neo-Nazi movements are drumming up anti-Semitic hatred. In Paris as well as rural France Jewish graves are sacked and swastikas painted on public buildings while neo-Nazi candidates win increasing support in national and local elections.

On the international scene, the United States remains determined to be the only superpower, in part because this gives it leverage over its major economic competitors in Western Europe and Japan. US military expenditures have been reduced by only 10 per cent since the days of George Bush and "Desert Storm." The US military budget is larger than that of the next ten major powers combined, all of whom are, or aspire to be, close friends of the United States.[28] Although there are no nuclear adversaries threatening the United States nor military threats of any type near the US borders, official defense policy doctrine under Clinton asserted that the United States must be prepared to fight two conventional wars at once.

There was an early perception that Clinton is a "domestic president," that he was less interested in handling foreign policy issues. But his deeds demonstrated that he is as committed as his predecessors to maintaining and expanding US interests abroad. In a major policy address to the United Nations in September 1993, Clinton made it clear that his administration would pursue an "activist" foreign policy designed to foment the continued expansion of "free market democracies." As the subsequent reneging on human rights issues with China revealed, the real priority is "free markets," not democracy.

This also explains why the Clinton administration continually supported the Yeltsin regime in Russia. It's democratic credentials were highly suspect to say the least, given Yeltsin's destruction of the Russian parliament in December 1993 and the war waged in Chechnya. But the United States was enamored by Yeltsin's commitment to a free market economy – he represented the best hope for the development of an economic system that will enable the United States and the multinationals to gain access to the vast markets and resources of Russia.

The interest in free markets is the same policy principle that has undergirded US policy since the declaration of the "Open Door policy" at the turn of the century. The Soviet Union may have collapsed but the United States is still driven to intervene on a global scale to assure that "disorderly" or non-capitalist forces do not gain the upper hand, thereby limiting US economic growth. Revolutions, social upheavals and radical reforms continue to be feared because they destabilize the economic environment for investors and market expansion. These fears, and not a fundamental commitment to democracy, explain why a "domestic president" has become involved in countries as diverse as Somalia, Haiti and the former Yugoslavia. Simply put, political and economic instability is anathema to US interests abroad.

Whither US society in the post-Cold War world?

For US leaders the end of the Cold War makes their task of ruling a more difficult one. For decades they were able to cover up critical internal problems by focusing public attention and consciousness against the Soviet threat and Third World challenges. Some of these conflicts, such as those in Vietnam and Nicaragua, divided the American people and precipitated internal political crises. But even the debate over different foreign challenges served to distract the American people from focusing on domestic issues and internal problems.

Now all that is gone. The war against Iraq enabled Bush to temporarily mobilize public support behind him, but it obviously did not enable him to win re-election less than two years later. And for Clinton is was difficult to use issues such as Somalia, Haiti or Bosnia to rally the American public behind him. The inability to find a foreign demon to replace communism has important, if undeterminable, consequences for the development of public consciousness and civil society. What does it mean that the bulk of the populace in the United States which grew up experiencing the Cold War and repeated foreign interventions and crises will no longer have their attention focused on these issues? Will they now be more concerned with domestic issues and try to organize and deal with them? Or will they follow the lead of bigots, reactionaries and groups on the right who try to divert attention from systemic problems by playing on racial and social differences?

Forces exist in the United States that feed each of these different tendencies. As a starting point, it has to be recognized that the majority of those in the United States are living the American materialist dream to one degree or another. They have fairly comfortable living conditions, conditions that are still the envy of people around the world. By and large most of the Americans in this well-to-do group are a conservative force. In a time of tightening budgets and a stagnant economy they defend their lifestyles against any incursions, throwing up legal and economic obstacles to minorities, immigrants and others who try to obtain what they have.

However, significant social fissures exist even within this large, materially prosperous sector. Since the 1960s many within the large middle class have rebelled against or questioned the existent order in the United States. It is noteworthy that most of the new social movements were overwhelmingly led by and composed of people with roots in the middle class. The other major movement that emerged full blown in the 1960s, the civil rights movement, had different social origins, but it ran parallel to and even sometimes overlapped with the middle-class social movements in the push for a more just and egalitarian society.

Today some of the historically progressive forces in the United States, like the labor movement, are clearly on the defensive. But other movements, like the gays, lesbians and environmentalists, are intensely pursuing their progressive agendas, having penetrated some of the highest levels of government and society with their ideas for building a more pluralistic and diverse America. If there is any advantage to having a Democratic rather than Republican administration in power, it is that there are always a few officials appointed who do respond to more progressive agendas. They are a minority and their voices are usually drowned out by the centrist and even conservative forces in the Democratic Party, but they do serve as gadflies often provoking public debate on issues that the party mainstream would like to ignore or cover up.

In the United States, the breakdown of traditional civil society by the onslaught of materialism has its positive as well as negative sides. The decline of traditional morals and forms of social interaction among much of the country's youth has not meant the end of the basic drive for social involvement. We are in fact witnessing the emergence of new forms of civil society in a wide range of areas. Youth gangs, hanging out in shopping malls, hip hop music and street smart culture – these are all forms of social interaction manifest among American youth that have both adverse and positive repercussions.

A new US civil society is in formation that is tremendously complex, comprised of a wide array of social microcosms. These include computer hack groups, sports and physical fitness enthusiasts, chess tournament players, elite social clubs, Hells Angels motor cyclists, golf players, Save the Wales groups, pro-choice activists, international solidarity organizations, and so on.

With the collapse of the old civil order, people have developed special interests and perspectives that take them away from traditional family and community values. Some of these groups and activities may have a reactionary impact, but there are many that reflect the human need for positive social and even political engagement.

The telecommunications and computer revolutions have at times fomented new forms of communication and interaction within the social movements and civil society. Many of the new groups and organizations are linked up or cognizant of each other through specialized newsletters, magazines, e-mail and the media in general. At times the existence of national media and communications systems has enabled groups like the African-Americans to unite nationally when they are threatened in one region or another. It was after all the national TV networks that enraged many in the United States with the bombing and murder of four black girls at a Birmingham Church in 1963. The disappearance and murder of the four civil rights workers in Mississippi the following year was also a political catalyst for many liberals and progressives. Both these events and the images they projected over TV helped galvanize a national reaction against the more vicious and horrifying forms of racism.

But the commercial exploitation of the mass media and technology has certainly had very adverse consequences. Many people feel powerless and victimized as they compare their own conditions with the "good life" portrayed through the media. Overwhelmed by what is going on in the world, large sectors of the population have simply "dropped out." Many African-Americans, Puerto Ricans, Latinos, Indians and others are angry, desperate and alienated. Some turn increasingly violent against each other, as well as against white America. It is this rage that exploded in its most bitter and vindictive form in the Los Angeles riots of May 1992. This is an unpredictable force, one that could appear again in an even more vitriolic and explosive form tomorrow, or it could lay seething and dormant for years to come.

It is also plausible to hope that forces like those unleashed in Los Angeles could be part of a process that provokes and develops a positive movement for creating a multi-cultured, democratic and pluralist society. The United States, unlike the other major capitalist powers, is a very diverse society, racially and culturally. The main issue is whether this diversity will be a source of strength or weaknesses. There is a distinct social and political tension in the United States which comes from this diversity. It produces continual controversy and challenges that sometimes degenerate into severe race and class conflicts. But at times this diversity provides an energy that drives the United States forward. If the trend of recent decades continues, in which more and more people are marginalized, while the rich continue to isolate themselves from the rest of society as they hoard more and more wealth, then urban upheavals, crime and social conflicts will only escalate. If, however, the diverse cultures and social movements from below are able to push their agendas forward, to demand and get a greater degree of social justice and participation, then it is conceivable that its cultural and racial diversity could enable the United States to move forward as a dynamic and creative society.

Fascism is probably not on the agenda in the United States. The minorities and distinct cultural groups in the United States are too diverse, too widespread and too deeply rooted to allow a fascist order to take hold. About one quarter of the US population is now non-white. However, the United States could become a society divided more and more along race/class lines. This would have severe economic consequences for the United States, especially in light of the underconsumption crisis that capitalism is facing. The past greatness of the United States has rested in large part on its ability to incorporate new immigrants and groups into the economic and social order. If this project of incorporation has come to an end, then the United States will continue its internal decay and social decline.

As Meredith Tax, a novelist and political commentator on US society, notes:

> We need a politics that links culture and economics, race and gender, fact and belief; that appreciates the need to listen as well as talk; that moves comfortably between the languages of policy and personal witness; and that sees the connection between large and small systems of exploitation and terror and is willing to stand up for justice in the home as well as justice in the world.[29]

Whether or not the United States can move forward depends in large part on the ability of the very diverse progressive forces in civil society to pull together around a common vision and political project. The United States is after all the country of George Washington, Abraham Lincoln, Franklin Roosevelt and Martin Luther King, Jr, a country that has at key moments broadened, rather than narrowed its political and economic base. The last three figures in particular advocated policies that sought to incorporate some of the most exploited and abused social sectors into the American Dream. Throughout US history these leaders and others have moved in tandem with popular movements to build a country that is more just and leads the world through example rather than military belligerence. Of course such advances have not come easily, usually occurring during periods of severe social and political conflict.

In the long term, the United States faces two distinct destinies. It could degenerate into a society of increasing strife in which race and social conflicts become increasingly destructive. The movie *Blade Runner*, with its two-tiered class society – one tier living in a high-tech world and the other inhabiting an impoverished and violent street society – may not be too far off the mark in depicting what will happen if this path is taken. Or the United States could be a creative and complex multiracial democracy that achieves a new dynamism on the global level and becomes a new "city on the hill" through its example.

CHAPTER 7

The Post-communist World: From Crisis to Catastrophe

> Other soldiers fought to save Russia. We fight to save Yeltsin.
> Sgt Vladimir Kalumin,
>
> Chechnya, 1995

> Liberal economics' devotion to personal egotism and avarice as the fundamental basis of social organization has been a persistent source of human misery and societal instability.
> Gabriel Kolko
> *Century of War*[1]

Much of the former communist world is experiencing a catastrophe of historic proportions. It is here that barbarism has emerged full blown just a few years after the collapse of communism. Whatever its flaws, the old system at least ensured that the bulk of the populace enjoyed an adequate standard of economic well-being as well as functioning health care and educational systems.

Now all that has ended with the imposition of economic policies beholden to neo-liberalism. Gangsters and mafia-like organizations control sizable portions of the economy and government bureaucrats enrich themselves as ever-increasing numbers of people find themselves homeless and without the minimal necessities. Diseases once regarded as conquered have reappeared: diphtheria, tuberculosis, polio and, in some regions, cholera. In Russia the population has fallen by 2 million as a result of a steep decline in the birth rate accompanied by an increase in the number of deaths. Although the educational and skill level of most of the region's peoples is quite high, economic disaster combined with disintegrating political systems have pushed many of the republics of the former Soviet Union and Eastern Europe into desperate conditions not all that dissimilar from those faced by a number of African countries.

The glitter of neo-liberalism

When the Soviet Union collapsed, the Russian authorities proclaimed that the country would be rapidly modernized and integrated into the "civilized world." The governments of other former Soviet republics promised the same, with the added caveat that "since we got rid of the Russians," all obstacles to prosperity have been removed and Western living standards are within reach. Then came the reforms. The strategy mapped out by Western advisers and Russian leaders was based on three very simple principles: liberalization of prices, minimization of government intervention – including the destruction of central planning and state welfare institutions – and the total privatization of the economy.

Though liberalization of prices was the first and most painful step, privatization became the core of the reform. A major problem was that while there were superficial similarities to privatization programs carried out in Britain and France in recent years, there was no domestic bourgeoisie in Russia capable of taking over and running the state properties. Privatization proved to be as extreme a process as the nationalizations that had once created the state-dominated economy. Its purpose was not just to make certain enterprises and institutions private, but to liquidate the very institution of state enterprise and ownership, even selling off economic sectors that in many capitalist countries remained publicly owned. To place some limits on the zeal of the privatizers, special decrees were passed stating that air and water could not be privatized.

While the Russian economy inherited many problems from the Soviet system, and the early process of price liberalization produced a certain economic disequilibrium, it was the privatization program that turned this crisis into the worst economic catastrophe in world history. In social terms, the years of reform in Russia have set the country back by decades, eliminating almost all the achievements of the post-Stalin period. The catastrophic fall in production and lowering of living standards during this period has brought Russia greater reverses than the four years of ruinous war with Nazi Germany.

By the end of 1992 inflation had wiped out the savings that people had accumulated over a lifetime. In the winter of 1993, the funds were often lacking to heat residential buildings. Huge factories stopped work and locally-produced goods disappeared from the shops. The buying power of most wages dropped to the level of the 1950s. More than half of the volume of industrial output has been lost and the technological level of Russian industry has fallen sharply. Every day, there are fewer buses on the streets. In place of public telephones, empty booths gape at would-be callers. Most Russian citizens simply lack the money to make major purchases. City streets have been turned into endless flea-markets as everything is bought and sold. People try to survive by selling off personal possessions or by becoming petty resale merchants, hoping somehow to stay afloat.

Barbaric bourgeoisie

In the world as a whole, the implantation of capitalism has normally been accompanied by the weakening or destruction of pre-capitalist structures. The primitive accumulation of capital took place at the expense of these structures. A predatory, "savage" capitalism was a natural phase of development, a normal pattern of behavior for a young bourgeoisie. But, however tragic the costs, in Europe or North America between the sixteenth and nineteenth centuries there was unquestionable progress. As technologically backward forms of production collapsed, they yielded their place to modern industry.

In Russia and the countries of Eastern Europe the maturing of capitalist entrepreneurship cannot be speeded up. It is impossible to carry out complex processes overnight that involve millions of people, including the transformation of cultures.[2] The new entrepreneurs are proving largely incapable of serious investment projects. In fact, the process is particularly unique in that for the first time in the history of capitalism, industries are being destroyed that are on a far higher technological level than those that are replacing them.

For all its weaknesses, the state sector in the former communist societies was generally recognized as having had a high level of technological development that allowed it to compete successfully with the West in some fields. This modern productive capacity is now being demolished in order to create favorable conditions for the development of private retail stores and commercial banks that so far have scarcely risen above the level of European merchant capital in the sixteenth century. If the communist state sector created hired workers with thoroughly modern habits and skills, the young capitalism is creating barbarian entrepreneurs whose intellectual, cultural, ethical and professional level is a whole epoch behind that of the people whom they set out to exploit. As a result, the implanting of capitalism inevitably involves regression in the social, cultural and technological spheres.

The superficial elements of modernization which accompany the activity of the new commercial structures do not change the essence of what is happening. The computers and fax machines with which these offices are filled, like the radio-telephones, fashionable ties and long-legged secretaries, represent no more than the kind of imitation of European luxury that was to be observed in the courts of barbarian chieftains from the epoch of the fall of the Roman Empire to early colonial times.

Privatization, which the representatives of the International Monetary Fund and the Russian authorities advertised as a miraculous remedy for any and all problems, has brought about a total economic collapse. Not only has privatization failed to help create a competitive market, but it has given birth to a system of rigid and uncontrolled monopolies exploiting the consumer and to a significant degree controlling the government. The performance of enterprises has deteriorated. The productivity of labor in the privatized sector has declined. Losses have increased, the competitiveness of production has fallen and foreign markets have been lost. The new private sector has sucked up huge subsidies and preferential credits from the government. Measures intended to encourage privatization have become one of the main sources of a colossal budget deficit, which in turn has contributed to uncontrolled inflation. At the same time the economy has fallen into an investment hole. Private capital investment in production has been practically non-existent.

With public investment abandoned and private investment missing, both privatized and public enterprises produce less and less. While the private enterprises enjoyed subsidies and cheap credits, the state-owned factories, which remain the only efficient element in the economy, have also had to slow down production. They were consciously strangled by government officials, who openly said that everything that cannot be privatized must be destroyed. The grim results of privatization are discussed in a report by the chair of the Privatization Commission, Vladimir Polevanov, who concluded that privatization in Russia created "pauper-proprietors" who "cannot survive without state protection."[3]

It is significant that an analogous picture is to be observed in almost all the countries of Eastern Europe, despite the various models of privatization and the differing scale of the process. In Poland by January 1993 the state sector, no longer dominant in the economy, was in practice providing the government with its sole tax base. In Hungary and eastern Germany the privatization of enterprises has been accompanied by their widespread closure and by the transfer of production to other countries. Even Western journalists who have scoured the countries of Eastern Europe in search of privatization success stories have been able to report almost nothing.

Economic subjugation and the new division of labor

Growing external indebtedness has become the curse of all the former communist countries, but nowhere has it led to such a clear and open dictatorship by the IMF as in Russia. The foreign trade of the Russian Federation has taken on all the features of colonial subjugation. The country exports fewer and fewer industrial products and more and more raw materials. Meanwhile, it imports low-quality mass consumption goods, obsolete and hence cheap technology, luxury items and radioactive waste.

In a new division of labor, the Baltic states are increasingly seeking to play the role of intermediaries between East and West, colonial trading stations on the frontiers of the barbarian world. The Baltic countries have been transformed into large-scale suppliers of non-ferrous metals to the world market, even though none of these metals is produced in the states concerned. All these materials are imported legally or illegally from Russia, Ukraine and Belarus, and then resold to the West. For such an economy, a strong convertible currency is more important than having its own production.

Owing in part to this new division of labor the governments of Estonia and Latvia have been unwilling to grant citizenship rights to the "barbarian" Russian population. The refusal of rights to Russians has a dual purpose. On the one hand, the national bourgeoisie in each of the Baltic countries is strengthening its monopoly on the new neo-colonial trade. On the other hand, the majority of the working class and of trade union members are excluded from participating in elections, since industrial production in these countries developed mainly on the basis of migrants from the old republics of the USSR. This has led in effect to the rebirth of apartheid in Europe at the same time as it is being dismantled in South Africa.

It is also significant that Poland and Hungary, despite suffering a serious decline in production, have nevertheless remained capable of exporting industrial and processing agricultural goods – the basis of some recent growth in their economies – while Russia has been transformed into a supplier of raw materials. In Russia, dependent capitalism is developing according to an African scenario, while in Eastern Europe the pattern is more akin to that in Latin America. As a result, the political system in the Eastern European countries is generally both more stable and more democratic than in the republics that have arisen on the territory of the former USSR.

At the same time, throughout Eastern Europe one can observe what might be called "Kuwaitization." Unable and unwilling to fully assimilate the entire eastern expanse, transnational capital is trying to establish its "strong points" in the East, raising certain areas to the level of the "civilized world." This coincides with the ambitions of the local elites. If the large countries are doomed to the role of being the periphery of the West, certain regions may rise to the level of the semi-periphery, with some prospect of eventual inclusion in the Western community of the wealthy. In order to create suitable conditions for this, the states or regions concerned need to separate themselves off from their less well-favored neighbors using state borders, customs duties and their own currencies. At the same time, they need to thwart all efforts to redistribute funds to the advantage of less developed regions.

It is this process, and not mythical outbursts of nationalism, that explains the disintegration of all the Eastern European federations. The collapse of the USSR created favorable conditions for the Kuwaitization of the Baltic republics. In Yugoslavia it was Slovenia that became "Kuwaitized." And after the disintegration of Czechoslovakia, the Czech Republic attained a privileged economic status compared to impoverished Slovakia. The possible disintegration of Russia could lead to resource-rich regions such as Yakutia becoming new Kuwaits.

Naturally, the process of disintegration has its own dynamic. This is the more so because the hopes that local elites associate with independence are not always borne out, as has happened in Croatia and the Ukraine. In Croatia, the collapse of the federation led to a prolonged war that undermined the economy, while the more prosperous Slovenia gathered in the economic fruits of independence. In the Ukraine, the precipitous collapse of industry after the disintegration of the USSR brought such an obvious and visible economic crash that all hopes of German investment came to nought.

The parasitic state and polarization

In the Ukraine, Russia, Romania and other countries the African scenario is giving rise to changes in the state structures themselves. If the state was earlier capable of carrying out bureaucratic modernization, it is now losing its sense of mission and becoming more and more parasitic; its dominant internal characteristics are chaos and unpredictability. This is a new state of affairs, even if we take into account the centuries-old traditions of bureaucratic arbitrariness and inefficiency in these countries.

Bureaucratism in the new Russia has reached heights never seen even in the Soviet period. In Moscow, where all the central ministries and departments remained after the collapse of the USSR, there is a shortage of government buildings. Corruption has become a part of everyday life and crime is growing at a catastrophic rate. This is not surprising in a country where the plunder of state property and the collapse of the constitutional order have together undermined all respect for the law. The new owners come from the mafia, from the old party and state bureaucracy, some are just successful Russian "yuppies," but all of them are united by the lack of roots and total disrespect towards any rules and laws as well as by the lack of even minimal moral constraints. In this sense Russian capitalism does not result in anything like the Protestant spirit of early Western capitalism or the Confucian ethics of Japan and Korea.[4]

It was not hard to predict that the people who had seized property, breaking all the rules along the way, would have trouble holding on to it. The new property owners have taught society an object lesson, demonstrating that might is right. It is for this very reason that they hold assiduously on to power, bent on allowing no political changes, even under a nominally democratic system. This was why Yeltsin's constitution concentrated unheard-of powers in the hands of the president and virtually ruled out any new attempts at political reform and any democratization of state rule. This proved to be a critical factor in his manipulation of the presidential elections in 1996. It is not beside the point to note that the Soviet dissident movement in its time demanded that the provisions of the constitution of the USSR should simply be carried out, while Academician Sakharov fought for the Congress of People's Deputies to be able to exercise its full powers. This is not occurring today.

Instead of the promised creation of a middle class, supposedly destined to become the basis for development and prosperity, we have seen a catastrophic polarization of society. Against a background of growing poverty, the luxury enjoyed by a tiny minority who have grown rich by speculating in privatized property and exporting mineral resources presents an outrageous spectacle. In 1993 sales of the most expensive and prestigious makes of Western cars in Moscow alone exceeded all the sales in Western Europe. Convinced that their capital is not safe in Russia, the new rich prefer to deposit it in Western banks. Press reports speak of $20 billion exported from the country every year by legal means alone.

But this is only the tip of the iceberg. The bulk of the funds that leave the country do so illegally, while Western financial aid often accumulates in the accounts of foreign firms or private individuals, never even reaching Russia. The present reformist project has been a total failure. It is not just individual crooked functionaries and entrepreneurs who are infected by corruption, but the entire political system of the new Russia and the country's ruling elite.

Popular discontent and the fractured ruling block

Russians are well known for their patience and submissiveness. However, it is one thing to make sacrifices in order to strengthen the country's economic might, and quite another to go without in order to secure the well-being of BMW owners. Consequently, it is not surprising that the great majority of the population regard the regime now in power in Russia with unconcealed hatred.

Among ordinary people, the phrases "economic reform" and "market economy" have the force of obscenities.

If the decades of the Cold War created in the Soviet population an enduring sympathy for and enthusiastic interest in all things Western, Western support for the Russian reforms has generated anti-Western and anti-American moods in the most diverse circles of society, especially among the less well-off members of the intelligentsia. The disappointment with the West has been aroused not only by hostility toward a pro-Western government. It is a sort of psychological compensation. The yearning for Western standards of consumption played a decisive role in securing the triumph of neo-liberalism in the East. In the late communist societies, where social bonds between people were extremely weak, citizens enjoyed considerable freedom in the sphere of personal life and consumption compared to the early decades of Soviet society and the immediate post-World War II years. The relative success of the Soviet system in competition with the West created numerous illusions, especially among the middle layers who believed that capitalism could offer even more. Thus, the modernization that had been promised by the neo-liberals was perceived by the majority of the population as the modernization of consumption.

The same happened as in the well-known story of the man who dreams of receiving 100,000 dollars, and whose wish is granted – at the cost of the death of his beloved son. The Western model of consumption finally triumphed, at least in the main cities. But for the majority of people, the price is that even the former Soviet way of life has become an unattainable dream.

Many Russian authorities try to link liberalization with modernization. But the Russian experience proves this is not true. As Vladimir Dakhin remarked in an influential center-left monthly *Svobodnaya Mysl,* in Russia it was always "liberalization for liberalization's sake."[5] These words were published in the same journal where Yegor Gaidar started his career as the editor of the economics section.

The anger of the population with the authorities and the new rich is not the only reason for the chronic instability of society. However paradoxical it might seem, another source of the volatility is the new elite itself. The ruling circles in Russia and in most "newly developing states" (this, for all its shortcomings, is the most accurate way of describing the post-communist world) are becoming more and more openly divided into two groups. On the one hand we see the formation of a bureaucratic bourgeoisie, only weakly linked to the West and without entrepreneurial dynamism, but striving for a certain stability. These people are conservatives and traditionalists. However, this is no longer conservatism in the old Soviet sense of supporting the Stalinist system, but in the Western sense: these conservatives seek a social order that will guarantee them the control and use of property.

Counterpoised to these people is a group of bankers and speculators who are seizing and parasitically eating their way through the country's resources. For this group, factories are no more than piles of scrap metal which can be sold off abroad at a profit. Real estate is worth more than infrastructure, the price of the dollar is more important than indices of production, and exporting oil is much more profitable than refining it. This is a comprador bourgeoisie with a lumpen-criminal psychology. Since the West is officially declared to be the bearer of all values and the source of all progress, social layers such as this are not only free from any pangs of conscience in delivering up their own country to be enslaved and exploited by foreigners, but even take a certain pride in doing so.

The two groups are united by corruption and by efforts to use the authority of the state to ensure their control over resources and property. But they are divided by a fundamentally different approach to the use of this property. All the Eastern European reforms were based on one or another formula for compromise between these two groups. But it was only in Russia following the collapse of the Soviet Union that the lumpen–comprador group triumphed completely. This created the preconditions for the African scenario that followed. Meanwhile, the reforms developed according to the bicycle principle: if you're not moving forward, you're falling over. For the new rich, stabilization meant collapse, since the lumpen-capitalist structures could not reproduce themselves on the basis of their own resources. They needed to continually seize new property and resources from outside.

Although the bureaucratic capitalism defended by the moderate section of the government and the "constructive opposition" based in parliament could not solve the country's problems, they at least required a certain nourishment in the form of relatively stable production. Here was the source of the irreconcilable struggle that divided the ruling block. This gave rise first to conflict with the parliament, culminating in the two-day civil war of October 1993. Then, after the population unequivocally rejected the neo-liberal course in the December 12 elections, the conflict came to be played out within the government.

Public opinion surveys showed that even those people who supported the reformers in December had turned against them by the spring of 1994. The groups that were going on strike by this time included doctors and teachers, who were simply incapable of surviving on their miserable salaries of $50–70 a month, as well as miners and workers in the oil and gas industries, that is, people who not long before had represented privileged layers. Irrespective of how events turn out in the long run, it was already possible by the spring of 1994 to state that capitalist modernization had once again failed on the expanses of Russia.

The combination of extreme backwardness with the outward signs of modernization and with dependency on a new big brother is creating a new and paradoxical situation, in which Moscow residents find it easier to make a telephone call to a small town in northern Texas than to St Petersburg. Nevertheless, the Western firms that are penetrating the boundless expanses of the former communist world are hostages of the conditions and culture that exist there. They are not only forced to confront the growing backwardness of technology and organization, but are themselves subject to barbarization.

American businessmen in Moscow constantly complain that, since the collapse of the USSR, doing business has become harder. But the West is quite unable to change this situation, since neither the funds, nor the technologies, nor interested investors exist for the large-scale modernization of the infrastructure. This could be done only by an indigenous state, which both the world and national bourgeoisie would seek to weaken by any means possible: foreign capitalists because they fear a dangerous potential competitor, and local ones because they have not reached the stage of being able to create their own state system.

The most important result of the global triumph of neo-liberalism in 1989 was to synchronize the social and economic processes unfolding in the world. In this sense, events occurring today in Moscow, New York and Mexico City are much more closely interlinked even than at the end of the 1980s. International communications systems have made Russia part of the global information system, and have made backward, barbaric Russian business a part of world capitalism. The question is whether the world system will be stronger or weaker as a result.

The altered social panorama

The offensive by the neo-liberal ideologues had been possible thanks to an exceptional combination of circumstances: the crisis and decomposition of the communist bureaucracy, the consumer expectations of the majority of the Soviet population, and the habit of most people in Soviet society of submissively following after the state authorities, wherever the authorities might lead them. Many Russians were bribed, intimidated and even terrorized in the 1996 presidential elections. Yeltsin repeatedly doled out favors to petitioners along the campaign trail, the full power of state was brought into play as the regional governors turned out the vote for Yeltsin, and much of the population was cajoled into believing they would loose what little financial security they had if the communists came to power. The West and its financial institutions, like the IMF, also played no small role in this process making it clear that under the communists no new financial assistance would be forthcoming to keep an economy afloat that was deeply mired in an economic crisis.

Meanwhile the divisions within the ruling bloc after the elections, maintained a relationship of forces which does not permit taking the reforms forward according to the original scenario. The ideologues of neo-liberalism originally anticipated opposition from pensioners, unskilled workers and relatively uneducated people who would be unable to prosper under free market conditions. In fact, the reforms at first found significant support within these very layers. The factors responsible included heightened consumer expectations, which are especially typical of these strata, and the habitual submissiveness to authority by members of this strata.

No less important was the fact that these were the social layers that were least dependent on productive investments. The collapse of production did not prevent them from finding new means of support through petty trade, participation in the informal economy, crime and sops from the local authorities. In those cases where the state social security system did not totally collapse, these groups benefited from the indexation of pensions and other welfare payments, and the fact that they sometimes still get clientelistic hand-outs from local political leaders.

The collapse of production has meant that highly skilled workers lost not only their incomes, but also their social status. Though a lot of discomfort is felt by the people in the lower reaches of society, it is the skilled working class that is totally frustrated and absolutely alienated by the regime.

The neo-liberal ideologues and politicians especially hoped for support from the youth and the intelligentsia. At first, both these groups gave real and enthusiastic support to the reforms, but then they soon found themselves among the primary victims of the reform process. There were no prospects for them in the shrunken, barbarized economy. Children cleaning cars on the streets in 1991 were seen as symbolic of the new entrepreneurship, but this activity soon came to be recognized as a sign of the inability of a collapsing society to offer the new generation any other work. Young people began filling the ranks of opposition movements of all types, from moderate left to extremist, although as the elections of 1996 revealed, many were fearful of the restoration of communism.

The capitalist project has thus come under dual pressure. On the one hand, it encounters continuing resistance from forces oriented toward the old, pre-capitalist way of life and, on the other hand, the new contradictions of capitalist development are giving birth to a new opposition among people who have assimilated the rules of the game but are dissatisfied with the results. Even small-scale entrepreneurs, supposedly a basic constituency of the new economic order, have become dissatisfied as they try to function in collapsing economies.

This growing pressure has already effectively paralyzed the neo-liberal project in the East by the end of 1993. Capitalist modernization had collapsed. Although its initiators had little hope of raising the peoples of the former communist world to the level of Western affluence, they had at least aspired to create in the East a significant-sized, stable minority capable of guaranteeing further capitalist development. This was achieved only to an insignificant degree in the Latin Americanized countries – Slovenia, Poland, Croatia, Czech republic and Hungary. In Russia, it was not achieved at all.

Russia will neither be part of the Western world, nor a banana republic. The reasons are not to be sought in the mysterious "Russian soul," but in the fact that the social and economic problems of this vast country simply cannot be solved through the recipes of the IMF and on the basis of free entrepreneurship. Democratic development is possible only on the basis of respect for personal interests and through taking into account established social and economic structures, accumulated experience and the existing culture. Ultimately, the Russians have reasons to take pride in their past, including the Soviet past. But any attempts to force Russia into the framework of the global Western project will sooner or later rebound on those in the West who have fed such illusions.

Under Gorbachev, inept attempts at saving the system simply had the effect of turning the crisis into the disintegration of the Soviet Union and brought to power intrepid children schooled on American textbooks. Today these children are no longer in favor, and the new authorities, as they try to overcome their crisis, are fussing about even more clumsily than the old ones.

The invasion of Chechnya

The crisis of the Russian regime, the economic collapse, and the unrelieved failures in all spheres of domestic and foreign policy forced Yeltsin's associates to look for a way out in late 1994. While the Yeltsin government had bungled all attempts at constructive activity, it had invariably emerged victorious from political crises. The closer the 1996 elections came, the more necessary it was to provoke a political crisis. A victorious little war in Chechnya seemed like an attractive way to increase the popularity of the authorities, to crush the opposition and, at the same time perhaps, to get rid of the faint-hearted within the government's own ranks.

On December 12, 1994 columns of tanks and 40,000 troops burst onto the territory of the mutinous Chechen Republic, along the way shooting up peaceful villages and killing the health minister of neighboring Ingushetiya. Aircraft and artillery dumped tons of bombs and shells on the capital of Chechnya, Grozny, founded by Russian generals in the nineteenth century in order to intimidate the Chechens.

Despite a television propaganda campaign by the government, the anti-war movement quickly gathered strength. The government's hopes of exploiting the racist prejudices of Russians against Chechens were not borne out. Surveys showed that the attitude of Russians toward Chechens, who had become the victims of aggression, became more favorable. Press reports of the bombing and shelling, from which the Russian population of Grozny suffered as much as anyone, played a considerable role.

Not for the first time, Yeltsin was supported by the far-right Liberal Democratic Party of Vladimir Zhirinovsky. Another person to declare his solidarity with the government was Aleksandr Barkashov, leader of Russian National Unity, the country's best-known neo-fascist group. In 1993 the presence of Barkashov's followers at the Moscow White House was enough for state television to accuse all supporters of the parliament of fascism. A year and a half later, Barkashov was speaking on state television in support of Yeltsin. Meanwhile the "democratic" mass media, which in October 1993 had been united in supporting Yeltsin, were subjected to fierce attacks from the authorities.

The weakest spot in the authorities' invasion of Chechnya was the lack of combat readiness of their own army – demoralized, poorly trained and without the slightest idea of why it was supposed to fight against citizens of its own country. The soldiers were going into battle beneath the automatic rifle muzzles of special forces troops. They refused to carry out orders, deserted and committed acts of banditry. While resourceful local residents succeeded in driving off some of the tanks and armored personnel carriers, federal soldiers and officers began fraternizing with the population. Warriors of the Russian army often began appearing in marketplaces in the suburbs of Grozny, where the besieged population fed them and gave them cigarettes. In ironic reference to Operation Desert Storm during the 1991 Gulf War against Iraq, military experts dubbed the Chechen operation "Bog Storm." "Super-accurate" laser gun-sights constantly failed to work. Bombs and rockets missed their targets sometimes by several kilometers, or even fell on the territory of neighboring Russian republics.

Failing to take Grozny with a lightning assault, the commanders of the Russian forces took out their wrath on the peaceful population, mounting an incessant bombardment of the city. The number of victims grew by the day. One of the first air raids on Grozny saw the devastation of Moskovskaya Street, where there was not a single military installation. The casualties included journalists who were in the battle zone. Although the whole world, including inhabitants of Russia, saw on television how Russian aircraft were dropping bombs on the city, the official Russian propagandists claimed to know nothing of any bombing, accusing the Chechens of engineering it themselves.

Just before New Year's Day Yeltsin promised to halt the bombardment of the Chechen capital. Immediately after the end of his speech, when residents of Grozny, whose hopes had been raised by the Russian president's promises, emerged from their bomb shelters, the most ferocious air raid of the entire war was unleashed. This was followed by a massed assault using tanks and infantry. The New Year attack on Grozny turned into one of the most shameful defeats in the history of the Russian army. The tanks that forced their way into the city were quickly cut off from the infantry and destroyed. The Russian forces retreated in disorder, even as the official propaganda was telling the world that the city had been taken and the presidential palace seized.

Following this debacle, the federal forces began systematically destroying Grozny. The attackers deliberately used artillery fire to demolish block after block, trying to make their way gradually toward the presidential palace. Meanwhile, almost the entire territory of the republic was engulfed in fighting. Skirmishes also began occurring in neighboring Daghestan. The drawn-out siege of Grozny allowed the Chechen fighters to develop a guerrilla war in the rear of the Russian forces. The Chechen volunteers fought professionally and with selfless courage, which is more than can be said of the Russian army. Federal soldiers refused to go into battle, deserted, and in some cases crossed over to the Chechens.

After arriving in the Caucasus and familiarizing himself with the situation, Deputy Commander of the Russian Land Forces Colonel-General Eduard Vorob'yev resigned his commission. Deputy Defense Minister General Boris Gromov came out with a public criticism of the war in Chechnya. Then national television showed the commander-in-chief of the Russian paratroop forces, General Podkolzin, delivering an anti-war speech at the funeral of a colonel killed in Grozny. Such statements by military officers in a country at war are virtually unknown, but perfectly natural in Yeltsin's Russia. After the country's ruling circles had spent five years destroying and humiliating their own military for the benefit of the West, they discovered to their surprise that the army was no longer willing or able to fight.

The war on Chechnya was illogical. The Russian government had spent three years allowing the Chechen regime of General Dzhokhar Dudaev to do whatever it liked. After proclaiming independence from Moscow, Dudaev did nothing to make independence a reality. Russian laws continued to be enforced on the territory of Chechnya, and the Russian ruble remained in circulation. The Chechen government did not set up its own customs system or institute border checks. The inhabitants of Chechnya remained Russian citizens, dealing with their problems through the relevant structures of the Russian Federation. Chechnya did not pay taxes, but other regions of Russia also refused to forward tax revenues from time to time.

The only thing that Dudaev did out of the ordinary was to set up armed formations under his personal control, a practice also followed by Yeltsin and Moscow Mayor Yuriy Luzhkov. In addition he delighted philatelists by issuing a series of Chechen stamps bearing his portrait, with a quality reminiscent of matchbox labels. It is quite clear that Dudaev was not so much seeking independence as trying to gain a special status for Chechnya within the Russian Federation or a future Eurasian Union, the need for which the Chechen general stressed repeatedly. The Moscow politicians for their part watched the events unfolding in Chechnya without particular alarm. The semi-independent republic was an ideal place for laundering millions stolen in the capital and for cutting deals in smuggled weapons, activities at which more than a few people from Moscow's ruling circles warmed their hands.

When military actions began in the Russian Federation for the second time in little more than a year, the nerves of many "democratic" politicians predictably gave way. Those who had been linked with Dudaev in earlier dealings were especially nervous. Neo-liberals in the Russian parliament began to protest but everybody remembered how they had supported the military suppression of Yeltsin's opponents in Moscow in October 1993. Against all their expectations, they found themselves in the same camp with leftists and communists. In the anti-war rallies red flags predominated, and the parliamentary liberals felt acutely uncomfortable.

For some psychologically incomprehensible reason the neo-liberals were sure in late 1993 that the crushing of the parliament, the shooting of demonstrators and the contempt shown for the law would have no bearing on their own rights. They saw nothing reprehensible in the fact that troops were opening fire with artillery in their own capital, nor in the fact that the representative organs of government had been turned into a pointless appendage of an uncontrolled executive power. It was only when these people saw the tanks in Chechnya on their television screens that they became outraged at the violence and arbitrariness of the authorities.

It is paradoxical that this time, unlike in 1993, Yeltsin acted strictly within the framework of his constitutional powers. The leading defenders of these powers once included Yegor Gaidar and other neo-liberal politicians. They, of course, imagined that these provisions would be used only against communists and leftists. But justice of a sort triumphed. The time came to recognize that to a police baton all heads are equal.

Whither national capital and the state?

It is obvious that under the rule of free competition the Russian banking sector would quickly fall under the control of Western capital. The same also applies to investment activity on the stock market. If there are no spokes thrust into their particular wheels, Western investors are able to establish control over any sector of the economy or the stock market in which they are interested. The Russian financial groups which in the course of voucher privatization seized control over a particular share of industrial capital discovered to their dismay that at the next stage they could be forced out with almost derisory ease by Western competitors. Because of their weaknesses Russian banks can only serve as dealers and subcontractors for Western ones. But to the surprise of their Western counterparts, Russian banks have begun trying to play the role of national capital, campaigning in favor of state protectionism. In response, Western financial interests have shown increasing aggressiveness.

The state is being called upon to defend young national capital. But how is this to be done, if in the course of primitive accumulation the state was stripped bare, deprived of property and of the elementary levers for influencing the economy? The question arose of writing off debts owed to the state by private banks, just as was done for industry and agriculture. But such once-only "emergency measures" merely serve to confuse the situation. The dependency of commercial banks on the state is increasing all the time, but the same cannot be said of the possibility of controlling the financial system. On the one hand, nothing can be done without the state, while, on the other, the ruling circles have not resolved on open nationalization.

The worst of all possible approaches is therefore being put into effect: indirect statization without nationalization. Maximum power is concentrated in the hands of particular financial bureaucrats, while society is not acquiring the possibility of controlling either these bureaucrats or the banks themselves. It is proving impossible to concentrate the resources required for investment, while the reorganization of the banking system remains an empty promise.

The need for a constant struggle against internal and external enemies is part and parcel of authoritarianism. This is why former allies and fellow-travelers of the regime have sooner or later become its victims. The circle has continually contracted. First the communists were defeated; then wavering democrats were thrown overboard; now the turn has come of the privatizing Westernizers themselves. The task of seizing property has been successfully fulfilled. The ideology of liberalism, which initially allowed the regime to create a mass base for itself, has been totally exhausted and discredited.

This has made the neo-liberal ideologues themselves unnecessary ballast for the regime particularly in the period leading up to Yeltsin's re-election. First these people were forced out of the corridors of power into the lobbies of a decorative parliament. Then even this parliament became a burden to the authorities, and the ideologues faced a new political catastrophe with the elections.

The idea of change is being replaced with the idea of order, and human rights by a police state. The situation is complicated, however, by the presence of democratic institutions. On the one hand, the new social order is incompatible with democracy, while, on the other, open dictatorship is impossible as well. Moreover, a certain heed must be paid to the West. The organs of repression, meanwhile, are unprepared for really rough and systematic work. They are capable only of episodic actions – raids, assaults and blockades.

With democracy impermissible, and dictatorship impossible, the Yeltsin regime is forced constantly to create democratic structures, and then when they had fulfilled their immediate purpose to abolish them. If these structures were to survive and acquire strength, they would be dangerous and destructive for Russian nomenklatura capitalism. The Duma is less dangerous than was the old Supreme Soviet, but it began to take on an independent significance as well.

The leaders of the Communist Party learnt a good deal from their earlier setbacks although not enough to overcome the power and perogatives of the Yeltsin regime in the 1996 elections. They understood that you cannot frighten the authorities with hysterical declarations and with little gatherings in Pushkin Square. In 1994, the Communist Party rapidly gained strength in the Russian provinces, acting as a democratic alternative along the lines of the post-communist parties in Poland and Hungary. The crisis in Chechnya confronted the communists with a new political situation. They lost some of their allies in the "patriotic" camp, but by speaking out against the war they once again acquired their own face as the leading left party.

The ever-deepening political and economic crises even pushed some of the authorities of the Yeltsin government to begin talking about selective nationalizations in 1994. Yeltsin's chief economic adviser Aleksandr Livshits was joined by the new head of the State Property Committee, Vladimir Polevanov, who declared that re-nationalization of the aluminum industry was possible "in the name of national interests." In response to this proposal, the newspaper *Segodnya* hurled thunderbolts, invoking "the sacred right to private property."[6] But the more practical-minded people in the government understand two points to which ideologues are oblivious: firstly, renationalization is absolutely indispensable in conditions where privatization has totally collapsed; and secondly, the predatory and economically ineffective approach to privatization in Russia has meant that renationalization cannot take any form apart from confiscation.

The faltering "royal" bankers

It is easy to understand the bankers, who are trying to secure their positions by feeding one group of politicians or another. In order to avoid putting all their eggs in one basket, the financiers are ready to befriend several rival groups simultaneously. But this, of course, also serves to devalue the bankers' friendship, making any mutual obligations extremely conditional. The politicians always win at this game. If the protector of one or another bank emerges triumphant from his or her struggles, the bank can expect to benefit, but this help merely strengthens the dependency of the financiers on state structures. If the bank loses its protector or finishes up linked to the losing side, it can expect to suffer. A raid by special forces troops on the bank's security guards is only the mildest form this pressure can take.

The politicization of the banks is opening the way for their nationalization. Moreover, this is occurring spontaneously and "from below." It is the banking circles themselves that are doing this, without any compulsion, for the simple reason that they cannot conceive of any other mode of behavior. The weakness of Russian finance capital cannot be overcome either through isolated emergency measures, or through cultivating the friendship of influential people.

The inability of Russian finance capital to act as the basis for a fully-fledged ruling class provides the preconditions for a new systemic crisis. It is now a common perspective to blame the hardships of present-day life on "primitive accumulation." But in so doing we forget that the merchants and bankers of the epoch of primitive accumulation had no pretensions to power, and could not have had. For centuries, they developed their businesses in the shadow and under the protection of a thoroughly non-bourgeois state. The same applied in the USSR during the NEP period, and applies today in China, where private business has acquired the possibility of a turbulent but organic development subject to the power of the Communist Party. One of the paradoxes of the Russian reform is that after more than half a decade of "building capitalism" this country has become less attractive for Western investors than China or even Cuba.

Today's Russian financiers, whether they like it or not, are becoming less and less like their present-day Western colleagues, and more and more like the bankers who extended credit to kings and princes in the late Middle Ages. This is politicized capital in the highest degree; it depends completely on the goodwill of the authorities, on their readiness to bestow privileges and commissions. It is significant that despite the vast accumulated funds at the disposal of the royal bankers of medieval times, the real entrepreneurial bourgeoisie in the West never arose out of financial empires of this type. On the contrary, it was always forced sooner or later to struggle against such formations. After weakening and undermining the old state economy and system of administration, the new capital in Russia has been unable to create its own substitute for them. The results include a constant investment crisis, a budget that is forever coming unraveled, and all-pervasive corruption, which remains in essence the sole mechanism of rational decision-making. The state, which on the whole was closely linked to the new structures, has been forced to stage frequent raids on them, instead of acting as their protector. Without these raids, the financial resources available to the authorities and their ability to exercise at least some degree of control would have been even less.

Instead of offsetting the financial and economic failures of the regime, the military adventure in Chechnya served to deepen them. The 1995 state budget, in which the government promised to renounce the practice of covering the deficit with credits from the Central Bank, collapsed even before the State Duma adopted it on the second reading. Inflation rose sharply. The financial crisis entered a new "military" phase; historians were forced to recall the collapse of the Russian economy in 1916 following the defeats suffered at the front in World War I.

The inconsistent and absurd attempts of the current regime to move a little to the left did not portend anything good. This pseudo-shift from above is accompanied by attempts to develop a compromise ideology, a mixture of liberalism and nationalism with collectivist traditions and the Russian love of authoritarian leaders. But it has not proven possible to graft this mixture onto popular consciousness, any more than it was possible with Gorbachev's efforts to mix democratic reforms with an authoritarian state. The efforts to achieve this have merely aided the spread in society of more radical versions of left ideology. If Gorbachev's semi-liberal version of communism aided the maturing of forces oriented toward an open transition to capitalist values, the present crisis is evidently preparing the way for society to return to collectivist and openly socialist ideas.

A renewed vision of Russian socialism

For Russia, the main lesson we could and should draw is the necessity of state ownership as a strategic alternative to neo-liberalism. Co-ops and workers' participation in property, which were supported by the Russian left in 1990–1 as a soft alternative to privatization, never worked. And they cannot work unless the key sectors of the economy become owned and formed by the state. This looks like a very traditional socialist approach and it is. And this is the approach now supported by a growing number of people in the former Soviet Union because it is the only realistic approach.

The only way to break the power of private monopolies is to nationalize them, whether under Yeltsin or a communist government. Nationalization enabled the old Soviet system in its best times to grow extremely fast and develop modern technologies.[7] Why are we afraid to discuss the real merits and advantages of the old communist system? Strategic planning is possible only by and through the state. And it is meaningless without state ownership. Even state indirect regulation is very weak and inefficient without public ownership. A mixed economy won't work. We support in Russia more co-ops within the state-owned and planned economy but not instead of it.

We must say what kind of state we want to have. The nature of state property will depend on it. If we don't recognize that and we don't support nationalization and expansion of the state sector, we take a position to the right of social democracy. At least in Britain in 1945 the state nationalized key sectors of the economy – even in Sweden there was some expansion of public enterprise. It is clear that without state enterprise there will never be any state capable of meeting the public's basic needs such as health care, education and employment.

We need to change the state, we need to democratize public enterprise but we have to stand firm against those postmodernists who argue for "stateless socialism." And that means that we need to reform traditional Marxism, not reject it. Every day of capitalist restoration in Russia or Eastern Europe proves that Marx and Lenin were right on capitalism and on the centrality of state property for any socialist project.

We have to be proud of our traditions and of our achievements as socialists and/or communists. A lot was said on reforming Marxism but up to now all real challenges to capitalism have been presented only by unreformed socialists and Marxists. Russian communism failed, it is true, but the French Revolution also failed, the Renaissance failed. We reject communism just as we reject Jacobinism, but we shouldn't forget how important their role was in changing the world.

CHAPTER 8

Visions: Old and New

When the gap between ideal and real becomes too wide, the system breaks down.

Barbara Tuchman,
A Distant Mirror[1]

History, far from coming to a stop is quickening its pace. But the left is bewildered. Its project has to be reinvented.

Daniel Singer[2]

The end of the twentieth century is not an easy historical moment. This is a world torn by conflict and upheaval, a world difficult to understand. Going far back in history, Barbara Tuchman, in one of her finest but lesser known works, *A Distant Mirror*, surveyed the wars, plagues and social upheavals that beset Europe in the fourteenth century. As suggested in the title, Tuchman believes there are parallels between this earlier period and our times. That century was afflicted with major calamities and had a certain millennial quality to it, and so does ours.

Gabriel Kolko in his seminal volume on the wars of the twentieth century concludes that:

There are no easy solutions to the problems of irresponsible, deluded leaders and the classes they represent, or the hesitation of people to reverse the world's folly before they are themselves subjected to its grievous consequences. So much remains to be done – and it is late.[3]

Many others continue to believe that humanity will somehow stumble through this period. After all, even the desperate century that Tuchman portrays gave way to the Renaissance and a new civilization. To understand what kind of world can be built, we first need to grasp the globe's astoundingly complexity. Five and a half billion human beings now live on the planet, approximately one out of fifteen human beings that have existed since the origin of homo sapiens as a species.[4] We are a tremendously diverse mix of societies, races and cultures, all in dynamic motion, far more active, more creative and more productive than our ancestors ever were. In spite of all the misery and exploitation that many suffer, the situation of the human species is far from hopeless. Unlike the fourteenth century, today's material foundation could enable us to create a world of freedom and happiness never known before.

But the contemporary world actually teeters on the brink of barbarism. Ideologically, the failure of socialism has been devastating. From the beginning of history, the diverse civilizations that emerged have possessed beliefs or values that guided their societies. Early in this century, socialism appeared to be the new ideology that would lead humanity forward. But even before the collapse of most of the communist societies from 1989 to 1991, "actually existing socialism" had already become a dream that failed. The regimes of Eastern Europe fell so quickly precisely because disillusionment, skepticism and alienation had taken hold among their peoples.

During the existence of a bipolar ideological world one could wish for the triumph of one system or another. The disgruntled living under communism could believe that Western-style democracy and/or capitalism would dramatically change their lives, while the disenchanted in the capitalist world could hope that "actually existing socialism" would be improved upon and open the door to a better world.

Now all that has ended. Today, most on the left are at a loss as to what humanity's societal destiny shall be. In the former Second World, the victory of capitalism has not meant a better life, but a world in which people are totally on their own, at the mercy of economic forces they have no control over. One of capitalism's salient features, rampant individualism, has spread like wildfire throughout the old communist world, isolating people at the very moment when the tremendous convulsions shaking the world drive people to seek mutual support and a system of beliefs that might unite them.

It was perhaps inevitable that with the collapse of communism there would be a resurgence of ethnic and religious beliefs. In Eastern Europe and the former Soviet Union, national rivalries are as intense as during the early decades of this century. Marxist-Leninist governments did put a lid on these conflicts with their multinational approach, but, as is now all too evident, communism never alleviated fundamental tensions among the different nationalities it governed. And when the regimes fell, the West's demands that the economies be rapidly privatized and incorporated into the "free market," lead to immediate hardship and growing inequalities for much of the population. This accentuated the old ethnic rivalries as first one group and then another began to look for scapegoats to blame for their difficult circumstances.

Of course not all the wars and conflicts of the 1990s have arisen out of the collapse of socialism and the resurgence of capitalism. In much of Africa and parts of Asia, many ethnic conflicts are related to the crisis of the twentieth-century nation states. Basil Davidson, in *The Black Man's Burden* argues that the Western powers foisted on the peoples of Africa and other parts of the world state structures and artificial boundaries that responded solely to Western interests and were out of touch with the community development and diverse tribal histories of the colonized countries.[5] The failure of these states to create stable and expanding economies soon led to conflicts among the different ethnic groups as they competed with each other for scarce economic resources and political power. In countries like the Congo, Zaire, Somalia, Liberia and Uganda these conflicts have led to the virtual collapse of the state.

The crisis will be a long one. We have by no means touched bottom. As billions of people find their very physical survival imperiled there will be increasing chaos and havoc on a worldwide scale. Political alliances will fragment, society will be increasingly anarchistic, there will be riots and civil wars. Tomorrow's societies are prefigured in today's science fiction. In the San Francisco of William Gibson's novel *Virtual Light*, or in the China and US east coast of his older novel (and subsequent movie), *Johnny Mnemonic*, the masses live in decomposing cities and are called "lowtechs" while private and public police forces become major areas of employment on behalf of the wealthy.[6]

The nature and depth of the Marxist crisis

The crisis of contemporary Marxism is not to be found in its analytical capabilities because it is a dialectical, open system of analysis that even allows us to dispute and discard many of the positions taken by Marx and Engels. As Paul Sweezy and Harry Magdoff declare, "Historical materialism ... is the firm foundation on which all that is best in social sciences has been and continues to be based."[7] It is rather the collapse of actually existing socialism that has thrown Marxism into a crisis that is profoundly different from any other in its century and a quarter of existence. Marxists may insist that their critique of capitalism is the most valid one around, but if they have no capacity to link up socialism with concrete experiments or broad-based social movements, then socialism or communism, as Marx and Engels described them in the *Communist Manifesto*, are in effect stripped of the social actors that moved these historic projects forward.

Some Marxists argue that the communist or national liberation movements were misguided or fundamentally flawed and thus socialism and Marxism deserve another chance. The reality however is that the mass of humanity is not interested in giving socialism that chance. From 1917 to 1991, history provided socialism with one opportunity after another to prove itself. The Bolshevik Revolution, the liberation of China and the subsequent Maoist experiment in permanent revolution, the Vietnamese war of national liberation, the Cuban Revolution, the liberation of the Portuguese colonies, the Nicaraguan revolution and even Gorbachev's efforts to reform communism from above – all these experiments and others sooner or later came up short and, because of this generalized failure, socialism as we know it no longer has any mystique or capacity to mobilize broad sectors of humanity.

As is frequently pointed out, these revolutions and experiments all occurred in underdeveloped or poor societies, not in the advanced capitalist countries where Marx and Engels predicted the first proletarian revolutions would occur. Even if we accept this as an explanation of what went wrong, it means nothing for the future of Marxism, since it is highly unlikely that future revolutionary socialist governments led by a proletariat will take power in any of the Western countries. The two largest parties on the left with ties to communism and the proletariat are the Democratic Party of the Left in Italy and the French Communist Party, both of which have renounced Marxism-Leninism. If they do come to power, they have made it clear they will not undertake any radical restructuring of their societies.

The left has to accept the fact that the Marxist project for revolution launched by the *Communist Manifesto* is dead. There will certainly be revolutions (the Iranian Revolution is probably a harbinger of what to expect in the short term), but they will not be explicitly socialist ones that follow in the Marxist tradition begun by the First International. It is this view of twentieth century history that led Marxist historian Eric Hobsbawm to declare in his monumental tome, *Age of Extremes*, that "the past ... has lost its role, in which the old maps and charts which guided human beings, singly and collectively, no longer represent the landscape through which we move."[8]

Gabriel Kolko in *Century of War* notes that socialism expanded dramatically as a consequence of the two world wars that were driven largely by the "egotism and avarice" of capitalism. But for Kolko the socialist alternative has also failed because

> the usages to which the word "socialism" have been put are so disparate, and make such a mockery of its original dedication to social justice, that the concept has been devalued to a very great measure, evoking well deserved cynicism from those who still believe in its simpler, broad goals.[9]

The process of globalization under capitalism is of course generating enormous misery, deprivation and violence. But it is highly unlikely that the new "wretched of the earth" will turn to

Marxism or the national liberation movements for salvation. We are in an age where a modern form of barbarism is a much more likely outcome of late capitalism's ruthless exploitation of the globe. As Eduardo Galeano notes, the "culture of violence" is rapidly assuming global proportions.[10]

Visions after Marx

To pull back from the descent into modern barbarism we need a new vision and an economic program for dealing with the impoverishment and destitution faced by ever-increasing numbers of the world's population. The resurgent religious movements respond in part to our ideological–spiritual needs, but most have no systemic understanding or program for dealing with the vast structural inequalities spawned by global capitalism. Communism theoretically bridged this gap but, as we now know, it came up short in both the ideological and material realms.

To end the growing sense of despair that runs through our societies, we have to be convinced that it is possible to change the world. But in order to do this we do need to construct a new unifying vision of what we are about. Neo-liberalism can only be effectively resisted and fought against with a new ideology that offers an alternative worldview. It will have to propose concrete alternatives to the present form of globalization while at the same time championing social justice. We cannot have a world where a minority enjoys a grand banquet while large numbers are castaways.

There will probably be no new Marx who comes out with the definitive opus for a new world. But we can and do have people advancing in different areas of thought, developing new ideas that can coalesce into a new system of values. Over the past quarter century there has been new and provocative thinking in the fields of literature, philosophy, geography, sociology and anthropology. What is lacking is the connection of these areas of thought and study with political practice and a mass base. The power of Marx's and Engel's revolutionary philosophy lay in their ability to dissect the exploitative working and living conditions of the proletariat and then to make the working class the motor of social transformation. This same task must be done with the masses of humanity today. Their interests and needs must be the driving force behind any new social theory. Only then can we generate a vision of what we are about.

Confronting neo-liberalism

Neo-liberalism has been astoundingly effective in erecting an economic ideology that makes us feel powerless, especially with the collapse of communism and socialism as alternatives. Throughout the world, neo-liberalism has generated a palpable feeling that participation in any movement or protest is futile. Voting does no good, since one set of politicians is the same as another, and labor unions are of no use since they have limited or negligible capacity to improve wages or benefits. Furthermore, cutbacks in social services, IMF monetary adjustment programs, corporate lay-offs and austerity measures imposed on even the largest countries by the financial markets also create a sense of powerlessness, a belief that we can do nothing to stop the onslaught of the market and financial forces that are beyond our control.

It is globalization, driven by neo-liberalism, that is pushing the peoples of the world into a sense of despair and hopelessness. States were once able to implement policies at a national level that would not be significantly undermined by global economic forces. Moderate, reformist governments, like those of the Christian Democrats in Chile or Italy in the 1960s could use the financial instruments of the state to stimulate employment, to carry out social reforms, and to increase the income of the poorest sectors without having to worry about international capital undermining them. But now that has ended with the rise of globalization and finance capital.

It is this despondency and despair of the popular sectors that we have to mobilize against. A program has to be put forward that confronts neo-liberalism head on, laying out alternatives to globalization and the class forces that stand behind it. Perhaps even more than that, in the arenas of political and social struggle what is needed is a certain "voluntarism." We have to believe that it is possible to change things, and acting on that belief we have to become involved politically. Neo-liberalism, the cult of consumerism, and the rise of globalization have all combined, almost conspiratorially, to made us feel impotent.

The popular sectors are riven with a profound sense of despair and nihilism. The poorest people – be they in the United States, Mexico, the Philippines or Great Britain – feel they are trapped, that neither they nor their children have any hope of escaping from a life of poverty. Besieged by the media hype that the "good life" of consumerism is the only way to live, the poor continually face those who are prosperous or well-to-do, those who have a piece of the modern material dream. This type of environment naturally breeds complete despair, and a turn to crime, alcohol and drug abuse.

There are of course less destructive versions of this pessimistic worldview around. Among the middle sectors who have access to much of the material world, there is a sense that one's life is controlled by a "deus ex machina" comprised of the "marketplace."

Many feel bound by a daily grind in which all they can do is try to survive through continual hard work. They have no time or space to improve the quality of their lives or that of their neighbors. Under globalization it is a dog-eat-dog world for much of humanity. Who can worry about the decline of the environment or unrepresentative political systems when it is difficult to eke out a living on a day-to-day basis?

Upending multiculturalism

As a starting point, any new or alternative approach that tries to grapple with this profound demoralization will have to be rooted in multiculturalism. What today's ethnic, tribal and national conflicts reveal is the existence of flourishing national movements. The shrinking of the globe has made people increasingly aware of their own distinctiveness and identity.

Any new ideology that tries to build a popular worldview without including these strong cultural and national impulses is destined to fail. Joanne Landy in 'Women and Nationalism' in the *Nonviolent Activist*, laments the "indifference and apathy" of many to the emergence of new states throughout the former communist world. She proclaims that progressives and leftists

> are doomed to be irrelevant or even counter-productive if we oppose legitimate self-determination struggles. The real question for democrats is how to build support for pluralistic, tolerant and democratic national self-determination and how to counter ugly, racist and pathological forms of nationalism.[11]

This view contrasts sharply with that presented by Benjamin Barber in *Jihad vs. McWorld*, which sees these forces assaulting the world's existent democratic institutions. "McWorld" signifies the multinationals and their insatiable demand for global markets, while "Jihad" for Barber embodies many of the nationalistic and identity movements of the planet. Jihad according to Barber is "a rabid response to colonialism and imperialism and their economic children, capitalism and modernity; it is diversity run amok, multiculturalism turned cancerous." For Barber, the common threat of Jihad and McWorld is that even though "they are antithetical in every detail," they "conspire to undermine our hard-won (if only half-won) civil liberties and the possibility of a global democratic future."[12]

The flaw in Barber's perspective is two-fold. He has on the one hand an antiquated, idealistic view of what democracy should be, and on the other he fails to understand that if new, more egalitarian societies are to be built they will have to come out of an amalgam of the different national, ethnic and cultural movements of the world.

These movements will not be nice quiet gatherings of middle and working class people who step forth to vote for the "common good" in peaceful elections. They will be messy and tumultuous movements, and they will have competing and often contradictory views of basic civil liberties and of what constitutes democracy.

Of course it needs to be recognized that some ethnic or national movements, like those of the Serbs or the Croats, have fallen under the control of leaders who are chauvinistic and revanchist. But by and large, the array of ethnic and multicultural movements that span the globe are resisting political and social oppression. Most of the diverse ethnic and identity struggles ranging from African-Americans in the United States to the Tibetans under Chinese rule, Indians in Mexico, and homosexuals (especially in the Latin and Anglo-Saxon cultures where virulent forms of homophobia are ascendant), are fighting for their basic human rights and an end to exploitation.

Many of the more visceral tendencies of the nationalistic movements are also counterbalanced by the growing strength of the international women's movement. The meetings at the women's official and unofficial gatherings in China in September 1995, represented an enormous advance for many progressive forces. Never in the history of humankind has such a diverse and democratic gathering occurred with delegations from all over the planet. The tremendous cultural and national differences, and even conflicting ideas over what constituted women's rights, led not to antagonistic and conflictual debates, but to a largely harmonious interchange of ideas and cultures. The globalism of the women's movement is important not only because it encompasses half of humanity but also because it helps sustain and foment other movements ranging from lesbian and gay rights to ethnic and cultural movements. The women's movement is a profoundly democratic force that confronts in many ways the patriarchal anti-democratic tendencies of virtually all societies.

These and the other movements in all their diversity constitute new social subjects for revolutionary change. Although each of these multicultural struggles have their own particular agendas, there is a certain cross-cultural awareness, and even interaction, among many of them. While multicultural movements emphasize the local and the specific, many of them constitute building blocks for a new internationalism. The Indian rebellion in Chiapas for example has reinvigorated the solidarity movement throughout the Americas and made peoples in diverse parts of the world aware that their own particular struggles against authoritarianism, racism and abusive state power are similar to what is happening in Chiapas.

The new ideologues of Eurocentrism

While these struggles advance, the ideologues of the Western Eurocentric worldview are trying to put an ideological spin on the rise of the ethnic and nationalist movements that covers up or ignores the problems of "actually existing capitalism." Samuel P. Huntington's essay in *Foreign Affairs*, 'The Clash of Civilizations?' argues that the West faces its gravest threat from other cultures. "The conflicts of the future will occur along the cultural fault lines separating civilizations," Huntington says. Immediate or potential challenges to Western civilization include those of Islamic fundamentalists, the Chinese or "Confucians," and the Russians as head of a Slavic bloc.[13] There are two major fallacies in Huntington's thesis. First he ignores internal discontent and strife within what he calls Western civilization. The plight of African-Americans for example goes unmentioned, as does the urban rebellion in Los Angeles in 1992. These are non-events because they do not fit into his effort to frame the major opposition to Western "democracies" as external. For Huntington it is a case of the "West versus the rest."

A second fallacy in Huntington's perspective is that he tries to ignore or obscure the reality that it is the very onslaught of capitalism, particularly Western capitalism, that is provoking a furious reaction on the part of many native peoples and nationalities. In Mexico for example, the indigenous rebellion in Chiapas is the result of the intensified exploitation that native peoples are experiencing as foreign and national capitalists tighten their hold on the Mexican state and produce an increasingly opulent and ever more corrupt ruling class that immiserates large sectors of the population, particularly the rural Indians. And if there is a challenge by "Slavic civilization" it will come primarily because the West has been so self-serving in its effort to reshape Russia in its own free-market image. The rise of an extremist figure like Vladimir Zhirinovsky is precisely due to Western capitalism's determination to impose shock therapy on the Russian economy and to force its markets open to multinationals and foreign capital.

What should we on the left do to counteract the efforts of Huntington and others to turn the current conflicts in the world into a battle of the West versus the rest? First we need to recognize our own past ideological limitations. Contrary to the assertions of many classical Marxists, the major tensions and conflicts in the world do not arise from a strict or narrow concept of class struggle. The "proletariat" which Marxists once saw as the ditch-diggers of capitalism are simply not going to overthrow capitalism on their own. Large sectors of the world's population, including many in the Western world, are suffering from exploitation and abuse by the capitalist system, but this exploitation often manifests itself in ethnic or gender issues.

It is in the arena of multiculturalism that the left must begin to construct a new ideology capable of galvanizing and unifying people. There are flourishing grassroots movements occurring around the world. People of color, indigenous people, religious people and social movements are defining themselves and their struggles for autonomy and freedom around issues of culture. They want and demand a world in which they are free to develop their own societies and communities – economically, culturally and politically. They may not characterize their struggles as contests with capitalism, but they are fairly clear that Western domination and the established political systems are by and large oppressive and need to be dramatically changed.

This principle of multiculturalism has important implications for the new political model that we try to construct. For one it means that there can be no single political prototype. The planet has been poorly served by the efforts of the communist and capitalist countries to impose their version of the nation state on the rest of the world. Each nation, culture or society will have to develop political institutions that respond to its unique historical and political development. If socialism is to be an integral part of this process, it will assume many forms. This is why we speak of "postmodern socialisms."

The small country of Eritrea, the only place in the 1990s to experience a successful political revolution under the leadership of a national liberation movement, provides some insights into how flexible forms of political and cultural organization can be wedded to a general socialist orientation. Governing three million people about equally divided between Christians and Muslims with nine different languages and at least as many cultures, the Eritrean People's Liberation Front (EPLF) has striven since 1991 to encourage local development rather than having the central government set out a masterplan. The villages and communities hold frequent local elections, sometimes as often as every six months. They use whatever resources are available to carry out their own economic initiatives, responding to what is needed at the local level.[14]

The central government has rejected proposals for assistance by the US Agency for International Development because of its rigid formula for privatization of the economy. Although per capita income is less than $150 and 80 per cent of the people earn their living from farming, the Eritrean government shuns aid and development projects that will not make its people self-sufficient. The President of Eritrea, Isaias Afewerki, states: "We have the capacity for self-sufficiency, we don't believe aid can solve our problems."[15]

Food aid is the major form of international assistance and this aid is channeled to local food-for-work programs to help build bridges, dams, schools and clinics, depending on community needs. The popular associations established by the EPLF during its years of war with the Ethiopian government – like women's and peasants associations, and trade unions – have been set loose from the dictates of the party. The priorities and activities of these organizations are determined largely at the community and regional level.

Due to the tremendous poverty of the Eritrian people, the country will hardly become a "model" for other countries to follow. But in a continent torn by ethnic and tribal wars, Eritrea is setting an example with its fostering of cultural diversity, its emphasis on local development and the central government's refusal to impose grandiose political or economic schemes on the country. Because of its exemplary role, the country's leaders have been mediating in neighboring Somalia and even among contending Ethiopian groups that the EPLF once fought against.[16]

Articulating the new project

A central task is that of articulating or giving a name to the new historic project or ideology that is emerging in the midst of the generalized crisis of the old system. Is it socialism, democratic socialism, libertarian socialism, or a new variant of communism? The problem is that the dominant forms of twentieth-century socialism, namely communism and social democracy, have failed, leaving the terms socialism and communism largely discredited among the popular sectors of the world. Other concepts like "radical" also have problems, given that there is a radical right as well as a radical left. The term "revolutionary" also has difficulties, given its historic identification with violence and the reality that people only overturn the existent political and economic orders when their situations are extremely desperate. Hopefully in the new epoch, there will be some largely peaceful, democratic, electoral paths to fundamental change that eschew bloody revolutionary upheavals.

In the long term, democratic socialism could be the most descriptive label for the new emerging ideology. However, until we come up with a label that has broad appeal, we prefer to use the concept of postmodern socialisms to discuss what we are about. It is the processes that are important rather than the defining terminology. Whatever the term, it will have to be developed through practice, rather than by proclaiming it as our banner from the start. We will have to stress the content of the new project and use specific, activating concepts such as participatory democracy, human rights, environmentalism, pacifism as an ideal, feminism, economic democracy, sexual freedom, social justice, ethnic liberation, local power, workers' power, and so on. The movement must also be multi-current, multicultural, and profoundly respectful of individual as well as group freedoms and liberties.

The political challenge for the left and progressives is daunting, given the ascendancy of liberal democracy. When we look back at the twentieth century we see that the major advances of socialism occurred because of the havoc and destruction wreaked by the two world wars. The other motors of socialism or national liberation movements were struggles against colonial rule and rebellions against dictators like Batista in Cuba and Somoza in Nicaragua. Now the types of political adversaries the left confronted in the past (such as the Tsar of Russia, Batista or Somoza) have become largely obsolete.

The hollowness of liberal democracy provides space for the left and progressive political activists, but the problem is that we have yet to come up with an alternative strategy and a new political system. The left has challenged and overthrown dictatorial or authoritarian regimes, but has never mounted an effective challenge to liberal democracy.

Today people are willing to fight and die for their ethnic and national identities. However, unlike the early and mid-twentieth century, few will fight for socialism. Only when new movements for social justice and postmodern socialisms have sunk deep roots around the globe and become wedded to people's most basic needs and interests will we have a powerful banner that mobilizes individuals to dramatically change the world they live in.

In a sense we have come full circle in the evolution of the struggle against capitalism. Marx originally thought that the first socialist states would emerge where capitalism existed, namely in Western Europe. Then when the Bolsheviks triumphed in Russia and the national liberation movements emerged in the Third World countries, the interpretation put forth by theorists from Lenin to Paul Baran was that imperialism enabled the capitalist powers to stave off internal contradictions and crises. They argued that socialism would take root in the colonial or underdeveloped capitalist countries and then encircle the core capitalist countries, bringing about their downfall. With the collapse of communism and most national liberation governments it must now be acknowledged that socialism could not really develop in the Third World or the weaker areas of the capitalist world. The economic dynamism, along with the adaptability and aggression of the dominant capitalist powers, overwhelmed the countries with socialist-oriented economies. Now in many ways we need to return to a view more akin to that of Marx and Engels in that we have to struggle directly against advanced capitalism as a globalized system.

Now the struggles are universal. Capitalist relations exist everywhere, be it Eastern Europe, Latin America, Africa and Asia or the United States and Western Europe. Every one of these regions has areas of ferment, discontent and even upheaval. These are not integrated or coordinated battlegrounds, and they are certainly not dominated by a revolutionary proletariat as Marx argued, but they are part of a global struggle that is challenging capitalism virtually everywhere it exists.

CHAPTER 9

The Long Transition to Postmodern Socialisms

We are the architects of our own houses,
The doctors of our sick people
Our children's teachers,
Our own building site engineers.

Popular course from the Peruvian barriadas[1]

If humanity is to have a recognizable future, it cannot be by prolonging the past or the present. If we try to build the third millennium on that basis, we shall fail. And the price of failure, that is to say, the alternative to a changed society, is darkness.

Eric Hobsbawm,
Age of Extremes[2]

We are indeed on the brink of a new millennium in which the prolongation of the past will only lead to more human disasters. The bastions of modernity and Western civilization are disintegrating. This will be a long period of transition as new societies and values slowly emerge out of the chaos and disorder of the old world. Late capitalism and liberal democracy, the economic and political bulwarks of modernity, have bequeathed virtually identical paradoxes – they have both triumphed globally, and yet they are both mired in difficulties from which they cannot escape. Capitalism has secured its global dominance as it propagates a large and diverse army of discontents while democracy has also triumphed globally and yet it has become a hollow system, largely under the control of special economic interests.

In principle, socialism should be able to take advantage of these limitations, implanting itself around the globe as the alternative to a capitalism that has run amuck by destroying the environment and begetting widespread alienation, poverty and despair. But the paradox of socialism is that just at the moment when capitalism has starkly revealed its flaws and blemishes to all of humanity, "actually existing socialism" has completely exhausted itself as an alternative.

With the collapse of the great socialist experiments of the twentieth century, we need to begin constructing a new historic project that arises out of the paradoxes and contradictions of capitalism, democracy and socialism. The starting point has to be the wreckage caused by late capitalism, particularly the increasing marginalization and exclusion produced by globalization. According to a study by Ray Marshall, a former US Secretary of Labor, almost one third of the earth's 2.8 billion workers are either jobless or underemployed.[3] In effect about one third of humanity is adversely affected since those who lack jobs and full-time work are linked to families and dependents in one form or another.

Late capitalism has also undermined the state, the principal institution that has demonstrated a capacity to deal with problems such as unemployment and marginalization. Now its powers are weakened, particularly by the ascent of finance capital. As *The Economist* pointed out in a special survey of the world economy in late 1995, "recent history is littered with examples of markets forcing governments to change policy," especially in the areas of fiscal policy, exchange rates and government spending on social programs.[4]

Another effect of late capitalism is the transformation of class struggle, particularly with the development of "flexible accumulation." The traditional agencies of class organization that have been so prominent in the development of industrialized societies in the twentieth century are severely weakened. Trade unions are gutted as corporations are downsized and manufacturing plants moved to cheap labor havens. The proletariat is overwhelmed in sheer numbers by the armies and masses of marginalized peoples who are difficult if not impossible to organize, at least by any organization emanating from the workplace. This also has consequences for the political arena, where mass parties with strong trade-union bases are no longer as capable of mobilizing men and women for electoral politics.

The new mode of production

Based on these trends it is inevitable that for years to come most societies will suffer from ever-increasing economic stratification and marginalization. But this very polarization is slowly begetting an alternative. What we labeled earlier as the postmodern economies, the diverse economic activities undertaken by the underemployed and the discarded sectors of society, will grow in importance. When one looks closely at the one third of humanity that is already adversely effected by the global economic system one sees a teeming array of human beings involved in all types of activities. Street vendors, micro-entrepreneurs, subcontractors, garbage scavengers and recyclers, petty drug dealers, all those who operate in the so-called informal economy – these and many other economic endeavors are at the heart of a new economy that has taken hold in diverse societies around the globe.

The conventional wisdom is that these are simply marginal economic activities at the bottom of the capitalist economic pyramid, or perhaps even activities that enable new entrepreneurs to emerge who will eventually find a niche higher up in the economic order.[5] Our argument however is that they are not a part of the existent system – they are part of an emergent mode of production. Late capitalism does not have the capacity to absorb these petty producers in any significant way. In fact their numbers will only swell as globalization, driven by ever more advanced forms of technology, requires fewer and fewer workers to turn out goods and services. The dominant economic system can certainly function without the excluded, indeed it discards them as redundant and useless. But there is another side to this rejection in that it turns the excluded into discontents who have no use for the dominant system. It gives them nothing and makes them potential insurgents.

Be it the impoverished towns and cities of African countries, or the inner cities of the United States, a wave of mercantile and petty-productive activity in taking hold in the age of late capitalism. All these simple economic ventures will gradually begin to coalesce with other popular economic endeavors like cooperatives, worker-run concerns and municipal or township enterprises. They will form a vast class of "associate producers." Marx used this term to describe the new relations of workers when they take control of the means of production in a socialist society. Here we use the term more broadly to include all those at the bottom who produce goods and services through their labors and economic endeavors. At some point in time these minions of associate producers will begin to overwhelm the system with their sheer numbers, the extensiveness of their economic activities, and their ability to confront the dominant state institutions.

When this happens it will be a classic case of one mode of production overthrowing another. As Marx noted, "At a certain stage of their development the material productive forces of society come into contradiction with the existing productive relationships." Whereas the existent laws and property relationships once served to advance "the productive forces, these relationships are [now] transformed into their fetters. We then enter an era of social revolution."[6] Marx of course was primarily writing about the development of a proletarian revolution in which the working class would overthrow the bourgeoisie. What we are arguing is that it will not be just the proletariat, but a much larger group of economic actors involved in an array of activities at the grassroots who will slowly shape a new alternative and carry out the new social revolution.

An important question is why won't these economic strata simply assimilate into the capitalist system as they expand in importance and size? After all our present system of what is often called "monopoly capital" – the domination of the economy by large multinational corporations – has its roots in a bygone age when small firms and enterprises were the norm. Here an important factor is that there is no room at the top, precisely because of the ascendancy of monopoly capital. Furthermore, the present system of corporate capital is restraining human development and economic creativity at the bottom. In the long term, small capital and the emergent system of associate producers can only eliminate the "fetters" imposed on them by organizing, or "associating" among themselves and engaging in a struggle against big capital.

The development of the ethnic and fundamentalist movements dovetails with the building of these postmodern economies. Most nationalist movements are opposed to the dominance of Western and transnational capital. They are demanding control of their own economic resources. The Indians of Chiapas, the Muslim Nation of Farrakhan and the Islamic movements in the Middle East are all resentful of the economic domination of their societies by foreign or outside interests. They often preach self-reliance, which sometimes appears as a separatist, or even conservative message. But this approach is necessary if they are to break with the historic tendency of outside capital to exploit their societies and economies. To the extent that these ethnic and national movements gain control of their lives and resources, they will be in a position to help construct a new global mode of production.

The lessons of the socialist collapse

As we try to envision the new societies, it is important to understand why the socialism of the twentieth century failed. Its principal flaw was that both its political and economic forms of governance were hierarchical and even authoritarian at times. The individual was subject to the "collective will" as determined by the leaders of the party and state. Democratic capitalism triumphed over socialism because it proved far more adept at placing the individual in the center of its system, and then endowing that individual with certain freedoms and liberties that were compatible with capitalist economic growth and expansion. Any new historic alternative to capitalism has to take this as its starting point, placing individual initiative, creativity and self-reliance at the center of the new project.

A related problem is that both the socialist governments and the national liberation movements placed the political system in charge of deciding how economic resources were to be allocated and how basic needs were to be met. With the state controlling the main centers of production, it also fell upon the state to discipline the workforce. But this posed another paradox, since socialist doctrine proclaimed that in the workers' societies everyone had a right to a job, a minimal income and basic social necessities like education and medical care. This made it difficult for state managers to impose discipline in the workplace and achieve maximum productivity, especially when the material incentives for those who did work hard were so limited. The neo-liberals have a certain element of truth in their argument when they assert that if people are not driven to work intensively to attain their basic needs, many will opt to work at a very lethargic pace or perhaps even do nothing at all. It is conceivable that the vast majority in a socialist society could be conscientious in their workplace activities, but if a significant minority chooses to opt out, the entire society will suffer from much lower productivity.

Most socialist countries did try to offer material incentives by providing higher earnings and more commodities to those workers who were more productive. But access to commodities beyond the minimal needs became the weak point of the socialist societies, particularly for the bulk of the population in Eastern Europe and the Soviet Union that was largely alienated from the political system. With the rise of globalization and the glitter of the cornucopia of goods produced by the Western world, it became almost inevitable that the people in the communist societies would become disenchanted with their governments and overthrow them. The revolutions of Eastern Europe were in some ways history's first consumer-led revolutions.

In contrast to the socialist economies, the genius of emergent postmodern economies is that they are not the creation of the state. They are based on individual or group initiative. It is the drive for survival that compels people to undertake simple mercantile activities or, at another level, to buy up floundering enterprises that are about to go bankrupt and lay off their workers. Once in control of their own economic destiny, these small producers and organized workers in large companies or cooperatives search for the most effective ways to hold their costs down and to maximize whatever earnings they can squeeze out of the economic activities they control.

Ideology and the new leadership

As under historic socialism, ideological consciousness of the new project is crucial. To mobilize and consolidate the diverse group of nascent producers a new ideology needs to counterpose grassroots economic development to the domination of big capital, just as

Marxist theory pitted the working class against the bourgeoisie. The mere existence of the new economic and social formations is not a sufficient condition for overthrowing the old order. A new ideology and a new leadership is needed that roots itself firmly in the economic and social transformations occurring in the postmodern societies and undertakes the long social struggle necessary to overwhelm big capital and the dominant order.

The Marxist tradition recognized the key role played by intellectuals, or an intelligentsia, in the building of a new society. The emergent postmodern societies already have an intelligentsia of sorts, not only among disenchanted intellectuals, but also among the middle sectors that are being expelled in ever increasing numbers from the "grand banquet." Many of these professionals will inevitably be driven to ally themselves with the more popular sectors.

The social movements, broadly defined, are the major ideological protagonists of the postmodern societies. The representatives of these movements and organizations have the potential to understand and articulate what is going on among the ever-swelling numbers of castaways of global capitalism. They already challenge neo-liberalism and globalization in many different ways. They fight to stop the destruction of the environment, they are anti-authoritarian and democratic in their structures and principles, they are generally opposed to the domination of multinational capital and they are based on grassroots activity. The women's movement, the ethnic rights movements, the human rights organizations, the gay and lesbian movements, the disabled, the Indians, the environmentalists, and so on, all demand fundamental changes in the existent world so that humanity can be liberated and freed from all forms of exploitation.

New leadership and values are also emerging from non-governmental organizations, especially in the underdeveloped world, and from progressive religious movements, particularly those rooted in exploited societies or ethnic groups. The goal of these social movements and organizations is not simply power, but the alteration of values at the level of civil society. They refuse to be controlled or contained. They provide alternatives to the bankrupt political parties and state authority.

Many of the leaders of these movements even question whether it is appropriate to hold state power at present, understanding the need to accumulate more forces, to develop more coherent ideas and values that can really change societies and the global economy. Communism failed in part because it was born prematurely. The same mistake shouldn't be made again, of launching a project of state power that will be stillborn or aborted because the full-blown elements do not exist yet for building a new society.

The new economic project

To advance towards postmodern socialisms, a new economic agenda will have to be developed that breaks not only with neo-liberalism, but also with the legacy of the old communist societies that tried to develop the economic order from the so-called "commanding heights of the state." The national liberation movements as well as the communist parties did not work intensively on developing the economic capacity of the working class and the popular movements. Economic plans and economic orders came from the top down – the workers implemented, but didn't really initiate.

Jorge Castañeda in *Utopia Unarmed* argues that in Latin America the only option for the left is to recognize the rules of the economic game as they exist under today's global capitalist system. He asserts that the left is limited to choosing what type of capitalist system it can buy into, whether neo-liberal, or closer to the more socially oriented models of Western Europe or Japan:

> By formally and sincerely accepting the logic of the market, and then immediately and equally sincerely endorsing the variations, regulations, exceptions, and adaptations the European and Japanese market economies have adopted over the years, the Latin American left can set the stage for the construction of a paradigm that is substantively different from the present state of affairs.[7]

Certainly, any emerging economic alternative will have to deal with the global market and the existing economic realities. But we need to go much further than simply adopting one capitalist model or another. What is necessary is a new economic philosophy that harnesses the individual drive to progress and get ahead with a broader social and political ideology that advances the common good. We have to combine elements of Adam Smith and Karl Marx. This is the dynamic and positive paradox of postmodern socialisms – they represent a synthesis of socialism and capitalism.

Adam Smith argued that the common good would be advanced simply by encouraging each individual to pursue his/her particular interests. This has proven true in the early stages of capitalist development, and it explains in part why China has been so successful up until now in developing a market economy. It has unleashed the peasantry and the urban populace to pursue their own interests. But what Smith failed to realize (and what bodes ill for the long-term development of the Chinese model) was that unless the state makes a determined effort to prevent the concentration of capital as the process of capitalist accumulation accelerates, those who have amassed the most wealth use that wealth to manipulate the state and to advance their own interests at the expense of the majority.

Now all that has to change. To break with both the contemporary system of capitalist accumulation and the command system of communism, progressives will have to focus on developing the popular classes as economic actors while constantly pressuring the state to limit the power of big capital. As members of political and community organizations, we can engage in providing business leadership to cooperatives, peasant organizations, housing construction projects and an array of other economic activities. The vast number of technicians, professionals and social workers who are disenchanted or alienated by the existent system are the new cadre who can make a living by assisting the development of worker-owned enterprises, by participating in educational programs that engage the poor and marginalized, and by fostering management and entrepreneurial skills at the grassroots level. The fomenting of these activities will help the entire left survive economically while developing a broader economic base for challenging the dominant system.

For years to come, the new economy will develop in an evolutionary, rather than a revolutionary manner. As Chapter 4 demonstrated, capitalism is experiencing fundamental problems from which there may be no exit. But this does not mean that capitalism will necessarily collapse. It could continue as the dominant economic order even in the midst of crisis. But it is precisely during cycles of slow growth and periodic crises that the left can more rapidly pursue alternative economic approaches, pushing from below for the advance of popular economic interests. At the same time we will need to advocate new legislation that empowers all forms of alternative production and commerce while undermining the ascendancy of finance and monopoly capital. Capitalism will enter into a definitive crisis only when enough alternative institutions exist to challenge it.

Worker-run enterprises

Historically, there has been a broad and diverse movement of workers and trade unions that have taken over and run their own factories and enterprises. As Assef Bayat points out in *Work, Politics and Power*, these movements have assumed a wide variety of forms and occurred under diverse political and economic systems.[8] In the nineteenth century Fabian and utopian socialists in Europe and the United States helped workers found their own factories and run their communities. The terrain shifted to Eastern Europe during the early years of the Bolshevik Revolution when workers' committees and soviets seized control of and ran many factories. Unfortunately in the case of the Soviet Union the state and the party stepped in to take control, and in countries like Hungary, the workers were violently expelled from their factories in 1919 by reactionary forces backed by the West.

In the early half of the twentieth century, cooperative movements sprang up throughout Western Europe, Canada and the United State and workers gained control of an array of enterprises in areas as diverse as finance, manufacturing and commerce. To this day cooperative enterprises are a little known but functioning sector of the economies of most advanced capitalist nations. Then in the second half of this century, Bayat notes that the Third World became the scene of intense struggles by workers to take over and run enterprises. Countries as diverse as Algeria, Egypt, Peru and Chile found workers in control of a significant number of their countries' manufacturing concerns.

In general, the Marxist left has put down these experiments, pointing to a variety of weaknesses. In the case of the capitalist countries, the cooperative movement and the employee self-managed enterprises have been criticized as being a mere extension of the capitalist system. Moreover, in many Third World countries the workers' experiences have been viewed as failures either because they were taken over by state bureaucracies (like Algeria), or because the right seized power and repressed the worker-run enterprises (as in Chile). But in the late twentieth century, there are a number of reasons for resurrecting the worker-owned enterprises as a centerpiece for fundamental change. For one, workers around the world are now better educated and better trained than ever before. Furthermore, there is no shortage of skilled engineers, accountants, technicians and even finance specialists who are willing to "sell" their skills and talents to the worker-owned enterprises or to directly join in running the enterprises with the workers. Another factor favoring worker-run enterprises is that even the capitalist world is now recognizing that worker involvement and participation leads to increased output and productivity. As *Business Week* pointed out in a special issue on this theme, corporations are increasingly "horizontal" in their structure.[9] Because of the spread of technology and the information revolution, workers have to participate in a variety of functions rather than being isolated cogs on assembly lines. Similarly, Japanese corporations have long been viewed as models of efficiency and productivity because they made their workers feel they are an integral part of the corporation.

The Third World is also the scene of continuing struggles over workers' control as local capitalists lurch from one crisis to another. In Nicaragua, workers and peasants have been especially active in taking control of farms and businesses since the electoral defeat of the Sandinistas in 1990. Some of these enterprises were previously owned by the state, others were abandoned by their old owners. In the rural and agro-industrial sector of the Nicaraguan economy, over 350 enterprises are now under the control of their workers.[10] And in neighboring El Salvador, cooperatives and small worker-managed businesses have begun to consolidate and expand their role in the economy since the end of the war. Co-ops and peasants are even linking up with small international financial firms and trading enterprises to break the stranglehold that the Salvadoran financial oligarchy holds in the commercial and export–import sphere.[11]

Another factor favoring worker-run enterprises is the bankruptcy of many regular corporations that can no longer compete in local or global markets. The steel industry in the United States is an example of where the workers have bought out companies like Republic Engineered Steels and turned them into successful enterprises. United Airlines is the most recent example of employees and unions taking over a large, financially troubled US company.

Gar Alperovitz of the National Center for Economic Alternatives in Washington DC points out that contrary to the neo-liberal assertion that only the traditional private sector can be economically viable, there are a number of municipal and worker-run companies operating successfully throughout the United States. Sewage plants, cable TV companies, methane plants, housing developments, football teams and even export-oriented companies are some of the examples of municipal or worker-owned enterprises that are turning a profit today.[12]

The peasantry and agroecology

The peasantry and small farmers of the globe will occupy an especially important role in any new, restructured economic order. In the Third World, where about 4 billion people live, roughly two-thirds of the people are classified as rural dwellers. And 36 per cent of them – over 950 million – live in absolute poverty.[13] The peasantry historically has been victimized by the rise of capitalist-driven industry that gutted rural-based societies through the promotion of cheap food policies that subsidized the growth of the urban areas. This led to a precipitous drop in rural living standards, thereby driving many of the peasants into the cities where they served as an enormous reserve army of labor holding down wages in the ever-expanding factories.

Because of their close relationship to the environment, these overexploited peasant and rural-based societies are critical in any effort to grapple with the physical destruction of the planet. A number of studies of peasant and small-farm units show that they produce about twice as much per acre as big farms while using only one-fourth to one-fifth of the purchased inputs.[14] Even more importantly, in a world where technology and automation are eliminating the jobs of tens of millions, small farms can be an area of labor absorption instead of expulsion due to their intensive use of labor to cultivate the land.

At present, many small producers adversely impact upon the environment because they cut down the rainforests or destroy whatever limited woodlands may exist on their plots of land. These practices are largely attributable to the impoverished state of the peasantry as they utilize whatever meager resources are at their disposal to survive. Agroecology, a new field of scientific study, demonstrates that these adverse practices can be changed when peasants gain access to external resources. Miguel Altieri and Susanna Hecht, two proponents of agroecology, declare that:

> It has become increasingly clear that improving the access of peasants to land, water and other natural resources, as well as to equitable credit, market, appropriate technologies, etc. is crucial to ensure sustainable development.[15]

Moreover, if this labor intensive sector of the economy receives its just share of resources, it can raise the standard of living of the entire countryside and generate a significant surplus for the rest of society. The development of the rural township enterprises in China from the late 1970s to the early 1990s demonstrates that the rural areas, when given access to financial resources and market incentives, can become centers of dynamic economic development. Organic agriculture with its intensive labor needs can also flourish in many parts of the world on small-scale agricultural units. It is big capital with its gargantuan high-energy inputs that does not have the capacity to adjust to the environmental needs of the planet in either the factories or the fields.

Altieri and Hecht also point out that "networking" among non-governmental organizations (NGOs), universities, community organizations and international research centers is critical to the development of a commercially-viable peasant-based agriculture. This dovetails with Michael Barratt Brown's contention that networking from the bottom up is the "third way" to build an alternative economy that is not controlled by the multinational corporations on the one hand nor by state planners on the other. Networking in the area of alternative trade in Europe has led to the formation of the International Federation for Alternative Trade, comprised of over forty trading organizations that purchase foodstuffs and commodities directly from peasants and small farmers at above average prices.[16]

Barratt Brown sees networking by consumer and community-based organizations as constituting an alternative to Ernest Mandel's call for a new economy dominated by workers' councils and federations. If economic decision-making is placed mainly in the hands of trade unions and workers' councils, then the interests of consumers and other social sectors, which increasingly outnumber the workers, are virtually ignored. As Barratt Brown points out, in our advanced societies there are many very specific interests such as "recreation, education, health, child care, housing, civil liberties, concern for the elderly, conservation and environmental protection, whole food, fair trade, etc."[17] These interests and needs can be represented and incorporated into the economy as they self-articulate by "networking" from the ground up.

In both the developed and developing countries, it also has to be recognized that there is a dearth of jobs in the manufacturing sector and the formal economy. As Jeremy Rifkin argues in *The End of Work*, the automation of industry along with "the globalization of the market sector and the diminishing role of the governmental sector will mean that people will be forced to organize into communities of self-interest to secure their own futures."[18] This is already occurring as workers are thrown out of regular salaried jobs and compelled to engage in other activities. Many of the discarded even organize among themselves, networking and linking together in small groups to advance their common interests. In northern California, the homeless organize to protest police abuse and to demand services. They even have a monthly newspaper, *Street Spirit*, that they hawk in the streets.[19]

In both the developed and underdeveloped countries, a wide variety of critical needs and interests are being neglected at the local level, including the building, or rebuilding, of roads, schools and social services. A new spirit of voluntarism and community participation, backed by a campaign to secure complimentary resources from local and national governments, can open up entirely new job markets and areas of work to deal with these basic needs.

All this means that in this long transitory period we will in effect be developing a mixed economy, one that includes cooperatives, joint ventures, small and medium sized private enterprises, consumer unions, worker self-managed and municipal enterprises. It is simply impossible to run a semi-complex modernizing economy as occurred under socialism where state bureaucracies dictate everything. Aside from questions of efficiency, there is also the strategic issue of whether the left can build a broad base of support if it simply expropriated large sectors of the economy and monopolized economic power. Under such conditions, the left would be driven in the direction of authoritarian control of the economy and society, just as the communist and national liberation movements were.

Control of the means of production by community and labor forces and a host of local interests must also be viewed as one way of dealing with the crisis of overproduction discussed earlier. The capitalist world today has more productive capacity than it can find profitable markets for. And the lack of markets is due to skewed income structures that make it impossible for hundreds of millions of the world's population to purchase what they need to survive. This problem would clearly be alleviated by placing manufacturing and agricultural production in the hands of the workers, communities and small-scale producers so they can expand their earnings and consume what they produce.

It is even possible to envision that the system of flexible accumulation discussed earlier could be stood on its head and turned to the advantage of the workers and a system of mixed ownership. Now flexible accumulation is beneficial to the multinationals, but the very fact that there are innumerable plants and businesses scattered around the globe that contract with and are formally "independent" of the multinationals means that these same enterprises could be run by the workers as part of a restructured system in which they would control the benefits and the profits. For example, there is no reason why workers and technicians could not manage and internationally market the production of an automotive parts factory in Matamoros, Mexico, or a microchip assembly plant in Seoul, South Korea.

When a major economic crisis strikes, like the Depression of the 1930s, the left and progressive forces will have more economic and political space to initiate and expand these new economic alternatives. The capitalist system will continue to exist during this transitional period but economic power could begin to pass to a wide array of participants. Ideologues for the capitalist system have in the past tried to argue that the widespread existence of stockholders and pension funds with investments in the stock market means that capital has been democratized. This of course is not the case. But if workers, small-scale producers, peasants, cooperatives and municipal enterprises can acquire an increasing stake in the productive system then they will in fact be democratizing the economy and be directly involved in the building of postmodern socialisms.

In the former Second World, the old communist state societies have helped prepare the conditions for this new economic project. The communist policies of industrial development did reduce the size of the traditional peasantry and produce a new working class.

But because of the nature of the model, top-down control, it was impossible for the new strata at the bottom to act autonomously or to develop dynamic civil societies. The old hierarchical state had to be eliminated first. Now, with the existence of new independent social actors, it is possible to develop the forces of production from below. In many of the former socialist countries, workers and peasants are in fact fighting the emergent capitalist classes for control of the old state enterprises.

The postmodern economies will be eclectic. They will assume a wide variety of forms. There can be few "laws" governing their functioning and development because of their very diversity. When the new popular interests finally do begin to influence governments, the power of the state should be used to control and contain the monopoly sector while the popular economy should be largely free to develop with government assistance (particularly through financing) but with limited direct government intervention.

Radical reformism

Given the incipient character of the new project, what is the appropriate political strategy to pursue? Here we would argue that we have to move in the "actually existing world," not wait for some ideal political conjuncture that may never arrive. In the short term reformism is the political scenario that the left has to work within as it struggles to articulate and consolidate a new historic project. Social explosions and upheavals will continue to occur but at this moment they do not appear destined to lead to revolutionary transformations in the traditional sense; there simply is no guiding political philosophy or revolutionary organization capable of assuming power. Thus reformism is the most viable path to pursue, a reformism however that needs to draw its force from the social upheavals and emergent postmodern societies of today's world.

The Marxist left historically has had difficulty relating to a reformist approach in the economy and in politics precisely because it has not understood how to begin changing society from the bottom up. Society could only be transformed by the seizure of complete state power. The revolutionary parties attacked social democrats and liberals for their reformism but never had an alternative other than state socialism. And when they held power they thought principally of dividing up the wealth of the bourgeoisie and the landowners under the direction of the state, not in terms of creating a new class of economic actors and producers at the bottom with autonomous power.

Along with the social movements, there are a number of left, pluralist political formations that could provide a basis for a radicalized reformism. These include the Workers Party of Brazil, the African National Congress in South Africa, the transformed Farabundo National Liberation Front in El Salvador, the Sandinista Front in Nicaragua and the Revolutionary Democratic Party in Mexico. An example in the developed world is the Democratic Party of the Left in Italy. These parties will not dramatically change their countries, but they may shift the balance of political debate and provide space for new ideas and approaches. And they can inspire other countries and movements to advance in a similar direction.

Many political opportunities will open up for these social movements and renovated political organizations to mobilize behind reformist projects. After all, our contemporary economic nemesis, neo-liberalism, is not able to create a stable world order. Governments driven by this economic philosophy often lose political power, particularly in the Third and former Second Worlds. The ups and downs of the capitalist business cycle also give reformists a number of openings for influencing political and economic struggles.

The advances of reformism in different societies will provide the left with a change to regroup and rebuild. Out of these experiences we can begin to assemble a new ideology that may be both revolutionary and non-violent. At some point a revolution with little or no bloodshed could occur. This is in effect what happened in Eastern Europe when communism collapsed. As the problems and paradoxes of capitalism and the actually existing democracies become increasingly obvious and a new ideology makes its appearance, it is conceivable that broad sectors of humanity could say *"basta"* ("enough") and turn the system upside down in relatively short order.

Ideologically, there will be a need to critique the existent order while enunciating basic ideals, such as those that go back to the French Revolution: liberty, equality and fraternity. We need to advocate and participate in a permanent democratic rebellion and, whenever possible, use government to this end. This may sound like a difficult endeavor given the state of the world. Yet the paradoxes of capitalism and liberal democracy with the end of the Cold War makes the dominant system more susceptible to challenge and gives us more ideological room for maneuver. It is more and more difficult for US and other Western rulers to cover over internal problems by mobilizing their peoples against external menaces; Russia, Nicaragua or El Salvador can no longer be portrayed as threats to the "national security" of the dominant powers like the United States.

Avoiding the social democratic trap

The problem of traditional social democracy is that it has become totally wedded to actually existing capitalism. There is little that distinguished the governments of Felipe Gonzalez of Spain or François Mitterrand of France from their more conservative counterparts in Europe. They accepted the rules dictated by a neo-liberal economic philosophy and allowed the demands of international capital to box in their governments.

As André Gorz points out in *Critique of Economic Reason*, social democratic governments

> had to confront not just their own national bourgeoisies, but the financial bourgeoisies and the central banks of all the industrialized capitalist nations. The opening up of national economies to the world market and the exacerbation of international competition thus became a sovereign weapon for the national bourgeoisies against a state interventionism operating only on the scale of a single country.[20]

Instead of challenging international capital, the social democratic governments caved in, curtailing the demands of trade unions and even cutting the social welfare states that they had been instrumental in creating during the post-war decades.

How will a new economic approach avoid the trap that social democracy fell into? While building a broad-based system of grassroots ownership involving workers, cooperatives, municipalities, small-scale producers and consumers, the left will have to fight for and insist upon a socially controlled and regulated mixed economy, both at the national and international levels. When in power or sharing power, the left will need to use the government to set the parameters and conditions for development while redirecting the resources of the international multilateral lending agencies. Ultimately, it is the state that controls and directs the capital accumulation process. It, more than any other institution, can facilitate the development of grassroots and popular-controlled enterprises through its credit and financial policies and its general regulation of the economy.

As the Fifty Years Is Enough campaign argues, there is no reason why multilateral institutions like the International Monetary Fund and the World Bank have to support and sustain big capital and neo-liberal economic policies. If their priority was to foment the development of an international system of associate producers, the enormous financial resources of these institutions could be used to counteract the efforts of finance capital to destabilize governments that pursue broad-based social policies.[21]

Another related point for the new postmodern economies is that they will have to be part of a global economy. Autarky is impossible in today's integrated world, if indeed it ever was feasible. Neither Russia nor China, Cuba nor Nicaragua can move forward without participating in the global economy. Machinery, technology and capital have to be mobilized on an international scale for any significant development effort. Of course the priority is the development of local material and human resources, particularly in the poorer regions of the world. But this can be done most effectively if there is an international injection of complementary, needed resources.

This approach to trade is exemplified by the networks and coalitions that came together in mid-1995 to oppose NAFTA, the North American Free Trade Agreement. On the eve of official negotiations for the entry of Chile, four national alliances and networks from Canada, Chile, Mexico and the United States representing over 170 organizations registered their opposition to any expansion of NAFTA in its present form. In a communique they declared:

> We are not opposed to trade and trade agreements, yet we are appalled by the growing gap throughout the Americas between the wealthy beneficiaries of deregulated integration and the growing numbers of poor people whose jobs are being displaced or eliminated and whose wages, rights, and environments are being eroded.

The declaration went on to call for a trade agreement "that places the rights of workers, indigenous peoples, farmers, consumers and women, as well as the protection of the environment at the center of the integration agenda."[22]

This leads to another principle – any new movement must be fundamentally internationalist. It needs to break with the confines and parameters set by the nation state while recognizing that national identities and the world can by no means be homogenized. The current form of globalization will have to be stood on its head so that it serves the masses of humanity and not the elites. Diversity, autonomy, local interests and self-determination constitute the building blocks of this new internationalism.

All this is part of the process of constructing postmodern socialisms. It will be a long transition, with many unforeseen twists and turns. It is evolutionary and revolutionary at the same time. No victories are certain. The final paradox is that in this political age where societies, cultures and economies are interlinked and impacted by globalism, the struggles for change are increasingly local. Now more than ever it is at the community level where we can all make a difference in changing the world. But this change will only occur if we decide to initiate this process by mobilizing ourselves as well as others, thereby constructing our new societies and ideologies in the process.

Notes

Introduction: Back to the Future

1. Bertrand Russell, *The Autobiography of Bertrand Russell: 1944–69* (New York: Simon and Schuster, 1969) p. 330.
2. Sigmund Freud, *Civilization and Its Discontents*, translated and edited by James Strachey (New York: WW Norton, 1962) p. 33.
3. For an earlier discussion of the New World Order and its relationship to globalization, see Jeremy Brecher, John Brown Childs and Jill Cutler, eds. *Global Visions: Beyond the New World Order* (Boston, Mass.: South End Press, 1993).
4. See Jacques Derrida, *Specters of Marx: The State of the Debt, the Work of Mourning and the New International* (New York: Routledge, 1994). It is an example of postmodernist thought that is extremely abstract and largely irrelevant, providing little or no insight into how we can move forward with the collapse of communism.
5. Walden Bello, *Dark Victory* (London and Oakland, Calif.: Pluto Press, Food First and the Transnational Institute, 1994) p. 111.
6. Ronald Aronson, *After Marxism* (New York: Guilford Press, 1995) p. 161.
7. Fredric Jameson, 'Actually Existing Marxism,' in *Marxism Beyond Marxism*, edited by Saree Makdisi, Cesare Casarino and Rebecca E. Karl (New York: Routledge, 1996) p. 54. See also Irwin Silber, *Socialism: What Went Wrong? An Inquiry into the Theoretical and Historical Sources of the Socialist Crisis* (London and Boulder, Col.: Pluto Press, 1994).
8. Serge Latouche, *In the Wake of the Affluent Society: An Exploration of Post Development* (London and New Jersey: Zed Books, 1993) p. 199.

Chapter 1: The New World Disorder

1. Paul Sweezy and Harry Magdoff, 'Notes from the Editors', *Monthly Review*, vol. 45, no. 9 (February 1994) p. 61.
2. Jeremy Rifkin, *The End of Work: The Decline of the Global Labor Force and the Dawn of the Post-Market Era* (New York: GP Putnam's Sons, 1995) p. 216.
3. See Walter Russell Mead, 'Forward to the Past,' *New York Times Magazine* June 4, 1995. He also argues that there are certain parallels in the period leading up to World War I, including "weak national states, free international capital flows and strong national passions."
4. Estimates are that over $1 trillion dollars in currency trading alone occurs on a daily basis. See *New York Times*, September 20, 1995, p. B3.

5. Worldwatch Institute, *State of the World 1994* (New York: WW Norton, 1994) p. 5. See also United Nations Development Programme, *Human Development Report 1992* (New York: Oxford University Press, 1992).
6. Worldwatch Institute, *State of the World 1990*, p.135.
7. Serge Latouche uses the terms "grand banquet" and the "castaways" in his provocative work, *In the Wake of the Affluent Society: An Exploration of Post Development* (London and New Jersey: Zed Books, 1993).
8. Worldwatch Institute, *State of the World 1990*, p. 135, and *State of the World 1994*, p. 1.
9. Worldwatch Institute, *State of the World 1990*, p. 148.
10. Robert B. Reich, *The Work of Nations* (New York: Vintage Books, 1992) p.208.
11. *Business Week*, 'The Rich are Richer – and America May Be the Poorer,' November 18, 1991, pp. 85–8. See also *Business Week*, 'Inequality,' August 15, 1994.
12. Alan Wolfe, *Whose Keeper?: Social Science and Moral Obligation* (Berkeley, Calif.: University of California Press, 1989) pp. 51–77.
13. See 'Introduction' by Philippe Bourgois in *Ninos Vulnerables*, edited by Franklin Alcaraz (La Paz: Direccion Nacional de Prevencion de Drogas, 1993).
14. Worldwatch Institute, *State of the World 1991*, p 3.
15. For an excellent discussion of how capitalism throughout this century has been the primary culprit in the destruction of the environment, see Victor Wallis, 'Socialism, Ecology and Democracy,' *Monthly Review*, vol. 44, no. 2 (June 1992) pp. 1–22.
16. Mikhail Gorbachev, et al., *Perestroika: Global Challenge*, edited by Ken Coates (Nottingham, England: Spokesman, 1988) p. 34.
17. Peter Rosset, Institute for Food and Development Policy, cited in Stephen Zunes, 'Will Cuba Go Green?', in *Context*, no. 40, p. 20.
18. Worldwatch Institute, *State of the World 1991*, p. 156.
19. Barry Commoner, *Making Peace with the Planet* (New York: Pantheon Books, 1990) pp. 157–68.
20. Ibid., pp. 217–19.
21. Leo Panitch, 'Globalisation and the State,' *Socialist Register 1994* (London: Merlin Press, 1994) p. 63.

Chapter 2: The Discontents

1. Citation in Serge Latouche, *In the Wake of the Affluent Society: An Exploration of Post Development* (London and New Jersey: Zed Books, 1993) p. 123.
2. Quote from Eduardo Galeano in a public address in Berkeley, California, June 1995.
3. Hernando Gomez Buendía, ed. *Urban Crime: Global Trends and Policies* (Tokyo: United Nations University, 1989) p. ix.
4. Ibid., p. 5.
5. Zbigniew Brzezinski, *Out of Control: Global Turmoil on the Eve of the 21st Century* (New York: Scribner, 1992) pp. 49–50.

6. Immanuel Wallerstein, 'The Collapse of Liberalism,' in *Socialist Register 1992* (London: The Merlin Press, 1992) p. 108.

7. Ernest Gellner, *Nations and Nationalism* (Ithaca, NY: Cornell University Press, 1983) pp. 44–5.

8. See Benedict Anderson, *Imagined Communities: Reflections on the Origins and Spread of Nationalism* (London: Verso, 1991).

9. Cited in Latouche, *In the Wake of Affluence*, unnumbered introductory page.

10. Wendy Harcourt, ed. *Feminist Perspectives on Sustainable Development*, (London and New Jersey: Zed Books in association with the Society for International Development, Rome, 1994) p. xiii.

11. Ibid., for example Raff Carmen, 'The Logic of Economics vs. the Dynamics of Culture: Daring to (Re)Invent the Common Future,' pp. 60–74.

12. Samir Amin, *Empire of Chaos* (New York: Monthly Review, 1992) pp. 92–3.

13. Special thanks to Franz Schurmann for his discussions and help with this section. There is very little available in the non-Arabic press that provides an unbiased view of what is happening in the Islamic movement.

14. See Karim el-Gawhary, 'Gama'at vs. Government in Upper Egypt,' *MERIP Report* (Washington DC: MERIP, July 1995).

15. Courtenay M. Sclater and George E. Hall, eds. *1995 County and City Extra: Annual Metro, City and County Data Book* (Lasham, Md.: Bernan Press, 4th edn., 1995) p. 832.

16. Special thanks to Fred Goff and the Data Center, Oakland, California, for research assistance for this section. See especially their collection, *Information Services on Latin America* (ISLA). Roger Burbach used it extensively to document the different uprisings and revolts in Latin America. I am also indebted to John Walton's work on urban protests in Latin America. See his article 'Debt, Protest, and the State in Latin America,' in Susan Eckstein, *Power and Popular Protest* (Berkeley, Calif.: University of California Press, 1988).

17. Richard Falk, *Explorations at the Edge of Time: The Prospects for World Order* (Philadelphia, Pa.: Temple University Press, 1992) pp. 206–13.

18. For a somewhat different, but complementary view of the impact and potentialities of globalization, see Jeremy Brecher and Tim Costello, *Global Village or Global Pillage: Economic Reconstruction from the Bottom Up* (Boston, Mass.: South End Press, 1994).

Chapter 3: The Crisis of Western Ideology

1. Newspaper interview, *El Nuevo Diario*, April 25, 1990, Managua, Nicaragua.

2. Immanuel Wallerstein, 'The Collapse of Liberalism,' in *Socialist Register 1992* (London: The Merlin Press, 1992) p. 108.

3. Francis Fukuyama, *The End of History and the Last Man* (New York: Free Press, 1992) p. 48.

4. Ibid., p. 45.

5. Cited in *Monthly Review*, vol. 33, no. 6 (November 1981) p. 10.

6. Wallerstein, 'Collapse of Liberalism', pp. 96–9.
7. See Giovanni Arrighi, Terrance K. Hopkins and Immanuel Wallerstein, *Anti-Systemic Movements* (London and New York: Verso, 1989) pp. 97–115.
8. See Perry Anderson, *Lineages of the Absolutist State* (London: Verso, 1974).
9. Samir Amin, *Eurocentrism* (New York: Monthly Review, 1989) pp. 89–118.
10. See Karl Marx, *The Eighteenth Brumaire of Louis Bonaparte* (New York: International Publishers, 1972).
11. Istvan Meszaros, *The Power of Ideology* (New York University Press, 1989) pp. 325–39.
12. For a discussion of conflicts among the colonists, see Jackson Turner Main, *The Anti-Federalists: Critiques of the Constitution* (Chapel Hill, NC: University of North Carolina Press, 1961).
13. In the case of the United States, see Ben H Bagdikian, *The Media Monopoly*, 3rd edn. (Boston, Mass.: Beacon Press, 1990).
14. Michael Ryan, *Marxism and Deconstruction: A Critical Articulation* (Baltimore, Mass.: The Johns Hopkins University Press, 1982) p. 1.
15. See David Harvey, *The Condition of Postmodernity: An Inquiry into the Origins of Social Change* (Cambridge, Mass.: Blackwell, 1989).
16. See Edward W. Soja, *Postmodern Geographies: The Reassertion of Space in Critical Social Theory* (New York and London: Verso 1989).
17. Richard A. Falk, *Explorations at the Edge of Time: The Prospects for World Order* (Philadelphia, Pa.: Temple University Press, 1992) pp. 49–50.
18 Samir Amin, *Empire of Chaos* (New York: Monthly Review, 1992) pp. 79–80.
19. See Arrighi, *Anti-Systemic Movements*.

Chapter 4: The Economic Shock of Globalization

1. Arthur MacEwan, 'Notes on US Foreign Investment in Latin America,' *Monthly Review*, vol. 45, no. 8 (January 1994) p. 16.
2. Percy Brazil, 'Memories of Carl Marzani,' *Monthly Review*, vol. 46, no. 10 (March 1995) p. 34.
3. *New York Times*, January 3, 1994.
4. See the pioneering work by Andre Gundar Frank, *Capitalism and Underdevelopment in Latin America: Historical Studies of Chile and Brazil* (New York: Monthly Review, 1969).
5. United Nations, *1990 International Trade Statistics Yearbook*, 1992.
6. For a discussion of this process in Latin America, see Roger Burbach, 'Ruptured Frontiers: The Transformation of the US–Latin American System,' *Socialist Register 1992* (London: Merlin Press, 1992) pp. 239–54.
7. David Harvey, *The Condition of Postmodernity* (Cambridge, Mass.: Basil Blackwell, 1989) pp. 201–326.
8. Robert B. Reich, *The Work of Nations: Preparing Ourselves for 21st Century Capitalism* (New York: Vintage Books, 1992) p. 81.
9. Ibid., p. 113.

10. *Business Week*, 'Why Downsizing Looks Different These Days,' October 10, 1994, p. 43.

11. Richard Barnet, 'Stateless Corporations,' *The Nation*, December 19, 1994, p. 755. See also Richard Barnet and John Cavanagh, *Global Dreams: Imperial Corporations and the New World Order* (New York: Simon and Schuster, 1994).

12. For an early discussion of this process see Roger Burbach and Patricia Flynn, *Agribusiness in the Americas* (New York: Monthly Review, 1980).

13. See Alejandro Bendaña, *Hegemonía y Nuevo Orden Internacional: Estados Unidos ante el Desafío de Alemania y Japón* (Managua: Centro de Estudios Internacionales, 1992).

14. Walter Russell Mead, 'Bushism, Found: A Second Term Agenda Hidden in Trade Agreements,' *Harper's*, vol. 285, no. 1708 (September 1992) pp. 37–45.

15. David C. Korten, *When Corporations Rule the World* (West Hartford, Conn.: Kumarian Press and San Francisco, Calif.: Berret-Koehler Publishers, 1995) p. 221.

16. *Business Week*, June 1, 1993.

17. Jeremy Rifkin, *The End of Work: The Decline of the Global Labor Force and the Dawn of the Post-Market Era* (New York: GP Putnam's Sons, 1995) p. xvii.

18. Paul Sweezy, 'The Triumph of Financial Capital,' *Monthly Review*, vol. 46, no. 2 (June 1994) pp. 8, 9.

19. Ron Martin, 'Stateless Monies, Global Financial Integration and National Economic Autonomy: the End of Geography?' in Stuart Corbridge, Ron Martin and Nigel Thrift, eds. *Money, Power and Space* (Cambridge, Mass.: Basil Blackwell, 1994) p. 256.

20. Ibid., p. 260.

21. Ibid.

22. *New York Times*, September 20, 1995, p. B3.

23. *San Francisco Examiner*, April 2, 1995, p. B-4.

24. Martin, 'Stateless Monies', p. 260.

25. Ibid., p. 261.

26. *Business Week*, December 26, 1994, p. 78.

27. Ibid.

28. *Business Week*, '21st Century Capitalism,' November special issue, 1994, p. 45.

29. Ibid., p. 25.

30. Cited in David Montgomery, 'What the World Needs Now,' *The Nation*, April 3, 1995, p. 461.

31. *United Nations Perspective on the World Economy: World Economic and Social Survey 1995*, p. 3.

32. See Rudolf Hilferding, *Finance Capital: A Study of the Latest Phase of Capitalist Development* (Boston, Mass.: Routledge, 1981).

33. *Business Week*, December 12, 1994, p. 71.

34. *Business Week*, November special issue, 1994, p. 48.

35. *San Francisco Examiner*, December 11, 1994, p. B-1.

36. *Business Week*, November special issue. p. 40.

37. Ibid., p. 50.

Chapter 5: The Trauma of the Third World

1. Ben Clarke and Clifton Ross, eds *Voices of Fire: Comuniques and Interviews from the Zapatista National Liberation Army*, translated by Clifton Ross, et al. (Berkeley, Calif.: New Earth Publications, 1994) p. 33.

2. Samir Amin, *Maldevelopment: Anatomy of a Global Failure* (Tokyo: United Nations University Press, 1990) p. 5.

3. Walden Bello, *Dark Victory* (London: Pluto Press, Food First and the Transnational Institute, 1994) p. x.

4. Guy Arnold, *The End of the Third World* (New York: St Martin's Press, 1993) pp. 1–3.

5. Robert D. Kaplan, 'The Coming Anarchy,' *Atlantic Monthly*, vol. 273, no. 2 (February 1994) p. 46.

6. Ibid., pp. 46, 49.

7. *World Tables 1994* (Published for the World Bank by The Johns Hopkins University Press, Baltimore and London, 1994).

8. Paul Kennedy, *Preparing for the Twenty-First Century* (New York: Random House, 1993) p. 23.

9. 'Agricultural Biotechnology, The Next "Green Revolution"?', World Bank Technical Paper Number 133 (Washington DC: The World Bank, 1991) p. viii. See also p. 6.

10. Michael Lipton with Richard Longhurst, *New Seeds and Poor People* (Baltimore, Mass.: The Johns Hopkins University Press, 1989) p. 3.

11. Ibid., p. 13.

12. Kennedy, *Twenty-First Century*, pp. 193–215.

13. Robert Weil, 'Somalia in Perspective: When the Saints Come Marching In,' *Monthly Review*, vol. 44, no. 10 (March 1993), pp. 1–13.

14. Amin, *Maldevelopment*, p. 5.

15. OECD, *Geographical Distribution of Financial Flows to Developing Countries 1987–1990* (Paris, France: OECD) p. 208.

16. See *Angola: An Introductory Economic Review* (The World Bank, Washington DC, 1991). See also *Angola: Economic Reconstruction and Rehabilitation* (United Nations Industrial Development Organization, September 1990).

17. 'Market Solution for the Americas? The Rise of Wealth & Hunger,' NACLA Report on the Americas, February 1993 (New York: NACLA).

18. *Business Week*, June 15, 1992.

19. Harry Magdoff, 'Globalization – To What End?' *Socialist Register 1992* (London: Merlin Press, 1992) pp. 52, 54.

20. Ibid., p. 55.

21. See Walden Bello and Stephanie Rosenfeld, *Dragons in Distress: Asia's Miracle Economies in Crisis* (San Francisco, Calif.: The Institute for Food and Development Policy, 1992).

22. Ibid., p. 11.

23. Manuel Castells and Peter Hall, *Technopoles of the World: The Making of Twenty-First-Century Industrial Complexes* (London and New York: Routledge, 1994) p. 105.

24. Bello and Rosenfeld, *Dragons*, pp. 201–2.

25. *World Tables 1994*, pp. 3–5. See also *The Europa World Yearbook 1994* (London: Europa Publications, 1995) p. 837.
26. This section is based on a series of interviews and discussions conducted by Roger Burbach in China in June 1994.
27. Immanuel Wallerstein, 'The Collapse of Liberalism,' *Socialist Register 1992* (London: Merlin Press, 1992) pp. 105–7.
28. For a more extended discussion see Roger Burbach, 'Roots of the Postmodern Rebellion in Chiapas,' *New Left Review*, no. 205, May–June, 1994, pp. 113–24.

Chapter 6: Decomposition in the United States

1. William Greider, *Who Will Tell the People: The Betrayal of American Democracy* (New York: Simon and Schuster, 1992) p. 415.
2. Cornel West, *Race Matters* (Boston: Beacon Press, 1993) pp. 7—8.
3. David Guterson, 'Enclosed, Encyclopedic, Endured: One Week at the Mall of America,' *Harper's*, vol. 287, no. 1719 (August 1993) pp. 49–56.
4. The Urban Coalition, *Profiles of Change: Communities of Color in the Twin Cities Area* (St Paul: The Urban Coalition, 1993) pp. 1, 15, 21.
5. John Kenneth Galbraith, *The Culture of Contentment* (Boston, New York: Houghton Mifflin Co., 1992) pp. 13, 55, 105–7. See also Kevin Phillips, *Boiling Point: Repubicans, Democrats, and the Decline of Middle-Class Prosperity* (New York: Random House, 1993) p. xxii.
6. *New York Times*, March 21, 1995, p. A15.
7. United Nations Children's Fund, *Progress of Nations* (New York: UNICEF, 1994) pp. 40–6.
8. Medea Benjamin and Devin Danaher, 'The Meaning of America,' *Global Exchanges*, issue 23, (Summer, 1995) p. 1.
9. Kim Moody, *An Injury to All: The Decline of American Unionism* (London and New York: Verso, 1988) p. 4.
10. Ibid., pp. 104–5.
11. Lester Thurow, *Head to Head: The Coming Economic Battle Among Japan, Europe and America* (New York: William Morrow, 1992) p. 168.
12. Robert B. Reich, *The Work of Nations: Preparing Ourselves for 21st Century Capitalism* (New York: Vintage Books, 1992) pp. 173–80.
13. Ibid.
14. William Julius Wilson, ed. 'The Ghetto Underclass: Social Science Perspectives,' *Annals of the American Academy of Political and Social Science*, vol. 501 (Newbury Park, Calif.: Sage Publications, 1989) p. 13.
15. Mike Davis, 'Who Killed L.A.? The War Against the Cities,' *Crossroads*, no. 32 (June 1993) p. 7.
16. West, *Race Matters*, p. 16.
17. Philippe Bourgois, *In Search of Respect: Selling Crack in El Barrio* (New York: Cambridge University Press, 1995) pp. 319–20.
18. Ibid., pp. 114–73.
19. Peter H. Rossi and James D. Wright, 'The Urban Homeless: A Portrait of Urban Dislocation,' *The Annals of the American Academy*

of Political and Social Science, vol. 501 (Newbury Park, Calif.: Sage Publications, 1989) pp. 132–42.

20. Thomas Bryne Edsall, 'The Changing Shape of Power: A Realignment in Public Policy,' *The Rise and Fall of the New Deal Order, 1930–80*, edited by Steve Fraser and Gary Gerstle (Princeton, NJ: Princeton University Press, 1989) p. 288.

21. Chip Berlet, 'The Rise of the Religious Right,' Public address before Brecht Forum, New York, September 28, 1994.

22. Figures from a radio program by Larry Bensky, KPFA, Radio Pacifica, April 28, 1995.

23. *Business Week*, April 3, 1995, p. 51.

24. *Business Week*, March 11, 1996, p. 98.

25. Reich, *Wealth of Nations*, pp. 282–92.

26. Gavan McCormack, 'The Price of Affluence: The Political Economy of Japanese Leisure,' *New Left Review*, no. 188 (July–August 1991) pp. 121–35.

27. Daniel Singer, *Monthly Review*, June 1995, p. 28.

28. Borosage, *Nation*, October 4, 1993

29. Meredith Tax, 'My Censorship – and Ours,' *The Nation*, March 20, 1995, p. 378.

Chapter 7: The Post-communist World

1. Gabriel Kolko, *Century of War: Politics, Conflicts and Society Since 1914* (New York: The New Press, 1994) p. 479.

2. Many reformers are quite aware of this. In 1994 Yegor Gaidar wrote in *Moscow News* that the theories for rebuilding the Russian economy on the basis of a private economy are "utopian." (*Moscow News*, November 8, 1994, no. 41.)

3. Report by V.P. Polevanov to the Prime Minister of the Russian Federation, V.S. Chernomyrdin, January 18, 1995, p. 8. For letting the cat out of the bag, Polevanov was sacked after only a brief reign as head of the Commission. See also *Nezavisimaya Gazeta*, January 26, 1995.

4. Jonathan Steele also notes the lack of any new values with the collapse of communism: "The removal of the pervasive ideology of Communism with its claim to be building a new structure of common values left a moral vacuum which could not easily be filled. The concept of public interest was virtually abandoned." See Jonathan Steele, *Eternal Russia* (London and Boston, Mass. Faber and Faber, 1995) p. 401.

5. *Svobodnaya Mysl*, no. 10, 1994, p. 8.

6. *Segodnya*, December 15, 1994.

7. It is noteworthy that this was also the conclusion of the Polevanov Report. See *Nezavisimaya Gazeta*, January 26, 1995.

Chapter 8: Visions: Old and New

1. Barbara Tuchman, *A Distant Mirror: The Calamitous Fourteenth Century* (New York: Knopf, 1978) pp. xix–xx.

2. Public statement by Daniel Singer.

3. Gabriel Kolko, *Century of War: Politics, Conflicts and Society Since 1914* (New York: The New Press, 1994) p. 483.

4. Massimo Livi-Bacci, *A Concise History of World Population*, translated by Carl Ipsen (Cambridge: Mass., Blackwell, 1992) p. 33.

5. See Basil Davidson, *The Black Man's Burden: Africa and the Curse of the Nation-State* (New York: Times Books, 1992).

6. See William Gibson, *Virtual Light* (New York: Bantam Books, 1993) and the film *Johnny Mnemonic*.

7. Paul Sweezy and Harry Magdoff, 'Notes from the Editors,' *Monthly Review*, vol. 47, no. 3 (July–August, 1995) cover page.

8. Eric Hobsbawm, *Age of Extremes: A History of the World, 1914–91* (New York: Pantheon Books, 1994) p.16.

9. Kolko, *Century of War*, pp. 474, 480.

10. Public address by Eduardo Galeano, Berkeley, Calif., June 1995.

11. Joanne Landy, 'Women and Nationalism,' *Nonviolent Activist*, July–August, 1995.

12. Benjamin Barber, *Jihad vs. McWorld* (New York: Times Books, Random House, 1995) pp. 11, 19.

13. Samuel P. Huntington, 'The Clash of Civilizations?' *Foreign Affairs*, Summer, 1993.

14. Dan Connell, 'Eritrea: A Revolution in Process,' *Monthly Review*, vol 46, no. 3 (July–August, 1993) pp. 7, 15–20.

15. *San Francisco Chronicle*, July 31, 1995, p. A8.

16. Connell, *Eritrea*, p. 14.

Chapter 9: The Long Transition to Postmodern Socialisms

1. Cited in Serge Latouche, *In the Wake of the Affluent Society: An Exploration of Post Development* (London and New Jersey: Zed Books, 1993) p. 127.

2. Eric Hobsbawm, *Age of Extremes: A History of the World, 1914–91*, p. 585.

3. Ray Marshall, 'The Global Jobs Crisis,' *Foreign Policy*, Fall, 1995, no. 100, pp. 50–68.

4. *The Economist*, October 7–13, 1995, Special supplement, p. 9.

5. See Hernando de Soto, *Caminando el otro sendero* (Lima: FUNDES, 1990). This is also the position of one of the contributors to this book, Boris Kagarlitsky.

6. As cited in Hobsbawm, *Age of Extremes*, p. 497.

7. Jorge G. Castañeda, *Utopia Unarmed: The Latin American Left After the Cold War* (New York: Alfred A Knopf, 1993) p. 432.

8. Assef Bayat, *Work, Politics and Power: An International Perspective on Workers' Control and Self-Management* (London: Zed Books, 1991).

9. See *Business Week*, 'The Horizontal Corporation', December 1993, no. 3351, pp. 76–81.

10. For an interesting proposal for reorienting the Nicaraguan economy around small and worker-run enterprises see *Propuesta del FSLN para Debatir la Orientacion de la Economia Nicaraguense* (Managua: Editorial El Amanecer, 1995).

11. Earth Trade, a publicly traded corporation in the United States, is working with co-ops and small producers to export organic crops as well as more traditional commodities in El Salvador, Nicaragua and elsewhere in Latin America. See Earth Trade, Common Stock Public Offering Prospectus, Oakland CA, 1995.

12. Gar Alperovitz, 'How Cities Make Money,' *New York Times*, February 10, 1994.

13. International Fund for Agricultural Development (IFAD), *The State of World Rural Poverty: A Profile of Latin America and the Caribbean* (Rome: IFAD, 1993) p. 1.

14. William Murdoch, 'World Hunger and Population,' in *Agroecology* by C. Ronald Carroll, John H. Vandermeer, Peter M. Rosset (New York: McGraw Hill, 1990) p. 11.

15. Miguel A. Altieri and Susanna B. Hecht, *Agroecology and Small Farm Development* (Ann Arbor, Mich.: CRC Press, 1990) p. 118.

16. Michael Barratt Brown, *European Union: Fortress or Democracy? Towards a Democratic Market and a New Economic Order* (Nottingham: Russell Press, 1991) p. 94.

17. Ibid., p. 116.

18. Jeremy Rifkin, *The End of Work: The Decline of the Global Labor Force and the Dawn of the Post-Market Era* (New York: GP Putnam's Sons, 1995) pp. 249–50.

19. See *Street Spirit* (Oakland, Calif.: Homeless Organizing Project, 1995).

20. André Gorz, *Critique of Economic Reason* (London and New York: Verso, 1989) p. 188.

21. See Kevin Danaher, ed. *Fifty Years is Enough: The Case Against the World Bank and the International Monetary Fund.* Preface by Muhammad Yunus (Boston, Mass.: South End Press, 1994).

22. See Letter to the Prime Minister of Canada and the Presidents of the United States, Mexico and Chile, June 7, 1995. Picked up on Internet Conference, Econ.Saps@igc.apc.org 'Chile's Entry into Nafta.'

Bibliography

Amin, Samir, *Empire of Chaos,* translated by W.H. Locke Anderson (New York: Monthly Review, 1992).

Amin, Samir, *Maldevelopment: Anatomy of a Global Failure* (Tokyo: United Nations University Press, 1990).

Anderson, Benedict, *Imagined Communities: Reflections on the Origins and Spread of Nationalism* (London: Verso, 1991).

Aronson, Ronald, *After Marxism* (New York: Guilford Press, 1995).

Arrighi, Giovanni, Terrance K. Hopkins and Immanuel Wallerstein, *Anti-Systemic Movements* (London and New York: Verso, 1989).

Bagdikian, Ben H., *The Media Monopoly,* 3rd edn. (Boston, Mass.: Beacon Press, 1990).

Barber, Benjamin, *Jihad vs. McWorld* (New York: Times Books, Random House, 1995).

Barnet, Richard J., 'Stateless Corporations: Lords of the Global Economy', *The Nation,* December 19, 1994, pp. 754–7.

Barnet, Richard and John Cavanagh, *Global Dreams: Imperial Corporations and the New World Order* (New York: Simon and Schuster, 1994).

Bayet, Assef, *Work Politics and Power: An International Perspective on Workers' Control and Self-Management* (London: Zed Books,1991).

Bello, Walden, *Dark Victory* (London: Pluto Press, Food First and the Transnational Institute, 1994).

Bello, Walden and Stephanine Rosenfeld, *Dragons in Distress: Asia's Miracle Economies in Crisis* (San Francisco, Calif.: The Institute for Food and Development Policy, 1992).

Bendaña, Alejandro, *Hegemonia y Nuevo Orden Internacional: Estados Unidos ante el Desafio de Alemania y Japon* (Managua: Centro de Estudios Internacionales, 1992).

Boff, Leonardo, 'Eo povo que se organiza para a libertacao,' *Jornal do Brazil,* May 3, 1981.

Bourgois, Philippe, *In Search of Respect: Selling Crack in El Barrio* (New York: Cambridge University Press, 1995).

Brecher, Jeremy, John Brown Childs, and Jill Cutler, eds. *Global Visions: Beyond the New World Order* (Boston, Mass.: South End Press, 1993).

Brecher, Jeremy and Tim Costello, *Global Village or Global Pillage: Economic Reconstruction from the Bottom Up* (Boston, Mass.: South End Press, 1994).

Brown, Michael Barratt, *European Union: Fortress or Democracy? Towards a Democratic Market and a New Economic Order* (Nottingham: Russell Press 1991).

Brzezinski, Zbigniew, *Out of Control, Global Turmoil on the Eve of the 21st Century* (New York: Scribner, 1992).

Burbach, Roger, 'Roots of the Postmodern Rebellion in Chiapas,' *New Left Review*, no. 205, May–June, 1994.

Business Week, *21st Century Capitalism*, (New York: A McGraw-Hill November, 1994).

Castañeda, Jorge G., *Utopia Unarmed: The Latin American Left after the Cold War* (New York: Alfred A Knopf, 1993).

Castells, Manuel and Peter Hall, *Technopoles of the World: The Making of Twenty-First-Century Industrial Complexes* (London and New York: Routledge, 1994).

Clarke, Ben and Clifton Ross, eds. *Voices of Fire: Comuniques and Interviews from the Zapatista National Liberation Army*, translated by Clifton Ross et al. (Berkeley, Calif.: New Earth Publications, 1994).

Commoner, Barry, *Making Peace with the Planet* (New York: Pantheon Books, 1990).

Cowhey, Peter F. and Jonathan D. Aronson, *Managing the World Economy: The Consequences of Corporate Alliances* (New York: Council of Foreign Relations, 1993).

Danaher, Kevin, ed. *Fifty Years Is Enough: The Case against the World Bank and the International Monetary Fund*, Preface by Muhammad Yunus, 'A Project of Global Exchange' (Boston, Mass.: South End Press, 1995).

Davidson, Basil, *The Black Man's Burden: Africa and the Curse of the Nation-State* (New York: Times Books, 1992).

Derrida, Jacques, *Specters of Marx; The State of the Debt, the Work of Mourning and the New International* (New York: Routledge, 1994).

Europa Publications, *The Europa World Yearbook 1994* (London: Europa Publications, 1995).

Falk, Richard, *Explorations at the Edge of Time: The Prospects for World Order* (Philadelphia, Pa.: Temple University Press, 1992).

Frank, Andre Gundar, *Capitalism and Underdevelopment in Latin America: Historical Studies of Chile and Brazil* (New York: Monthly Review, 1969).

Fraser, Steve and Gary Gerstle, eds. *The Rise and Fall of the New Deal Order, 1930–80* (Princeton, NJ: Princeton University Press, 1989).

Freud, Sigmund, *Civilization and Its Discontents*, translated and edited by James Strachey (New York: WW Norton, 1962).

FSLN, *Propuesta del FSLN para Debatir la Orientacion de la Economia Nicaraguense* (Managua: Editorial El Amanecer, 1995).

Fukuyama, Francis, *The End of History and the Last Man* (New York: The Free Press, 1992).

Galbraith, John Kenneth, *The Culture of Contentment* (Boston and New York: Houghton Mifflin, 1992).

Gellner, Ernest, *Nations and Nationalism* (Ithaca, NY: Cornell University Press, 1983).

Gibson, William, *Virtual Light* (New York: Bantam Books, 1994).

Gomez Buendía, Hernando, ed. *Urban Crime: Global Trends and Policies* (Tokyo: United Nations University, 1989).

Gorbachev, Mikhail, et al., *Perestroika: Global Challenge*, edited by Ken Coates (Nottingham: Spokesman, 1988).

Gorz, André, *Critique of Economic Reason*, translated by Gillian Handyside and Chris Turner (London and New York: Verso, 1989).

Greider, William, *Who Will Tell the People: The Betrayal of American Democracy* (New York: Simon and Schuster, 1992).

Griffin, David Ray and Richard Falk, eds. *Postmodern Politics for a Planet in Crisis* (Albany: State University of New York Press, 1993).

Guy Arnold, *The End of the Third World* (New York: St Martin's Press, 1993).

Harvey, David, *The Condition of Postmodernity: An Inquiry into the Origins of Cultural Change* (Cambridge, Mass.: Basil Blackwell, 1989).

Hobsbawm, Eric J., *Nations and Nationalism Since 1780: Programme, Myth, Reality* (New York: Cambridge University Press, 1992).

Hobsbawm, Eric, *Age of Extremes: A History of the World, 1914–91* (New York: Pantheon Books, 1994).

International Fund for Agricultural Development (IFAD), *The State of World Rural Poverty: A Profile of Latin America and the Caribbean* (Rome: IFAD, 1993).

Internet Conference, Econ.Saps@igc.apc.org, 'Chile's Entry into Nafta,' letter to the Prime Minister of Canada and the Presidents of the United States, Mexico and Chile, June 7, 1995.

Kennedy, Paul, *Preparing for the Twenty-First Century* (New York: Random House, 1993).

Kolko, Gabriel, *Century of War: Politics, Conflicts and Society since 1914* (New York: The New Press, 1994).

Landy, Joanne, 'Women and Nationalism,' *Nonviolent Activist* (New York: Magazine of the War Resisters League, July–August, 1995).

Latouche, Serge, *In the Wake of the Affluent Society: An Exploration of Post Development*, introduced and translated by Martin O'Connor and Rosemary Arnoux (London and New Jersey: Zed Books, 1993).

Lipton, Michael with Richard Longhurst, *New Seeds and Poor People* (Baltimore, Mass.: The Johns Hopkins University Press, 1989).

Livi-Bacci, Massimo, *A Concise History of World Population*, translated by Carl Ipsen (Cambridge, Mass.: Basil Blackwell, 1992).

Makdisi, Saree, Cesare Casarino and Rebecca E. Karl, eds. *Marxism Beyond Marxism* (New York: Routledge, 1996).

Marshall, Ray, 'The Global Jobs Crisis,' *Foreign Policy*, Fall, 1995, no. 100, pp. 50–68.

Martin, Ron, 'Stateless Monies, Global Fiancial Integration and National Economic Autonomy: the End of Geography?' in *Money, Power and Space*, edited by Stuart Corbridge, Ron Martin and Nigel Thrift (Cambridge, Mass.: Basil Blackwell, 1994).

Miliband, Ralph and Leo Panitch, eds. *New World Order? Socialist Register 1992* (London: The Merlin Press, 1992).

Miliband, Ralph and Leo Panitch, eds. *Between Globalism and Nationalism, Socialist Register 1994* (London: The Merlin Press, 1994).

Moody, Kim, *An Injury to All: The Decline of American Unionism* (London and New York: Verso, 1988).

Murdoch, William, 'World Hunger and Population,' in *Agroecology*, edited by C. Ronald Carroll, John H. Vandermeer and Peter M. Rosset (New York: McGraw Hill, 1990).

Nugent, Daniel, 'Northern Intellectuals and the EZLN,' in *Monthly Review: In Defense of History, Marxism and the Postmodern Agenda*, July–August, 1995.

Phillips, Kevin, *Boiling Point: Repubicans, Democrats, and the Decline of Middle-Class Prosperity* (New York: Random House, 1993).

Reich, Robert B., *The Work of Nations: Preparing Ourselves for 21st Century Capitalism* (New York: Vintage Books, 1992).

Rifkin, Jeremy, *The End of Work: The Decline of the Global Labor Force and the Dawn of the Post-Market Era* (New York: GP Putnam's Sons, 1995).

Ryan, Michael, *Marxism and Deconstruction: A Critical Articulation* (Baltimore, Mass.: The Johns Hopkins University Press, 1982).

Sclater, Courtenay M. and George E. Hall, eds. *1995 County and City Extra, Annual Metro, City and County Data Book* (Lasham, MD: Bernan Press, 4th ed., 1995).

Silber, Irwin, *Socialism: What Went Wrong? An Inquiry into the Theoretical and Historical Sources of the Socialist Crisis* (London: Pluto Press, 1994).

Soja, Edward W., *Postmodern Geographies: The Reassertion of Space in Critical Social Theory* (New York and London: Verso, 1989).

Soto, Hernando de, *Caminando el Otro Sendero* (Lima: FUNDES, 1990).

Steele, Jonathan, *Eternal Russia* (London and Boston, Mass.: Faber and Faber, 1995).

Sweezy, Paul M., 'The Triumph of Financial Capital,' *Monthly Review*, June, 1994.

The Urban Coalition, *Profiles of Change: Communities of Color in the Twin Cities Area* (St Paul: The Urban Coalition, 1993).

Thurow, Lester, *Head to Head: The Coming Economic Battle Among Japan, Europe and America* (New York: William Morrow, 1992).

Tuchman, Barbara, *A Distant Mirror: The Calamitous Fourteenth Century* (New York: Alfred A Knopf, 1978).

United Nations, Department for Economic and Social Information and Policy Analysis, *World Economic and Social Survey, 1995, Current Trends and Policies in the World Economy* (New York: United Nations, 1995).

United Nations Development Programme, *Human Development Report 1992* (New York: Oxford University Press, 1992).

United Nations Industrial Development Organization, *Angola: Economic Reconstruction and Rehabilitation* (New York: United Nations Industrial Development Organization, September, 1990).

Walton, John, 'Debt, Protest, and the State in Latin America,' in *Power and Popular Protest*, edited by Susan Eckstein (Berkeley, Calif.: University of California Press, 1988).

Wendy Harcourt, ed. *Feminist Perspectives on Sustainable Development* (London and New Jersey: Zed Books in association with the Society for International Development, 1994).

West, Cornel, *Race Matters* (Boston, Mass.: Beacon Press, 1993).

Wilson, William Julius, ed. 'The Ghetto Underclass: Social Science Perspectives,' *Annals of the American Academy of Political and Social Science, 501* (Newbury Park, Calif.: Sage Publications, 1989).

Wolfe, Alan, *Whose Keeper?: Social Science and Moral Obligation* (Berkeley, Calif.: University of California Press, 1989).

World Bank, 'Agricultural Biotechnology, The Next "Green Revolution"?',
    Technical Paper Number 133 (Washington, DC: World Bank, 1991).
World Bank, *Angola: An Introductory Economic Review* (Washington DC:
    World Bank, 1991).
World Bank, *World Tables 1994* (Baltimore, Mass.: The Johns Hopkins
    University Press, 1994).
Worldwatch Institute, State of the World 1990–5 (New York: WW Norton
    1990–5).

Index